LIBRARIES WITHOUT WALLS 5

the distributed delivery of library and information services

Libraries Without Walls 5

the distributed delivery of library and information services

Proceedings of an international conference held on 19–23 September 2003, organized by the Centre for Research in Library and Information Management (CERLIM), Manchester Metropolitan University

Edited by

Peter Brophy
Shelagh Fisher
Jenny Craven

Published by
Facet Publishing
7 Ridgmount Street
London WC1E 7AE

Facet Publishing (formerly Library Association Publishing) is wholly owned by CILIP: the Chartered Institute of Library and Information Professionals.

First published 2004

British Library Cataloguing in Publication Data
A catalogue record for this book is available from the British Library.

ISBN 1-85604-511-0

Typeset in 10/13 Caslon 540 and Zapf Humanist from authors' disk by Stephen York.
Printed and made in Great Britain by MPG Books Ltd, Bodmin, Cornwall.

Contents

Contributors

A. Anneli Ahtola, Library Development Officer, Tampere University Library, Finland

Susan Ashworth, Team Leader, Biomedical Sciences, Glasgow University Library, UK

Coral Black, User Services Manager, Learning Services, Edge Hill College of Higher Education, UK

Marié Botha, Technikon Southern Africa, Gauteng, South Africa

Peter Brophy, Professor and Director, Centre for Research in Library and Information Management (CERLIM), Manchester Metropolitan University, UK

Geoff Butters, Research Associate, CERLIM, Manchester Metropolitan University, UK

Julie Carpenter, Director, Education for Change Ltd, London, UK

Andrew Comrie, Assistant Principal, Lauder College, Scotland, UK

Andrew Cox, Research Student, Department of Information Science, Loughborough University, UK

Penny Dale, Subject Librarian, Bournemouth University, UK

Susan Eales, Programme Manager X4L, JISC Executive, King's College London, UK

Maurits Ertsen, Faculty of Civil Engineering and GeoSciences, Delft University of Technology, The Netherlands

Emmanouel Garoufallou, Lecturer, Department of Library Science, Higher Technological Educational Institution of Thessaloniki, Greece

Fraser Hamilton, Senior Research Consultant, City University, London, UK

Dick Hartley, Professor of Information Science and Head of Department, Department of Information and Communications, Manchester Metropolitan University, UK

Kees Hopstaken, Utrecht University Library/Verwey-Jonker Institute, The Netherlands

Michelle Kelly, Research Associate, CERLIM, Manchester Metropolitan University, UK

Neil King, Researcher, Centre for HCI Design, City University, London, UK

Oluwatoyin O. Kolawole, Customer Services Manager, British Council, Lagos, Nigeria

Jan Kooistra, Faculty of Social Sciences, Utrecht University Library, Delft University of Technology, The Netherlands

Nils Lagerweij, Faculty of Social Sciences, Utrecht University Library, The Netherlands

Irene Lopatovska, School of Library and Information Sciences, University of North Texas, USA

Terry Hoi-Yan Ma, Research Assistant, Centre for HCI Design, City University, London, UK

William E. Moen, Principal Investigator, ZLOT Project, Texas Center for Digital Knowledge, University of North Texas, USA

Kay Moore, Information Specialist, Sheffield Hallam University, UK

Anne Morris, Reader, Department of Information Science, Loughborough University, UK

Kathleen R. Murray, Associate Fellow, Texas Center for Digital Knowledge, University of North Texas, USA

Gill Needham, Learner Support Services Manager, the Open University Library, UK

William Nixon, Deputy Head of IT Services, Glasgow University, UK

José Miguel Baptista Nunes, Lecturer, Department of Information Studies, University of Sheffield, UK

Bo Öhrström, Deputy Director, Danish National Library Authority, Denmark

Helen Petrie, Professor of Human Computer Interaction (HCI), City University, London, UK

Maria Carla Proença, José Saramago Public Library, Loures, Portugal

Sue Roberts, Head of Learning Services, Edge Hill College of Higher Education, UK

Lynne Rutter, Student Support Lecturer, Bournemouth University, UK

Non Scantlebury, Team Leader and Subject Information Specialist, Arts, IET and Maths and Computing, Open University Library, UK

Rania Siatri, Librarian/Researcher, University of Macedonia, Greece

Liz Stevenson, Electronic Publications Librarian, Edinburgh University Library, UK

Franco Toni, Biblioteca dell'Istituto Superiore di Sanità, Rome, Italy

Sirje Virkus, Research Student, Department of Information and Communications, Manchester Metropolitan University, UK

Margaret Wallis, Head of Social Informatics Research Unit, University of Brighton, UK

Caroline Williams, Library Services Manager (Electronic Services Development), Manchester Metropolitan University, UK

Panayiotis Zaphiris, Lecturer, Centre for HCI Design, City University, London, UK

1

Introduction

Peter Brophy, Shelagh Fisher and Jenny Craven

The fifth Libraries Without Walls (LWW5) conference was held in Lesvos, Greece, from 19 to 23 September 2003. It continued the tradition of the LWW conferences by bringing together international perspectives on the delivery of library and information services to users who are not in the physical library. When the first LWW conference was held in 1995, the focus was primarily on distance learning and geographical dispersion. Since then, however, rapid advances in the development of information and communications technologies (ICTs) based infrastructures and services have led to a situation where many library users now routinely access services remotely – even when 'remotely' means 'within sight of the library building'. As a previous conference attendee observed, 'we are all distance learners now'. LWW5 was concerned with innovative ways of delivering library and information services in this new environment

In his keynote paper ('Beyond the Mainstream', Chapter 2) Peter Brophy reflected on the focus of the LWW conferences since 1995 when the first LWW conference was held to disseminate findings of the BIBDEL project in which three university libraries had worked together to explore the delivery of library and information services 'at a distance' through the use of information technology (Irving and Butters, 1996). Brophy noted that in the second LWW conference held in 1997 (Brophy, Fisher and Clarke, 1998) the remote delivery of information services was a subject that had seen rapid growth as an area of specialist interest, so that by the third conference (Brophy, Fisher and Clarke, 2000) the topic had moved into the mainstream of information service delivery and, by the fourth conference (Brophy, Fisher and Clarke, 2002) in 2001 the topic was actually driving the mainstream. In his paper Brophy raised critical questions about the notion of the 'library' as an appropriate construct and about the need to develop a new model of 'libraries without walls'.

Subsequent papers that were delivered at the conference all contributed in some way to addressing these questions by articulating the findings of new research and the evaluation of novel practices in remote delivery in the context of education and lifelong learning. The themes of the conference were:

- the integration of library services and virtual learning environments (VLEs)
- the relationship between user needs, information skills and information literacies
- usability and accessibility of digital library services
- designing the information environment: national and institutional perspectives
- the creation of digital resources by user communities.

Within the first theme – the integration of library services and virtual learning environments – Black and Roberts (Chapter 3) explored the twin subjects of the integration of library services within VLEs and the design of information environments to support staff within this rapidly changing context. Staff at Information and Media Services at Edge Hill College of Higher Education (Ormskirk, UK) have developed a 'life cycle' approach to support staff in the development of their awareness and skills to support online learning. The paper reviewed the identification, development and evaluation of a number of e-support mechanisms that have equipped staff with the skills and confidence to support e-learning developments. The paper concluded by identifying the need to take an holistic approach to developing 'staff without walls' who need to work across conventional boundaries. Kooistra et al. (Chapter 4) presented the results of work being undertaken at universities in Delft and Utrecht in the Netherlands in which the aim is to initiate networks or working groups that serve as virtual centres of knowledge and experimentation on specific themes, in order to advance education and research. The concern here is with web-based applications that provide access to information for a certain professional field to stimulate user communities. The contention is that the roots of these user communities lie on campus and it is valuable for the student and the university to develop peer-driven, information-based networks during the study period, to continue them after graduation and to involve existing experts.

Findings from the UK Joint Information Systems Committee (JISC) funded DEViL (Dynamically Enhancing Virtual Learning Environments from within the Library) project undertaken with pilot courses at the University of Edinburgh and Open University were presented by Scantlebury and Stevenson (Chapter 5). The project focuses on pedagogical, cultural and institutional factors influencing course team decision-making with regard to incorporating library services in the production of VLE courses. Here it was concluded that, in a world of increasing competition for e-learning services, it is even more imperative that librarians become fully engaged with the crafting of the content, and play a key role in supporting learning through greater facilitation. Ahtola's presentation (Chapter 6) discussed the methods adopted in Tampere University Library in Finland in developing the library as a physical and virtual learning environment, in integrating digital services into virtual learning strategies, and in improving the usability and accessibility of library services. Ahtola concluded that academic libraries can no longer afford to be silent partners in their learning communities. They cannot just ask to be trusted, but instead they have to show how they can be integral parts of academic communities, and partners worth trusting. Finally, under this theme, Garoufallou, Siatri and Hartley (Chapter 7) reviewed the developments that have occurred in Greek academic libraries in the last decade, while noting that support and promotion of VLEs within Greek universities is now seen as a task for academic libraries. They concluded that although the current technological infrastructure in Greece might not support heavy use of VLEs, and that there are gaps in the knowledge of librarians, Greek academic librarians have already demonstrated a capacity for rapid development of library services. Active involvement, or even adopting a leadership role in the creation of VLEs, can only further enhance the role of librarians in Greek higher education.

In exploring the relationship between user needs, information skills and information literacies (the second conference theme), Moore started with the premise that encouraging student engagement with information skills teaching has always been difficult and that transferring this to the impersonal context of virtual learning is even more challenging (Chapter 8). She described the curriculum-based approach taken at Sheffield Hallam University (UK) to deliver information skills in the virtual learning environment and drew on some of the lessons learnt from this experience. Rutter and Dale (Chapter 9) showed how a 'student perception' approach to information skills teaching was used to engage two very different groups of 'widening participation' students. The two case studies demonstrated how a bespoke service and a set of interventions enabled deeper and more independent learning. In examining information literacy and learning, Virkus (Chapter 10) took a more theoretical stance from the position that the concept of 'information literacy' is ill-defined. She concluded that there are many definitions and meanings of information literacy and that its nature is complex and difficult to capture. In designing instruction in information literacy, library and information professionals should also know what happens in education and the developments in research in this field. In the final paper under this theme Needham described the results of an evaluation of an Open University (UK) course on information literacy (Chapter 11). Data was collected from over 600 learners to find out what factors had led them to undertake the course, whether they had achieved their objectives and what could be learned from this group about the value placed on information literacy by a wider population of learners.

The third theme of the conference was 'Usability and accessibility of digital library services'. The five papers within this theme tackled a spectrum of issues from the micro to the macro. For example, King et al. posited a framework for evaluating digital libraries from the perspectives of usability and accessibility (Chapter 12), while, in stark contrast, Kolawole (Chapter 13) presented the constraints faced by Nigerian professionals in using libraries. Noting the diverse needs within the group, she suggested that libraries might best demonstrate their relevance to this group by providing a blended information service with an appropriate mix of innovative on-site resources and networking activities complemented by off-site, remote access to virtual content, leaving the choice of method of access to the user. Toni (Chapter 14) evaluated remote access to e-documents, their impact on the general use of the library and changes in user practices at the Biblioteca dell'Istituto Superiore di Sanità, Rome, the most important biomedical library in Italy. Botha (Chapter 15) recounted issues concerning access to the internet in Africa and summarized the steps being taken to allow students access to a virtual library (ADL) that is available to inhabitants of Africa, free of charge. The final paper (Moen, Murray and Lopatovska, Chapter 16) within this theme provided an overview of the Library of Texas Resource Discovery Service, its development and current status. Usability issues of such resource discovery services were identified and possible approaches for improving and optimizing user and search interfaces were suggested.

In the fourth theme of the conference the focus was on designing the information environment from national and institutional perspectives. Williams (Chapter 17) presented an institutional perspective on designing the information environment. This consisted of elements in which the context of library electronic development at Manchester Metropolitan University (UK) was described; the meaning of the information environment at the university was articulated and the value chain model illustrated. Current and future innovation in creating the university library information environments was demonstrated and links were drawn between the UK national and university perspectives. Proença and Nunes (Chapter 18) presented the findings of an evaluation study undertaken at the University of Sheffield aimed at investigating the use of internet services by Portuguese public libraries that are members of the Portuguese National Network of Public Libraries. The paper identified the current state of the web presence and services of Portuguese public libraries and reported on the impact of disintermediation. The paper also presented a critical review of how these libraries were meeting the challenges presented by the information society. From a national perspective, Öhrström recounted the way in which Denmark's Electronic Research Library (DEF in Danish) changed from a five-year national project to a permanent activity in 2003, fulfilling a vision of building one virtual research library in Denmark (Chapter 19). Wallis and Carpenter (Chapter 20) outlined the current and future information needs and user patterns of the UK academic research community based on the key findings from the national study Researchers' Use of Libraries and other Information Sources. The Research Support Libraries Group (RSLG) was established in 2001 with a remit to make proposals for a national strategy to ensure that all UK researchers continue to have access to world-class information sources. The final report was published in Spring 2003 (Research Support Libraries Group, 2003) with the recommendation to establish the Research Libraries Network, which was to develop, prioritize and lead a UK-wide strategy for research information provision.

The final theme of the conference focused on the creation of digital resources by user communities. The paper by Kelly and Butters (Chapter 21) described the EC-funded COINE (Cultural Objects In Networked Environments) project which is rooted in the idea of digital cultural heritage being driven by these user communities. It embraces the possibility of a 'two-way' flow of information and cultural heritage resources. The idea here is that no longer should it only be museums, libraries and archives that create the digital content for remote users, but these institutions should also present the opportunity for the users themselves to be active in this creative process using information technology to improve the sharing of and access to community heritage, collections and personal stories. Ashworth and Nixon's paper (Chapter 22) described the DAEDALUS project and its role within the context of a 'crisis' in scholarly communications. The paper detailed how research produced by higher education institutions in the UK is increasingly difficult to access, particularly by communities outside the system, and described one different model for dissemination of that research. Cox and Morris reported on a study of one online user community, using Wenger's concept of the 'community of practice' as a theoretical perspective (Chapter 23). The analysis suggested ways of evaluating such communities and measuring their value. It also clarified the challenge to librarians of supporting such informal, dynamic groups. The final paper, by Eales and Comrie (Chapter 24), explained the work of the JISC-funded Exchange for Learning Programme – a £4 million programme of projects providing tools, case studies and exemplar materials to help teachers and information professionals to locate, assemble, use and share learning materials of direct relevance to curriculum needs. The paper focused on one of these projects, Healthier Nation, which is looking into the use of accessibility metadata as part of its work.

There is significant evidence in the papers in this volume that the delivery of information services to remote users is occupying practitioners and researchers in library and information management across the globe. Key issues affecting the definition of the 'library' are being addressed and new models of information service delivery are being developed. At this conference the elements of new 'mainstream' emerged, and in answer to the question posited by Brophy in his keynote paper, it is at this conference we might look to find models on which to build and aid understanding and development of the 'library without walls' of the future.

References

Brophy, P., Fisher, S. and Clarke, Z. (eds) (1998) *Libraries Without Walls 2: the delivery of library services to distant users*, London, Library Association Publishing.

Brophy, P., Fisher, S. and Clarke, Z. (eds) (2000) *Libraries Without Walls 3: the delivery of library services to distant users*, London, Library Association Publishing.

Brophy, P., Fisher, S. and Clarke, Z. (eds) (2002) *Libraries Without Walls 4: the delivery of library services to distant users*, London, Facet Publishing.

Irving, A. and Butters, G. (eds) (1996) *Proceedings of the first Libraries Without Walls Conference*, Mytilene, Greece, 9–10 September 1995, Preston, CERLIM.

Research Support Libraries Group (2003) *Final Report*, www.rslg.ac.uk/final/final.pdf.

2

Keynote paper: beyond the mainstream of library services

Peter Brophy

Introduction

The ideas behind the Libraries Without Walls series of conferences, of which this is the fifth, can be traced back to a number of different roots. Some of these were concerned with the ways in which information technology might be used to deliver library services – and as such they go back at least to the early 1970s. Other ideas concerned the delivery of education, and especially experiments and services that sought to deliver to the learner rather than expecting the learner to come to an institution – distance learning concepts that can be traced back even further, and were well developed in many countries by the middle of the 20th century. Yet other concepts arose from beliefs in the importance of widespread participation in society and thus in learning, and the imperative to find ways to involve the disenfranchised. Draw these together – technology, delivery and universal participation – and the stage is set for new ways of thinking about library services.

One result of this kind of thinking was that by the early 1990s most libraries had come to accept that their role was better described as the provision of access to information sources than as the custody of physical artefacts – although of course there were exceptions, for example among national and highly specialist libraries. But as the access paradigm started to dominate, new methods of service delivery began to appear. The question became whether remote delivery, digitizing content, deploying electronic networks and exploiting the ever more widespread ownership of personal computers could offer a new way to think about, conceptualize and run the library.

It was at this point that the BIBDEL project was conceived. Funded by the European Commission's Libraries Programme it brought together three academic libraries – those of the University of Central Lancashire (UCLAN) in the UK, Dublin City University (DCU) in Ireland and the University of the Aegean (UAe) in Greece – to explore the potential of electronic delivery of library services to distant users. The co-ordinating partner, UCLAN, worked with students taking university courses at small, remote colleges across the north-west of England. DCU, acting as a kind of open university for Ireland, identified a number of individual students who had access to their own computers at home or at work. UAe developed infrastructural services to enable island campuses to be linked and to share resources electronically.

It had been agreed that at the end of the project there would be an international conference to share results and to engage with a wider professional audience. Thus were the Libraries without Walls conferences born – the first in 1995 (Irving and Butters, 1996).

At LWW2 in 1997 (Brophy, Fisher and Clarke, 1998) it became clear that a considerable number of professionals were engaged in exciting new methods of delivery to distant users. While the topic might be a niche one, generally serving quite small numbers of students, it was growing in importance and many institutions were devoting considerable resources to it. We had not yet detected the important insight that it was the *library* that was remote, rather than the user, but this kind of thinking was starting to influence service development.

By 1999 the concept of a 'library without walls' had entered the mainstream of professional thinking (Brophy, Fisher and Clarke, 2000). The remarkable growth of web-based services, including library catalogues and a wide variety of information services, coupled with the seemingly unstoppable rise of Google and other internet search engines, meant that users increasingly expected desktop delivery of library services. In other words, the library was becoming just one of a range of services that students and other users drew on. The imperative was the integration of these IT-based approaches with the traditional library service – while trying to integrate them with other desktop environments that were not designed with library services in mind. In the UK this was the era of 'hybrid library' experiments (see, for example, Breaks, 2001).

The fourth Libraries Without Walls conference, in 2001 (Brophy, Fisher and Clarke, 2002), reflected that 'the topic of library services to remote users . . . has now become a matter of widespread interest and concern' (Brophy, 2002a). Information and communications technologies (ICTs) were by now almost universally adopted, so that more and more users were accessing services remotely. The conference organizers chose the theme 'Driving the mainstream' to reflect the way in which the needs of users who were outside the library building were now a principal driver for the development of all new library services. In her keynote address, Liz Burge urged delegates to confront this new situation by:

- thinking sideways
- thinking creatively
- thinking critically
- thinking transformatively (Burge, 2002).

The conference attracted a number of papers describing case studies of the application of new approaches and new technologies, while a few papers began to debate the theoretical basis for what was being seen by some as a fundamental shift in the purpose of the library – if it has a future at all.

Libraries Without Walls 5: beyond the mainstream?

So we come to the fifth conference. The organizers have again set out themes they believe summarize key issues that we are facing as a profession. In brief these are:

- the integration of library services and virtual learning environments
- the relationship between user needs, information skills and information literacies
- usability and accessibility of digital library services
- designing the information environment: national and institutional perspectives
- the creation of digital resources by user communities.

I want to suggest that these headings can give us a single, challenging, theme to consider – and that is that the 'libraries without walls' concept has moved 'beyond the mainstream'.

In the reminder of this paper I will try to suggest where we might find promising lines of enquiry to pursue, using the conference themes as headings.

The library and virtual learning environments

It is striking that the concept of learning dominates a great deal of debate at national and international level, and not just among public bodies. The idea of the 'learning organization' has been around for a long time now (for example Pedler, Burgoyne and Boydell, 1991) and has proved popular among commercial and industrial organizations. National policies frequently stress the importance of skills development and more general learning to economic prosperity, while other contributions stress that social cohesion and cultural identity are dependent upon the ability of citizens to become lifelong learners. In educational institutions we are seeing the widespread adoption of virtual learning environments. These provide a rich, technology-based environment that is particularly conducive to distance learning, including elements of time-shifting, which may be attractive to those with a busy lifestyle, for example part-time learners, such as those in full-time work and single parents.

Librarians have noted the need to integrate information resources into these virtual learning environments (VLEs). However, it is arguable that we have not yet grasped the full impact of these approaches. The pedagogical theories that are underpinning current educational practice do not always find their way into delivery of services in libraries. I have argued elsewhere that libraries have a tendency to approach learning from an objectivist point of view:

> [objectivism] views the world as an ordered structure of entities which exists and has meaning quite apart from the observer or participant. Much of science and technology is taught on this basis: what needs to be achieved by learning is a closer and closer approach to complete (and thus 'correct') understanding . . . in this understanding 'the goal of instruction is to help the learner acquire the entities and relations and the attributes of each – to build "the" correct propositional structure' (Duffy and Jonassen, 1993, 3) . . . very often an underlying assumption of information and library service delivery can lie very much within this frame of reference – references to 'bibliographic instruction', for example, reveal an objectivist approach in which the student is instructed in the 'correct' view of the world – perhaps that devised by Melvil Dewey! (Brophy, 2001, 136)

Or, perhaps more graphically:

> Take young children:
> - Open up the tops of their heads
> - Pour in all the information they are ever going to need to know to get along with life
> - Continue as long as possible – for 12 to 20 years
>
> Now let them loose upon society, to spend the next 60–80 years as productive citizens, never having to be educated again. . . . A very simple scheme, practiced by nations throughout the world (Norman, 2001).

Have we yet taken on board the challenge of alternative constructivist approaches to learning? Bednar and his colleagues present the argument:

> learning is a constructive process in which the learner is building an internal representation of knowledge, a personal interpretation of experience. This representation is constantly open to change, its structure and linkages forming the foundation to which other knowledge structures are appended. Learning is an active process in which meaning is developed on the basis of experience. This view of knowledge does not necessarily deny the existence of the real world . . . but

> contends that all we know of the world are human interpretations of our experience of the world. ... learning must be situated in a rich context, reflective of real world contexts for this constructive process to occur (Bednar et al., 1993, 19).

So the question that we have to ask is, how does the library support and enhance the rich context in which constructive learning takes place? Do we have sufficient understanding of the process of learning to design our contributions to the VLE?

User needs, information skills and information literacies

There are a number of linked questions that are subsumed under this heading. The first is whether librarians have yet, despite a considerable number of studies, developed sufficient understanding of the needs of users. Although there has been excellent work in the past, for example by Dervin (1976), Kuhlthau (1991) and Wilson (1999) – see also the excellent recent overview of information seeking needs and behaviour by Case (2002) – we have in recent years entered a new age of networked information in which user needs may be quite different. Most obviously, we are now in an era of information plethora, in which a major problem for most users is information overload. Students, for example, may be more interested in finding any one resource from among the many that can support a particular task, rather than the definitive paper or a comprehensive list of everything published on the topic. Furthermore, all of our users are bombarded with a wide variety of information sources, such as e-mail (including discussion lists), alerting services of various kinds, and services such as news feeds delivered via portals. Libraries have traditionally concerned themselves with only a subset of the information resources now widely available. Do we know how the material that we wish to deliver to our users fits into this overall information landscape?

A related question, although the relationship is not often made explicit, is why there are so many non-users of libraries. Public libraries have shown particular concern about this in recent years, not least in reaction to statistics showing, in some countries including the UK, that the number of books issued is in fairly rapid decline. A similar trend can be found in academic libraries, where the number of physical visits to the library is declining. Clearly one of the reasons for these trends is that there is more use of the virtual library, and libraries' very success in delivering resources electronically is bound to have had an effect on visitor numbers. But, leaving this issue aside, it is still clear that many people manage their lives, including their learning, with very little recourse to formal, library-type resources. There is a need for a systematic research to explore this question further in the current, ICT-rich context.

Still within this general area, we also need to ask whether our users, or potential users, are being disadvantaged through a lack of appropriate skills and literacies.

There is now a very considerable literature on information literacy and information skills, but as yet little on how information and other kinds of literacy are related. Undoubtedly there are aspects of information literacy that are covered in other approaches. For example the European Computer Driving Licence (ECDL, www.ecdl.com/main/index.php) contains some elements of information handling. The concept of functional literacy, which is used by the United Nations as a Human Development Indicator (www.undp.org/hdr2003/indicator/indic_29_1_1.html), also contains elements of information skills, for example the ability to read and interpret the instructions on, say, a bottle of medicine. In seeking to place information literacies in this broader context we also need to consider whether these, and other literacies, are best understood as 'situated'. By this is meant, does the literacy required to operate effectively depend on the situation in which the individual person finds him or herself? To what extent can these literacies be transferred from one situation to another? Are we justified in assuming that information literacies are generic?

Usability and accessibility

In CERLIM we have long had an interest in the accessibility of information resources to blind and visually impaired people (see, for example, Craven and Brophy, 1999). In a real sense this issue is simply one aspect of the broader concern to ensure the usability of information services, although we believe that disabled users have a right to special consideration. The subject of usability has a huge literature, with contributions from many different disciplines including human-computer interaction, psychology, graphic design and language engineering. But in essence it is the science of fitting system functionality to user needs – so again it helps if we understand what those needs are. The work of Jakob Nielsen, perhaps the leading usability 'guru', has provided inspiration for many designers. As he said in a recent publication,

> Usability is a quality attribute that assesses how easy user interfaces are to use. . . .
> Usability has five quality components:
>
> - Learnability: How easy is it for users to accomplish basic tasks the first time they encounter the design?
> - Efficiency: Once users have learned the design, how quickly can they perform tasks?
> - Memorability: When users return to the design after a period of not using it, how easily can they re-establish proficiency?
> - Errors: How many errors do users make, how severe are these errors, and how easily can they recover from the errors?
> - Satisfaction: How pleasant is it to use the design?' (Nielsen, 2003).

Using this definition we can see that usability is closely linked to user satisfaction, a topic that has received considerable attention in the professional literature of librarianship. What we have not achieved, so far, is an integrated approach that links together initiatives such as the Association of Research Libraries' LibQUAL process (ARL, 2003) with library system design. Forging this link could help us deliver more services more appropriately.

Designing the information environment: national and institutional perspectives

It is now clear that very few libraries are able to operate as independently as they have in the past. While there has always been a measure of co-operation between libraries, for example in the deployment of interlibrary loan services, the advent of network services, where a single database may provide access for libraries and their users worldwide, introduces a new imperative for collaboration. We need to ask ourselves which services should remain essentially local and which should be planned, and perhaps delivered, regionally, nationally or internationally. Because these services are shared and because they sit alongside other similar services a critical issue is that of interoperability. The only way in which it is likely that we will be able to assure the required level of interoperability is through the adoption of an agreed standards framework. Over the past few years libraries have become used to the need for adherence to technical standards, for example through the use of Z39.50 for search and retrieval, but this activity needs to move up to a new plane. Not only do we need a much more complex framework for libraries to work within, but that framework has itself to interoperate with those providing kindred services such as VLEs. Nor is this solely a technical issue. We need to determine the appropriate economic and service models that will enable us to provide integrated services that enable our users to operate without detailed knowledge of each of the underlying datasets. At a conference such as this, it is also appropriate to ask whether new models are needed in order to secure international collaboration.

The creation of digital resources by user communities

The final theme of this conference suggests that libraries need to develop services that enable and encourage users not simply to be passive receptors of information, but themselves to create new information and other objects that they can share with their worldwide community. In CERLIM we are currently leading a European Commission funded project called Cultural Objects in Networked Environments (COINE), which is developing software to enable ordinary citizens to tell their own personal stories, embedding images or other digital objects (Brophy, 2002b). They will then be able to publish the stories either within a local domain or for a worldwide audience. In this way the library's role ceases to be that of an endpoint in the information chain but rather becomes the mechanism that 'closes the loop', linking information access and use back to information creation and publication. By enabling ordinary citizens to express their creativity the library can find at least part of its new role within the networked society. The COINE project is described in greater detail in one of the conference papers (Kelly and Butters, 2004).

Conclusion

The mainstream of library professional practice needs to move in new directions if a viable role is to be found for the future. New models of the library are required. McLean and Lynch (2003) have suggested that what is needed is 'a conceptual shift away from a traditional systems architecture viewpoint to one where applications become defined by the services provided and the services that can be accessed'. We should perhaps go even further than this. In a recent CERLIM report we have written that what is required is 'an architectural design which is driven by the tasks and activities which users perform or wish to perform' (Brophy et al., 2004). Taking this viewpoint will help us to contribute to the continued relevance of libraries and to define new kinds of service, which we may hope the mainstream of professional practice will adopt, adapt and make its own.

References

Association of Research Libraries (2003) LibQUAL+, www.libqual.org/; see also www.arl.org/stats/newmeas/newmeas.html

Bednar, A., Cunningham, D., Duffy, T. and Perry, J. D. (1993) Theory into Practice: how do we link? In: Duffy, T. and Jonassen, D. (eds), *Constructivism and the Technology of Instruction*, Hillsdale, NJ, Lawrence Erlbaum Associates.

Breaks, M. (2001) The eLib hybrid library projects, *Ariadne*, **28**, www.ariadne.ac.uk/issue28/hybrid/.

Brophy, P. (2001) Networked Learning. *Journal of Documentation* **57** (1), 2001, 130–56.

Brophy, P. (2002a) Introduction. In Brophy, P., Fisher, S. and Clarke, Z. (eds), *Libraries Without Walls 4: the delivery of library services to distant users*, London, Facet Publishing, 1–6.

Brophy, P. (2002b) Cultural Objects in Networked Environments – COINE, *Cultivate Interactive*, **7**, July 2002, www.cultivate-int.org/issue7/coine/.

Brophy, P., Fisher, S. and Clarke, Z. (eds) (1998) *Libraries Without Walls 2: the delivery of library services to distant users*, London, Library Association Publishing.

Brophy, P., Fisher, S. and Clarke, Z. (eds) (2000) *Libraries Without Walls 3: the delivery of library services to distant users*, London, Library Association Publishing.

Brophy, P., Fisher, S. and Clarke, Z. (eds) (2002) *Libraries Without Walls 4: the delivery of library services to distant users*, London, Facet Publishing.

Brophy, P., Fisher, S. M., Jones, C. R. and Markland, M. (2004) EDNER Project: final report, Manchester, CERLIM.

Burge, L. (2002) Keynote Paper: behind-the-scenes thinking: key factors for librarianship in distance education. In Brophy, P., Fisher, S. and Clarke, Z. (eds) *Libraries Without Walls 4: the delivery of library services to distant users*, London, Facet Publishing, 7–15.

Case, D. O. (2002) *Looking for Information: a survey of research on information seeking, needs, and behavior*, London, Academic Press.

Craven, J. and Brophy, P. (1999) *The Integrated, Accessible Library: a model of service development for the 21st century: the final report of the REVIEL (Resources for Visually Impaired Users of the Electronic Library) Project*, British Library Research and Innovation Report 168, Manchester, CERLIM, Manchester Metropolitan University.

Dervin, B. (1976) The Everyday Information Needs of the Average Citizen: a taxonomy for analysis. In Kochen, M. and Donahue, J. (eds), *Information for the Community*, Chicago, American Library Association, 23–35.

Duffy, T. and Jonassen, D. (eds) (1993) *Constructivism and the Technology of Instruction*, Hillsdale, NJ, Lawrence Erlbaum Associates.

Irving, A. and Butters, G. (eds) (1996) *Proceedings of the first Libraries Without Walls Conference*, Mytilene, Greece, 9–10 September 1995, Preston, CERLIM.

Kelly, M. and Butters, G. (2004) Cultural Objects in Networked Environments (COINE). In Brophy, P., Fisher, S. and Craven, J. (eds), *Libraries Without Walls 4: the delivery of library services to distant users*, London, Facet Publishing.

Kuhlthau, C. (1991) Inside the Search Process: information seeking from the user's perspective, *Journal of the American Society for Information Science*, **42**, 361–71.

McLean, N. and Lynch, C. (2003) Interoperability between Information and Learning Environments – Bridging the Gaps. A joint White Paper on behalf of the IMS Global Learning Consortium and the Coalition for Networked Information, www.imsglobal.org/DLims_white_paper_publicdraft_1.pdf.

Nielsen, J. (2003) Usability 101, www.useit.com/alertbox/20030825.html.

Norman, D. (2001) The Future of Education: lessons learned from video games and museum exhibits, www.jnd.org/dn.mss/NorthwesternCommencement.html.

Pedler, M., Burgoyne, J. and Boydell, T. (1991) *The Learning Company: a strategy for sustainable development*, London, McGraw-Hill.

Wilson, T. D. (1999) Models in Information Behaviour Research, *Journal of Documentation*, **55** (3), 249–70.

Theme 1
The integration of library services and virtual learning environments

3

Staff without walls: developing library and information staff for e-learning

Coral Black and Sue Roberts

Introduction

Recent research and case studies have predominantly focused on the integration of resources into virtual learning environments (VLEs) or on the development and adaptation of services for the e-learning environment. This paper argues that such integration presupposes the successful development of library and information services staff, with awareness, new skills and new roles simply a given. The findings of the *Investigating Portals for Information Resources and Learning* (INSPIRAL) report (Currier, 2002) point to new staff development needs and the emergence of new roles and more complex teams in response to the e-learning imperative. However, these issues have not been explored and articulated in any great depth or detail. Staff development within this context is a significant challenge and requires creative and flexible approaches that are not simply based on technology or competencies. This paper discusses the current e-learning context in relation to staff roles, the skills required and potential staff development strategies, with a particular focus on one case study where e-learning and e-skills are embedded within the staff development life cycle. The paper argues for a lifecycle approach rather than 'one off' training sessions, and explores the characteristics of an appropriate learning environment – both real and virtual – to support and develop staff in such a demanding context.

Context

E-learning and UK higher education

E-learning has rapidly become an integral feature of UK higher education whether for distance or blended learning approaches or as a supplement to face-to-face learning. Library and information services staff became involved in e-learning initiatives and developments at an early stage in some institutions. While this is far from consistent either within or across higher education institutions, staff are undoubtedly becoming increasingly involved in e-learning at all levels, for example in the discovery and embedding of electronic resources, design of materials, e-support and tutoring. Allan's (2002, 1) judgement that 'E-learning is becoming an increasingly important approach to user education, information literacy and also staff development' can now almost be viewed as an underestimation of the pervasive impact of e-learning. Such developments could also potentially lead to a crisis in library and information services management. Student and academic staff expectations are beginning to stretch the limits of services, resources and roles, with support and resources demanded via the VLE when required regardless of time or place. As users increasingly use VLEs their expectations of what technology can achieve also increases, with the gap between expectations and the resources available ever widening. Martin (2002) convincingly argues that it is not simply a resources gap but a skills gap: 'there is a pressing need to increase the . . . knowledge and skills base of all staff'.

This scenario of a crisis of expectation becomes positively utopian in comparison with the contrasting scenario where library and information services are bypassed completely. In the e-learning environment 'many of the established mechanisms that were once in place to support teaching and learning have been compromised, or overlooked . . . In many instances this has included the library' (Fletcher and Stewart, 2001, 213). As Fletcher and Stewart reassure us, 'it does not necessarily have to be like this', but we must shift from 'the traditional role of support to one that is active, adaptable and "in-your-face"'.

E-learning and library and information staff roles

From the Follett and Fielden reports of the 1990s (JFCLRG, 1993a; 1993b) a body of literature has emerged that has focused on the changing roles of the academic librarian, especially in relation to information and communications technologies (ICTs), networked learning and learning and teaching. For example, Stoffle (1996) and Stoffle et al. (2000) argue for the need to develop strategic partnerships and engender a broader educational role and Burge, L. (2002) discusses the need for library and information professionals to become consistently proactive educational partners. The most significant research on professional roles and ICT, pre-empting the emergence of e-learning as a major factor in role transformation, is Fowell and Levy's work (Fowell and Levy 1995; Levy, 1997; Levy, 1999) on networked learner support. Taking their cue from Follett and Fielden, they reflected further on the impact of the electronic library and the new educational spaces created by local and global networks. While pointing to the emergence of flexible working and 'boundary crossing' they do not, understandably, anticipate the full significance of the impact of e-learning on roles in the 21st century.

The pace of change over the last five years is evident, with information professionals undertaking work and roles that 'only tenuously relate to the training they received at the start of their careers' (Biddiscombe, 2002, 228). The emergence of learning support roles, whether real or virtual, has led to new and rewarding (or terrifying?) career paths as staff must be 'equipped to provide the glue of the educational world, making links, connecting ideas and individuals' (Biddiscombe, 2002, 235). Consequently, there are new ways of working, new opportunities, new partnerships for library and information professionals as a result of this changing learning environment. Traditional roles are disappearing, new hybrid and blurred roles emerging, and it is becoming increasingly obvious 'that to remain relevant and even viable' staff must 'anticipate trends, seek new alliances and consider new ways of doing things' (Fletcher and Stewart, 2001, 215). Not only must staff update skills in relation to the technology (in using VLEs) but they must adopt ever-changing approaches to work, new partnerships and a flexible view on role development. Allan (2002, 247) identifies six areas in which e-learning is affecting individuals:

- new learning opportunities
- new employment opportunities
- development of new skills
- new roles and responsibilities
- teleworking
- life–work balance.

Although hers is a very positive spin, it should not be assumed that all staff view these changes in the same light. This context does present opportunities, but clearly also barriers to overcome: a major question is how can staff best be prepared to take advantage of these opportunities?

The staff development imperative

The provision and approach to staff development within UK higher education has increased in sophistication and importance over the past decade. Human resource strategies are now the norm and human resource management and planning is now in vogue, stressing the proactive, developmental management of people as a major resource for the achievement of organizational objectives. As Oldroyd (1996, x) states, staff development must be an integrated part of human resource management (HRM) in a context of relentless change, and must be consciously planned for staff at all levels and at every stage of their working life, from appointment to retirement. Consequently, staff development has a crucial purpose in enabling staff not only to acquire new skills and knowledge but to be comfortable with the fact that this skills set will change and evolve continuously throughout their working lives (Jordan and Lloyd, 2002, 183). Staff development strategies have also had to change with the changes in the profile of the workforce, working patterns and roles.

E-learning and staff development

The INSPIRAL study investigated and critically analysed the non-technical, organizational and end-user issues relating to the linking of digital libraries with VLEs. Interestingly, the issue of staff development was raised at every juncture during the research and identified as a vital part of the success of e-learning and digital library development. The major staff development issues were highlighted as:

- ongoing support and training, and this means more than just teaching staff to use the technology – new skills and new roles must be incorporated
- pedagogical issues need to be included to ensure academic validity
- staff development must be applied to *all* staff (Currier, 2002).

It is clear that staff development for e-learning and related emerging roles presents a challenge to library and information services, demanding not only skills-based training but ongoing awareness and the development of new approaches to how we support and advance learning and teaching. Salmon (2002) suggests that 'for staff development to be successful, training needs to be rooted in the peculiarities and requirements of the online learning environment itself'. E-learning is not simply a training issue; the tool itself can be harnessed as one possible solution. The VLE as both medium and message is leading services to design information environments to support, develop and train staff in a variety of ways. The use of VLEs to deliver staff development specifically for e-learning skills and more generically can be seen at Newcastle University (Bent, 2002), as well as the case study represented in this paper.

Skills and approaches in the new environment

The skills, approaches and roles needed within this new environment have already been partially indicated; it is important, however, to attempt to capture and summarize the defining elements in all their complexity and diversity if only to emphasize the challenges for the profession and for staff development. Individual practitioners and researchers have highlighted different skills. Biddiscombe (2002) identifies pedagogic skills, computing skills and an understanding of VLEs and managed learning environments (MLEs), while Levy (1997) emphasizes teamworking in the research stemming from the NetLinkS project on continuing professional development and training needs for staff engaged in networked learner support.

What emerges relates not purely to skills but to a combination of skills and ethos and approaches. These are far more difficult to inculcate and are not unique to the LIS profession; issues around cultural change, professional identity and boundary crossing are becoming increasingly recognizable across higher education. Perhaps new models of learning are only possible if the divisions between staff disappear but this points to an increasingly unstable and unfamiliar working environment not necessarily suited to all staff nor to department and institutional structures and cultures. The following case study illustrates the strategies adopted by one institute of higher education to develop an e-learning ethos, awareness and skills in a wide range of staff.

The case study

Edge Hill and WebCT

Edge Hill College of Higher Education is a higher education institution in the north-west of England, with 9000 students on a range of degree and diploma courses and a further 6000 on continuing professional development courses, particular in education and health-related areas. Edge Hill has strong centralized academic support structures enhanced by the recent formation of the Learning Services department. Introduced in 2000, WebCT now supports over 110 courses delivered across the curriculum and currently has 5200 registered users studying on a range of courses, both undergraduate and postgraduate. The concept of blended learning is gathering momentum with many students experiencing mixed mode teaching. The administration, development and support for the VLE are managed within Learning Services with staff working closely with academic colleagues.

Learning Services

Learning Services incorporates learning resource centres and information provision, learning support, ICT user support for learning and teaching, e-learning development and support, media services, and disability and dyslexia support. Staff are fully engaged in curriculum developments in a variety of roles with e-learning, electronic information, e-literacy, distributed services and support and learning technologies as key drivers. Staff in learning support and learning technology roles are particularly heavily involved in these developments, working closely with educational developers and teaching staff. However, e-learning is not viewed as simply the remit of these two distinct groups, as it influences the wider team.

Staff development within Learning Services

There is a strong commitment to staff development and training within Learning Services by the senior management team and the wider staff team. A staff development policy is in place providing a framework for staff to operate within and a separate budget is identified for this activity. All staff undertake an annual performance review, a process that allows a more formal discussion about training and development needs. This is underpinned by ongoing discussion with staff around changing roles and team approaches to their work. Priorities are also identified at a strategic level in line with institutional, teaching and learning, and departmental changes. The development of e-learning has had a huge impact not only on staff in learning support and technology roles, but also staff who provide front line support on help desks or through off campus support services. Consequently, this area has been identified as a human resource management priority within the service strategy.

The staff development life cycle approach

Within Learning Services the approach to supporting staff with their e-learning role is to start from day one, irrespective of job role. A cyclical approach has been developed with a number of e-support mechanisms providing frameworks for the development of awareness and skills at various points in the staff life cycle. All staff are expected to reach a certain level of understanding of e-learning while developing skills in using WebCT. For specific roles in learning support this is reinforced by project and team work to enable staff to put skills into practice and to discuss issues with a wide range of colleagues.

Two e-mechanisms have been developed within Learning Service to enable this to take place, providing staff with a foundation of understanding and skills as well as embedding WebCT within professional practice. These should not be viewed in isolation as they form part of a wider strategy to inculcate a conducive learning environment and a culture that embraces e-learning and its related challenges.

ProVIDE – Providing a Virtual Induction and Development Environment

Initially a project, ProVIDE was developed to enable staff to actually use WebCT within their everyday role. The project was funded by the SCONUL (Society of College, National and University Libraries) Staff Development Award for innovative practice in 2001. ProVIDE is a secure web-based information base for all Learning Services staff regardless of role or position within the department. It provides staff with equal and flexible access to information, support, guidance and training opportunities. It is also a key tool for all staff induction and has embedded the institutional VLE within the staff development programme. It allows all staff to experience WebCT and the online environment at a very basic level while developing navigational and information retrieval skills.

ProVIDE coverage

ProVIDE has the following information (see Figure 3.1).

- **Read Me** is an introduction and 'how to' guide to ProVIDE. It provides the context and explains how to use the WebCT tools and navigation within the pages of text.

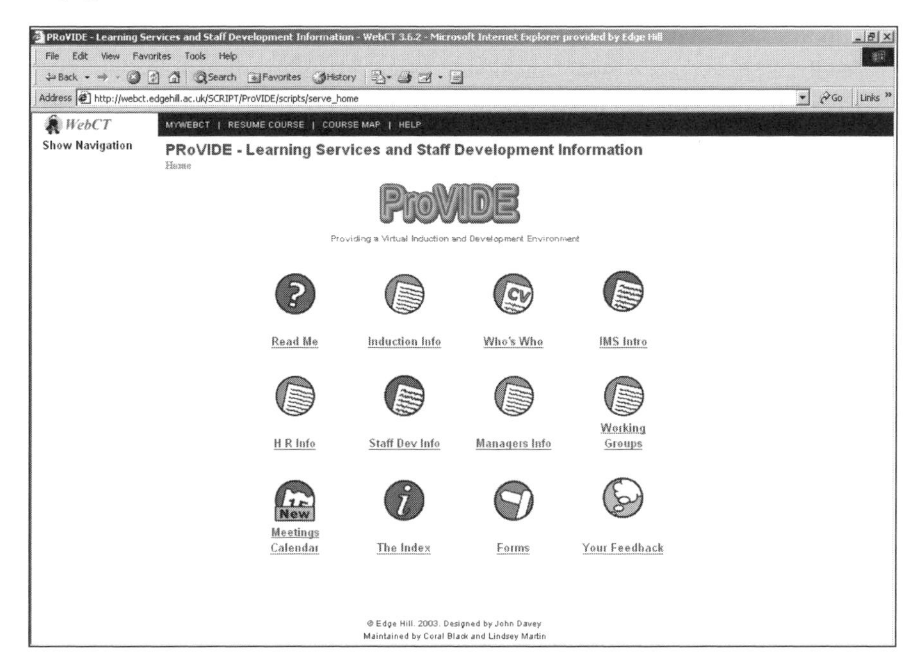

Figure 3.1 Design and layout of main areas of ProVIDE

- **Induction Info** contains information about staff induction within Learning Services and the wider institution. It is customized to the extent that new staff can view their personal induction timetables and task information, which ensures that staff navigate the resource and obtain details about induction.
- **Who's Who** is the profiles section within WebCT. Staff create a personal home page complete with a photograph.
- **Learning Services (IMS)** provides an overview of the service and staffing structures.
- **HR Info** contains information such as salary details, annual leave and sickness monitoring.
- **Staff Dev Info** contains the staff development and mentoring policies plus information about training within Learning Services.
- **Managers Info** contains guidance information for new managers on the management aspect of their role.
- **Working Groups** provides details of the formal meetings structure with details of group membership.
- The **Meetings Calendar** provides details of training sessions and meetings.
- An **Index** is provided to help with navigation.
- **Forms** are provided electronically for efficiency. Examples include staff development applications, leave, additional hours payment.
- **Your Feedback** encourages users to give essential feedback – the resource is only useful if it meets the needs of its target audience and, to this end, a feedback mechanism was considered essential. All staff will be asked to complete an evaluation of the resource at the end of their induction process.

Four-week module – the Supporting Online Learning course

Prior to the development of ProVIDE a short introductory online course was developed specifically aimed at front-line staff. The primary aim was to expose staff to the e-learning experience while also learning about the pedagogy and technology. Staff developed an understanding of the types of support and skills required to learn in this environment and began to realize what it felt like to be a student studying online. The course runs over four weeks starting with a face-to face session and a further drop-in session. Staff have needed to commit approximately 2–4 hours per week to complete the course and produce the final portfolio. Learning Services staff deliver the course thus further developing their e-facilitation and e-tutoring skills.

Supporting Online Learning content

The module contains:

- An introduction: this provides a general overview of the module with aims and objectives, course structure, learner guidelines and assessment information.
- Module 1: an introduction to online learning looks at 'what is online learning', 'what is a VLE' and 'how will it affect me'.
- Module 2: this provides a closer look at online learning, covering online interaction, online communication systems, advantages and disadvantages of them and success factors.
- Module 3: this covers ways of assisting online learning, looking at the use of online resources, skills supporting ICT and information, and tutor support.

The communication systems are:

- Mail: an internal e-mail system allows students to send completed work to the facilitator.
- Discussion forum: this allows students to post comments and work to all the course members.
- Chat: this area allows real-time discussion to take place with all students logged on.
- Profile: this is used as part of the assessment with students creating their own personal website.

Embedding within the service

Both ProVIDE and the Supporting Online Learning course have now moved from being time-limited projects to part of the service and support available to all staff. Staff now rely on ProVIDE to find information, support and guidance about the department, staff development activities and other staff details. As part of staff induction all staff are introduced to using ProVIDE during the first week of employment with a short training session and follow-up tasks to complete. They are then enrolled onto the Supporting Online Learning course, which they complete within the first 6–8 months of starting work.

Further training and development

With all staff completing the four-week course and then using ProVIDE regularly, a basic level of awareness and skills are developed across the staff base irrespective of role or seniority. For those staff in learning support and learning technology roles, further training and development is available to complement project work:

- an eight-week Developing and Delivering Online Learning course
- additional specialized workshops – e-facilitation, e-moderating, technical skills

- information skills online to support staff in help desk roles
- external joined-up activities, for example internally with academic staff, externally with other higher education institutions.

Evaluation and feedback from staff

Extensive evaluation has been obtained in a number of ways, though verbal feedback, ongoing monitoring of usage and questionnaires. This has allowed Learning Services to review and make improvements in a number of areas such as technical matters, design, content, page structure and length. Staff have also identified additional information that they would like available on ProVIDE.

On the whole the feedback has been very positive both from new and existing staff. Staff found ProVIDE easy to navigate, they liked the design and structure, information was easy to find and they liked being able to access ProVIDE from any location, some even from home. Staff found the course enjoyable and useful and felt they had gained a good understanding of the topics covered and e-learning generally. Interestingly, during the pilot 66.7% said 'they would choose to take another online course' and 55.5% 'found it easy to learn online' (Forsyth, 2002).

An inclusive approach has ensured that all staff now have a basic awareness of WebCT and e-learning, with those in first line support roles confident in dealing with student queries. In addition, learning support staff have developed both pedagogic, technical and design skills required to work in the online environment. With the continuing need to review and evolve staff roles in this dynamic environment, staff have recently undertaken a short questionnaire focusing on the following key areas:

- current role and activities
- changes of the last two years
- staff training and development undertaken, and its value
- identification of further activities.

This has provided more formal feedback on staff perceptions on role changes and how staff feel they have been supported to undertake this change. This feedback will influence future strategies and developments in relation to roles, skills and e-learning.

Conclusion: strategic issues and challenges

The strategic management of human resources and staff development within this context raises considerable challenges as e-learning influences all areas of service operations. INSPIRAL provided a vision for the linking of libraries and online learning, drawn from the input of learners, librarians, learning technologists, academics and commercial interests; it also identified staff development as a potential barrier.Tellingly, the majority of the INSPIRAL case studies focus on services and resources, not staff roles, development and identity, which must surely underpin any progress towards such a vision. The vision for staff roles and professional identity is strikingly absent, yet crucial.

Preparing staff for ever-changing roles as e-facilitators, e-designers, e-tutors and e-managers is not just about formal courses and training; action learning and self-development can be extremely valuable as can the involvement of staff in project work, task force membership and new hybrid teams. The greatest challenge is in creating a professional environment that engenders an ownership of e-learning and which empowers staff with the skills, strategies and confidence to work across (and even destroy) conventional boundaries. This cannot be achieved through formal training and courses alone; however, initiatives such as ProVIDE and Supporting Online Learning embed e-learning within the daily routines and culture of a service, forming a strong foundation on which to base the development of new teams and roles. If higher education is to truly develop 'new academic teams' (Association of University Teachers, 2001) which are viewed by some as the only approach to contemporary challenges in learning and teaching, such methods must form part of a larger strategy for staff development, role development and human resource planning. This begins with the recognition that we need not only services but staff without walls in order to maximize the opportunities that e-learning brings.

Bibliography

Allan, B. (2002) *E-learning and Teaching in Library and Information Services*, London, Facet Publishing.

Ashton, S. and Levy, P. (1998) Networked Learner Support in Higher Education: initiatives in professional development and research for a new role, *Journal of the American Society for Information Science*, **49** (9), 850–853.

Association of University Teachers (2001) *New Academic Teams*, London, AUT.

Bent, M. (2002) Blackboard and Staff Development at Newcastle University Library, *SCONUL Newsletter*, **25** Spring, 13–14.

Biddiscombe, R. (2002) Learning Support Professionals: the changing role of subject specialists in UKM academic libraries, *Program*, **26** (4), 228–35.

Bruce, C. (2001) Faculty–Librarian Partnerships in Australian Higher Education: critical dimensions, *Reference Service Review*, **29** (2), 106–16.

Burge, L. (2002) Keynote Paper: behind-the-scenes thinking: key factors for librarianship in distance education. In Brophy, P, Fisher, S. and Clarke, Z. (eds) *Libraries Without Walls 4: the delivery of library services to distant users*, London, Facet Publishing, 7–15.

Currier, S. (2002) *INSPIRAL: Final report,* Strathclyde, Centre for Digital Library Research, www.inspiral.cdlr.strath.ac.uk.

Fletcher, J. and Stewart, D. (2001) The Library: an active partner in online learning and teaching, *AARL*, September, 213–21.

Forsyth, A. (2002) *Exploring New Learning Landscapes: Edge Hill's Supporting Online Learning module*, Edge Hill College of Higher Education, unpublished.

Fowell, S. and Levy, P. (1995) Developing a New Professional Practice: a model for networked learner support in higher education, *Journal of Documentation*, **51** (3), 271–80, www.aslib.co.uk/jdoc/1995/sep/4.html.

Joint Funding Councils' Libraries Review Group (1993a) *Report*, Bristol, HEFCE (The Follett Report).

Joint Funding Councils' Libraries Review Group (1993b) *Supporting Expansion: a report on human resource management in academic libraries*, Bristol, HEFCE (The Fielden Report).

Jordan, P. and Lloyd, C. (2002) *Staff Management in Library and Iinformation work*, 4th edn, Aldershot, Ashgate Publishing.

Levy, P. (1997) Continuing Professional Development for Networked Learner Support, *International Journal of Electronic Library Research*, **1** (3), 267–82.

Levy, P. (1999) An Example of Internet-based Continuing Professional Development: perspectives on course design and participation, *Education for Information*, **17** (1), 45–58.

Levy, P. (2000) Information Specialists Supporting Learning in the Networked Environment: a review of trends and issues in higher education, *New Review of Libraries and Lifelong Learning*, **1**, 35–64.

Martin, L. (2002) Redesigning Support Structures: a strategy for developing learner support staff to work in a virtual learning environment, *8th International Conference of European University Information Systems,* 19–22 June, University of Porto, Lisbon.

Oldroyd, M. (ed.) (1996) *Staff Development in Academic Libraries: present practice and future challenges*, London, Library Association Publishing.

Salmon, G. (2002) Pedagogical Requirements of Virtual Learning Environments (VLEs): pets & planets: the 24 hour university: stretching the limits, *UCISA TLIG-SDG User Support Conference,* Leeds, April, http://wwtweb.open.ac.uk:8282/oubs/gilly/download/Salmonleeds.htm .

Stoffle, C. (1996) The Emergence of Education and Knowledge Management as Major Functions of the Digital Library, Follett Lecture Series, University of Wales Cardiff, 13 November 1996, www.ukoln.ac.uk/services/papers/follett/stoffle/paper.html.

Stoffle, C., Allen, B. Fore, J. and Mobley, E. R. (2000) Predicting the Future. What does academic librarianship hold in store? *College and Research Libraries News*, **61** (10), 894–901.

4

Supporting information-based networks in higher education

Jan Kooistra, Kees Hopstaken, Maurits Ertsen and Nijs Lagerweij

Introduction

With the development of information and communications technologies (ICTs) classic library practice has become digitized and at the same time has evolved into the practice of information skills. Digitizing practice has greatly increased the quality of instruction. Apart from the standard advantages that employing ICT brings, such as improved facilities at the work place, speed and time independence, the biggest advantage could be the potential to demonstrate exactly how different library systems work, from information seeking to lending. It is possible to serve users by offering them the necessary skills to approach library systems properly and to make their visits to libraries more successful. Many good examples of such programmes, the so called self-explanatory libraries, are available nowadays – for example, the Wageningen Desktop Library (http://library.wur.nl/desktop/direct/), The Personal Composer (http://search.library.tudelft.nl/pcom/) (both from The Netherlands), LUMINA (www.lib.umn.edu/), The Data Genie (www.lib.calpoly.edu/research/data_genie.html) and, of course, MetaLib (www.exlibris.co.il/metalib/overview.html). With the rise of electronic learning environments, however, one is forced to proceed a stage further. This is a move from information skills to 'dealing with' digital scientific material. 'Dealing with' implies more than 'possessing skills'. It involves working according to the rules and methods that determine the exchange of scientific knowledge. The question is no longer how to understand the library system or even how to use it, but knowing how to deal with scientific material as it presents itself through the e-platform both socially and with respect to content. By 'socially' we mean that through use of the e-platform it is possible to engage with the scientific network that provides information, which enables us to evaluate it. Dealing with the content of scientific material means that it is now possible to have direct access to the information itself so the information has great influence. Thus, in order to make the package of library functions compatible with and work with an e-platform, the library will need to develop new forms of service and interactive systems that contribute to the possibility of being at the right knowledge centre at the right moment.

Ommat and DelftSpecial

To achieve this end, in 1998 Utrecht University started to develop an interactive program for searching, exchanging and sharing information called Ommat (Omgaan met Wetenschappelijk Materiaal) (Kooistra and Hopstaken, 2000). In 2001 Delft University of Technology joined the program with the DelftSpecial (Delft Student Personal Education Coach for Information Alerting and Learning) project. Altogether three versions are being developed: a *training version* to help users and students become familiar with working in an information environment, a *support version* related to the open internet version for everyday information searching and a *portal version* to store, exchange and share information. Within the portal program are instructional scenarios to share and moderate information. The program is also developing technical and social procedures to transfer students' final products from the e-platform environment into open internet environments supported by the library. The transfer of information from the e-learning platform to the open internet environment marks the end of the educational path. The student is entering the domain where professional rules are applied. The kind of professional domain we are referring to here is called a virtual knowledge centre (VKC). A virtual knowledge centre exists to provide user-focused integrated access to a substantial number of information resources and to facilitate sharing of the knowledge contained within the user group. Ultimately, the aim is to initiate networks or working groups within an integration of education and research, which serve as virtual centres of knowledge and experimentation on specific themes, in order to advance education and research.

This paper has three parts. First we will describe the educational and strategic elements of the program. (Note that if we are speaking about the program in this article we are referring simultaneously to the Ommat program as well as to the DelftSpecial program. They are to a large extent identical and the result of the same drive of the same research team.) We will explain the ideas that we put into practice in the program. In the second section we will report on our experience, especially about the two portal pilots: the Integrated River Basin Management project at the faculty of Civil Engineering at Delft University of Technology and the Writing a Scientific Essay project at Utrecht University's Faculty of Social Sciences, Department of Anthropology. In both pilots educational ideas of working on an e-platform are tried out. In Delft the transfer of students' work into an open internet environment (VKC) has also been tested. Some test results of research by means of the Subjective Computer Experience Scale (SCES) and the Subjective E-platform Experience Scale (SEES) are presented. The scales were used to monitor students working at the portals in the projects at Delft and Utrecht.

In the third part we present our observations. Analysing the problems of being at virtual knowledge centres, we conclude that libraries must address the consequences of the rise of electronic learning environments. It is not enough any longer to teach students how to use the library: the library has moved beyond merely providing students with information skills. Soon libraries will have to support scientists at work by providing them with the detailed information that they ask for.

Theoretical notions

Dealing with digital scientific information

The program described here can be characterized as an ICT-supported program to explore the question of how to deal with digital scientific information. The program is intended for use in close relationship with an e-platform. It can be used by students both as a stand-alone application and an integral part of an educational program. It employs a network model for the dissection of all processes involved in the use of information – its collection, registration and exchange with the environment. The design is such that it enables students to carry out practical exercises in the processing of information that are directly related to their study on a specific project, while simultaneously offering them an opportunity to work on the development of a scientific network. This network is of importance to and necessary for students' ability to validate, maintain and expand the information they have acquired by holding discussions with others and making use of their knowledge. The underlying assumption is that it is worthwhile for students to work on the construction of (scientific) networks during their study, for them to build up internal and external networks, and to continue to use these networks after they graduate. ICT plays an important facilitating role in this process. Most databases and full-text files are accessible only on the campus, and consequently the library intends to play a pivotal role in the development of methods for the permanent provision of important information resources to the networks, for example by means of alumnae membership of specific campus-only resources.

The program comprises a training version, a support version and a portal version, which are related to each other.

- Students follow the *training version* to become familiar with working in an information environment. The training course is made available on the e-platform (Blackboard) and is linked to and integrated in one of the existing educational units also running on the e-platform. Students learn how to make use of a combined search engine and information-processing program while simultaneously using the same platform to work on a specific study assignment.
- The *support version* constitutes the basis of the program; it is the open internet version intended for everyday use. The program includes numerous direct links and useful hints for professional users of information resources. Parts of this version are used in the training version.
- The *portal version* comprises a specific virtual environment, which is provided with computer-mediated tools that students can use for their digital studies. Students can use the portal to store and exchange information on the theme they are working on with others, and to store their personal and shared databases. The portal also extends to the information and communications systems, and it can employ detection and signalling systems to collect and channel (and personalize) internal and external flows of information. Students can also use the portal to grant others access to their knowledge for the purposes of exchange of knowledge and joint work on new projects.

The relationship between training, support and portal can be understood as the organic modelling of science at work. The program instils users with the frame of mind to be able to deal with scientific information in their daily work. Once used, the program becomes a way of thinking. One gets the program into one's head.

Science is open correspondence about references

The fundamental aim of the program is to obtain insight into how science works in the active sense of the word, making use of and being influenced by information and communications technologies (ICTs). The program studies ideas that the team has put forward in earlier work:

> in the near future anonymous and unfinished material [data] will go round ready to get a push by someone as a ball in the pinball machine . . . that we are in need of an outward oriented ICT-methodology which could handle the situation of being connected the digital way, a methodology which has its own pragmatics which will process people into a new system . . . that the consequence of the ICT methodology will be that one is persistent at an address in a process of growing intelligence. (Kooistra et.al., 2001; Kooistra and Hopstaken, 2002).

The program realizes that the library's original linear process – the selection, acquisition and classification of information, followed by making the information accessible and available to users – is increasingly being sub-divided into distinct and potentially independent dimensions that increasingly observe their own specific rules. These dimensions – quality-based selection, information logistics and information mediation – are the point of departure of the program.

From the perspective of ICT a library is not autonomous but a part of the procedure of science at work. The program's methodology (didactics and strategies) restores the responsibility of seeing to these dimensions to the user. Students will become their own librarians and their knowledge will develop throughout their life. So, under the surface of the tools provided, the program is made up of procedures that lead students from the area of traditional information literacy skills into the area of strategic searching. Strategic means obtaining insight about the laws that rule the area which the student is exploring at that moment. To be (and belong) somewhere is very important.

Quality-based selection means the possibility of having access to a network that can give an opinion about the value of information a student is finding. The pragmatic consequence of the use of ICT is that students become correspondents at a far earlier stage. They understand that all the books and articles they have to take in are actually meant to be disassembled into their references and that these sources of information are only valuable through this activity. Libraries are like freezers. They keep the information that is assembled into books deep frozen until their moment of consumption – or until the moment their storage life is over. The use of ICT means speeding up knowledge and reducing the need for the kind of packing and the type of storage that we hold to be normal and necessary in a library. Science is open correspondence about references. Libraries store pre-packaged references calling them journals and books .

One of the biggest problems at the moment is the fact that librarians still think that they have the task of educating their users. Because librarians observed that they could help their users to get better results, they welcomed the idea of information literacy. Information literacy provided a way out of the problems they were faced with in the 1980s: the explosive growth of science, immense piles of paper, linear retrieval systems and being cursed with the assumptions of librarians. Librarians were now able not only to help their users to get better results, they could also join the faculty, having their own scientific discipline and thus their own educational task. So the revolution of information literacy resulted in a teaching model in the mind and the practice of librarians (Marcum, 2002). This was not without justification. Teaching was the right answer to the linear knowledge system in use. The fact that someone knowledgeable about how information actually behaves can get better results is based on the fact that the system in charge does not allow you to get your information unless you follow the system (you have to know this before you can know that, and so on). In the meantime, with the introduction of ICT we have control of other complex and adaptive systems. So we can locate where the clash between information literacy and education is happening.

One of the main problems of educational systems is their ambiguity when it comes to sharing information. On the one hand the student has to learn to share information openly. Science is open correspondence about references. On the other hand educational systems are set up to isolate and individualize students for the sake of testing their knowledge. Even if students and teachers have had to face this ambiguity of educational systems, the library has not. Education about information redoubles the problem – the library has to be beyond educational programmes. ICT shows the difference. The library has 'simply' to support science at work with the detailed information that is asked for. If librarians are horrified by what they call the indolence of students who are only 'googling around' for information, they are in fact confusing the system that is used to get information with the educational system that is meant to control what has to be learned from this information.

Shared database and virtual knowledge centres

When speaking about speeding up knowledge we should recognize that the educational elements of the program must meet the standards that academic professionals have to deal with. Modern university graduates need to process huge amounts of information. This information is produced, communicated and validated within peer networks. It is valuable for students to develop and learn to work within these peer-driven, information-based networks during their period of study, to continue their involvement after graduation and to involve other experts. Libraries could play a central role, as they have the expertise and means to support information-based networks. The program recognizes this dimension as a part of its strategy. It focuses (next to training and daily support) on the development of scientific networks (scientific communities) through offering the student membership of a shared database (Utrecht) or one of the virtual knowledge centres (Delft).

The objective of a shared database and a virtual knowledge centre is to create and maintain open user communities in a specific course (Utrecht) or in a specific discipline (Delft). Both are designed to promote the exchange of knowledge. They offer users an opportunity to search for information in an efficient manner, to keep up to date in the field, and to locate students or experts (colleagues) within the course or discipline. A large number of sources are accessible solely via the campus network, and consequently a search is currently under way for a formula whereby alumnae are offered specific forms of membership (life-long membership of the library) that will enable them to continue to make use of the information network.

Experiences and evaluation: training, support and portal

The training version

In Utrecht the training version of the program was introduced in 1999 together with the introduction of the e-platform, Blackboard (http://studion.fss.uu.nl). It was integrated in the courses of five disciplines at the Faculty of Social Sciences. Since that year about 2000 students have been linked to the program while studying their own discipline: psychology, sociology, general social sciences, anthropology or education. What these undergraduate and postgraduate students have in common is that they have to perform the same kinds of assignments at several occasions during their study. They have to accomplish the design of a research project on a topic and have to write papers and extended essays. On these occasions the students work together in project groups (of 20 persons) divided into sub-groups (of four or five persons). However, in most cases they have to complete an individual paper or extended essay on a topic. The time required to complete the Ommat program within a course varies from 20 to 60 hours. Proportionately this is between 10% and 30% of the total course size. In the case of an investment of 60 hours the students learn to provide their essay with a series of correct references by using the support version of the program; they learn to review the essay of a colleague student, paying attention to the use of references; and they learn to share information on the topic that they choose.

Sharing happens by building a collective database in the group or sub-group discussion board of the e-platform. In the case of a 20-hour investment, training stresses the use of the support version and the processes of validating the information found by the students. In this case the students are performing a so-called 'network exercise'. In Delft the training version started in 2002 at the Civil Engineering and Technology, Policy and Management faculties. To date it consists of training on a small scale (10 hours of investment).

The support version

Building the support version of the program has taken a lot of preparation and is still causing considerable problems. Three main issues appear to have been solved. They are, in ascending order of difficulty:

- defining search profiles and corresponding operations of deep linking into databases
- developing user profiles and corresponding research into agent technology
- defining the position of the library and corresponding discussions about policy and the role and activities of current library departments.

Search profiles

To get an efficient support system one needs a good impression of the different search profiles that can be used. To give the right support it is necessary that the databases should be accessible via different search paths, for instance by the kind of publication one is searching for, by the approach one wants to employ, by the type of information or by type of publication. Support at this level also implies that one gets help to evaluate the information that is found or that one can get an update of the information one already has. In addition, support supposes that there will be an 'organic' connection between the support version and the training version. The support version is meant for everyday use but has to offer also the possibility of looking at the instruction material.

Examples of how we currently organize these profiles can be found at http://ommat.library.uu.nl (Ommat) and www.library.tudelft.nl/ctkc/Information_skills/DelftSpecial/delftspecial.html (DelftSpecial).

User profiles

To provide efficient support the system should have the capacity to recognize different kinds of user profiles and the ability to recognize an individual user. We made an inventory of the kinds of software we should have to buy (or otherwise acquire) to be able to provide personalized support to users. Currently Delft is offering MetaLib to a selected group of users of the project in Civil Engineering. In the meantime it became clear that offering the possibility of personalization to users has to go hand in hand with the development of virtual knowledge centres. Membership of a virtual knowledge centre or scientific community stimulates the user or member to activate a personal profile that in turn could provide the agent the kind of information that is needed for further accurate provision of information (Zhang and Nunamaker, 2003).

The hierarchical position of the URLs in support versions

The difference between the hierarchical position of the URLs of both support versions reflects the state of the discussion about policy at the two libraries. It is clear that the positioning of Delft Special within the Delft library website has been more problematic than in Utrecht where Ommat has achieved a higher positioning and level of accessibility. One of the bigger problems is to divest oneself of the 'teaching mode', not only in the mind of the librarian but also in the knowledge systems that are in use. The introduction of learning content management systems will help to overcome this problem.

Evaluation support

Presently both support versions, at Delft and at Utrecht, are running as pilots and are being evaluated by their users. It is mainly a question of time to complete both versions. An investment in agent technology will have to be made once the policy on virtual knowledge centres is clear.

Portal version

Delft

The first pilot trial with the portal version took place in Delft in the period March–April 2002 and was completed with a follow-up study between September 2002 and June 2003. The pilot trial tested the concept of a portal and the technology and instructional philosophy of a shared digital information-rich environment. The pilot trial focused on a fourth year final project, the Integrated River Basin Management (IRBM) project, which was carried out within the context of the Civil Engineering curriculum. A group of 23 students was divided into sub-groups, each working on a study assignment on basin management of the River Meuse and River Rhine within the scope of the new European directives. The students worked on the portal during the period assigned to the project (seven weeks). The work on the project was managed by means of the teaching system of the program, which focused on the provision of instruction and the organization of the exchange of information between the sub-projects. The customary physical project-group setting remained intact during the course of the project, and project-group meetings were held in a lecture room at weekly intervals. Results of the trial IRBM project are available from www.library.tudelft.nl/ctkc/Information_resources/Specific_information_resources/Water_management_and_Hydrology/Integrated_River_Basin_Managem/integrated_river_basin_managem.html.

Utrecht

Another pilot trial with the portal version took place in Utrecht from November 2002 to March 2003. The pilot trial tested the concept of a portal, the technology and the didactics of a shared digital information-rich environment. The pilot trial focused on an undergraduate project – writing a scientific essay – within the context of the Anthropology curriculum. A group of 60 students were divided into sub-groups of four or five persons, which worked together on a study assignment on writing a scientific essay on a topic chosen by the sub-group. While members of the sub-groups wrote their own essays, it was the task of sub-group 1 to build up a shared database out of the individual search operations, of sub-group 2 to exchange information, of sub-group 3 to review the essay of a colleague student, including its use of the database, and of sub-group 4 to present at the end of the course a 'cleared database' representing the state of the art on the topic.

Part of the assignment required the use of metadata. The sources that a student decided were worthwhile to be included in the database were completed with extra metadata, which gave other students information about the suitability of the source in question and its qualities as an inspirational source on the topic. The students worked on the portal during the period assigned to the project (ten weeks). The work on the project was managed by means of the teaching system of the program, which focused on the provision of instruction and the organization of the exchange of information between the sub-projects. The customary physical project-group setting remained intact during the course of the project, and project-group meetings were held in a lecture room at two- week intervals. These meetings capitalized on the writing process itself.

(We are currently carrying out a more systematic study of the use of metadata at the Faculty of Architecture at Delft University of Technology. The project is called InfoBase. For further details see Kooistra, Stouffs and Tunçer, 2003.)

Evaluation of the portal

Issues of perception involved in collaboration in an information-rich digital work environment were investigated by means of surveys employing two scales. The surveys were carried out before and after the projects in Delft and Utrecht. These measurements were made using the Subjective Computer Experience Scale (SCES) (Smith, Caputi and Rawstorne, 2000) and the Subjective E-platform Experience Scale (SEES). (The Subjective E-platform Experience Scale is a scale that measures subjective perceptions associated with the use of an e-platform. The SEES scale is currently in a development phase – the scale differentiation is not yet entirely definitive. Cluster and item analyses being used in an investigation of the scale will provide information about any modifications to the scale that may be required.)

The SCES scale

The SCES scale encompasses 25 items, which make a differentiation between five factors. The factors are frustration, independence (autonomy), training, enjoyment and negative self-efficacy. Measurements were effected using a five-point Likert scale, expanded with the option of a 'not applicable' score.

Results of SCES

The results of the survey are shown in the Appendix on pp. 46–7. Taking into account the fact that the survey was carried out among a small number of respondents (Delft Civil Engineering n = 20, Utrecht Anthropology n = 41–47) it is possible to conclude the following.

In the IRBM project at Delft frustration decreased; the tendency to adopt an independent approach (autonomy) remained unchanged; the importance attached to a training course increased; the enjoyment obtained from working with a computer increased; and the idea that 'others exhibit a greater performance with the computer', the negative self-efficacy, remained unchanged. The mid-point of the scale is represented by a grade of 3. The results reveal that the score for frustration is significantly lower than the mid-range score, and that the scores for enjoyment and negative self-efficacy are significantly higher. A striking feature of the results is the large variation in the scores awarded for each factor; it should also be noted that, with the exception of the negative self-efficacy score, the variation in the scores for all factors is smaller in the second series of measurements.

The Cronbach alphas that Smith found are solid. The alphas we found in the factors training and negative self-efficacy are comparable with those of Smith. The alphas we found in frustration, independence and enjoyment are weak. We think that this is probably the result of the small number of respondents.

In the scientific essay writing project at Utrecht there was a slight decrease in frustration; the tendency to adopt an independent approach (autonomy) slightly increased; the importance attached to a training course increased; the enjoyment obtained from working with a computer increased; and the idea that 'others exhibit a greater performance with the computer', the negative self-efficacy, remained unchanged. The mid-point of the scale is represented by a grade of 3. The results reveal that the score for frustration is significantly higher than the mid-range score, and that the scores for enjoyment and negative self-efficacy are also significantly higher. A striking feature of the results is the large variation in the scores awarded for each factor; it should also be noted that the variation in the scores for frustration, enjoyment and the negative self-efficacy increase and those of training and autonomy decrease in the second series of measurements.

The Cronbach alphas that Smith found are solid: the alphas we found at all factors are comparable with those of Smith.

Comparison between the studies at Delft and Utrecht

Students in Utrecht scored significantly higher on frustration (average 3.27) than the students in Delft (average 2.3) and significantly lower on enjoyment (2.73 in Utrecht versus 3.60 in Delft). The negative self-efficacy is significant lower in Utrecht (3.24 in Utrecht versus 3.99 in Delft). In both studies (Delft and Utrecht) the correlations between frustration, enjoyment and negative self-efficacy are significant at the 0.01 level.

This might be explained by the average age of the students, as the average age of the Delft students is almost four years higher than that of the Utrecht students.

The SEES scale

The SEES scale encompasses 65 items, which provide differentiation between four factors that in combination represent the subjective perception of working with an e-platform. The items themselves represent the tools and the possibilities offered by working on an e-platform. The factors are: confidence, worthwhile, liking and believing. Measurements were effected using a five-point Likert scale, expanded with the option for a 'not applicable' score.

Results of SEES

The results of the survey are shown in the Appendix on p. 48. Taking into account the fact that the survey was carried out among a small number of respondents (Delft Civil Engineering n = 20, Utrecht Anthropology n = 41–47) it is possible to conclude the following.

In the IRBM project at Delft we conclude that on average the students greatly appreciated working on the e-platform. Moreover all the scores exhibited a shift to the favourable side of the scale in the 2nd measurements series (taken at the end of the IRBM project, whereby note should be taken of the minimum and maximum scores), and the scores remained above 3. An important point is that the students find working on an e-platform more worthwhile and more enjoyable. Moreover both factors exhibit a somewhat smaller variation. The belief that working on an e-platform has a beneficial effect on co-operation also increases, although the variation remains large. The Cronbach alphas of the SEES factors that we found are very solid.

In the scientific essay writing project at Utrecht we conclude that the scores of confidence, liking and worthwhile exhibited a shift to the favourable side of the scale in the 2nd measurements series. The score on believing decreased slightly. An explanation is that the project in Utrecht took place with undergraduate students and that a shared database using the intranet is less appealing to students' imaginations and offers less functionality than a virtual knowledge centre using the internet. An important point is that the students find working on an e-platform more worthwhile and a little bit more enjoyable. There is a strong mutual correlation (each at 0.01 level) between the four factors. The figures indicate that the factor 'worthwhile' is the key figure. If the use of an e-platform is found more worthwhile the other factors follow. The Cronbach alphas of the SEES factors that we found are very solid .

Portal student evaluation

The students on the IRBM project (at Delft) were interviewed during the project itself and five months later. During the project, the students had the feeling that they were required to comply with other standards and need to carry out more work on the project in comparison with their colleague students using a traditional approach. The students appreciated that the increased number of direct and interactive opportunities offered for collaboration and the mutual comparison and assessment (peer reviews) of project material is an inherent and pragmatic consequence of the use of an e-platform. Although the students appreciated these opportunities, they also complained about the additional burden and about the absence of the relevant standards (extra awards, and extra supervision).

After five months the students were asked which functionalities the VKC should offer to make visiting the site worthwhile and what they found important about their own IRBM section of the VKC. The results are shown in Tables 4.1 and 4.2.

Table 4.1 Desired functionalities of the VKC (five-point scale)

> 4	overview experts; access to experts; access final reports; alerting system.
> 3.5 < 4	access library; membership VKC; discussion facilities and discussion board; personalization by agents; access research programs; access concept reports

Table 4.2 Important functionalities of the VKC after five months

> 4	presenting results IRBM project; presenting home pages of members project
> 3.5 < 4	presenting concept reports; presenting project design

Discussion

The development of the Ommat and DelftSpecial programs during the last five years, the evaluations of these programs, the pilot projects in Civil Engineering and more recently in Anthropology, and our scale research lead us to make assumptions about the implications of large scale use of e-platforms in education and research.

With the rise of electronic learning environments, e-platforms such as Blackboard and Web-CT, the library is forced to proceed with the move from 'the solution' of teaching information skills to 'the solution' of dealing with digital scientific material. This solution concerns learning how to work according to the rules and protocols that determine the exchange of scientific knowledge, making use of and being influenced by ICT. This solution no longer forces users to understand the library system or even use it, but means that they have to know how to handle scientific material as it presents itself through the e-platform, both socially and with respect to content.

Using e-platforms does not change the nature of the scientific process, which continues as usual – this is perhaps the most important assumption that we make. The academic ways of doing things are as old as science itself and independent of paper or electronics. From the beginning the 'economy of science' means developing active relationships between references in networks. In this tradition, libraries have become reservoirs of scientific information, even if their books and journals remain unmoved on the shelves. Through metadata (f)actual relationships are enabled. Opening and re-ensuring traceability of scientific material through the use of metadata therefore shapes the most fundamental of the tasks of a librarian. Science communicates through metadata and the librarian guides that process. To consider scientific study as a stable system in which knowledge is dealt with according to academic standards is a clear point of departure. Science is science. Nothing changes it.

Even so, the use of e-platforms as information-rich environments can be considered as revolutionary. Our assumption therefore can also be considered as a paradox. Many changes do occur simultaneously. With the Ommat and DelftSpecial programs we shape again the relationship of references according to what is still academic behaviour. It centres on scientific correspondence within the boundaries and conditions set by an e-platform in which the processes of seeking, communicating, distributing and validating electronic scientific material occur simultaneously. With Ommat and DelftSpecial we have focused strategically on the concept that the intentions of scientists will not change, even if the environment in which they work changes drastically. Thus, Ommat and DelftSpecial focus on the pragmatic consequences of the use of ICT for all stakeholders.

What does it mean for the library when the continuous relationship of references is no longer shaped through static products? Circulation speed, the extent of robustness, the management of and exercise of authority over knowledge – suddenly everything follows, pragmatically, the laws of ICT. Here the most important difference between the concept behind information skills and dealing with scientific material becomes apparent. Where in the first case (information skills), the library forces users (for their own good) to learn how library systems work, in the second case the roles switch. The library must seek connection with the hectic pace of an information exchange system in which the knowledge that was formerly stored or contained in books is suddenly released from the shelves. Knowledge runs, accelerates and sings interactively in the circle of those who formerly could be defined as readers, but now suddenly have become the network that exercises authority over the very same knowledge by itself. In the Ommat and DelftSpecial projects and programs we have gained the necessary experience (in higher education) in use of e-platforms enabled with integrated procedures and facilities for the processes of seeking, communicating, distributing and validating electronic scientific material. *De facto* it centres on developing so-called virtual knowledge centres.

Despite the work that we have invested in building websites with training modules, portals and support systems, the most difficult task has been developing a strategic educational scenario with which the traditional handling of scientific material could be shaped and interconnected with the objectives of education and research as they are expressed in the curricula of the departments. Furthermore, we also encountered many difficulties in tempting library personnel to leave behind the old positions and tasks that they traditionally fulfilled for the library and to use their skills in ways appropriate to an e-platform. But it is not only the library personnel: working with an ICT program that accommodates new ways of dealing with scientific information causes a lot of uproar in the whole academic educational system. Common sentiments expressed by faculty members are 'e-platforms are awful, let us go back to the goose quill'; 'Why introduce such a complicated system when you can go to the library and borrow a book?'; 'Dealing with electronic scientific information takes a lot of time, it is an attack on our course'. Questions such as: 'Who are these people talking about growing intelligent agents and virtual knowledge centres?'; 'Is Ommat a new brand of washing-powder?' are asked frequently.

But! The development of virtual scientific communities supported by the library seems as inevitable as it is problematic. Ommat and DelftSpecial are exponents of a development that cannot be stopped. Virtual knowledge centres must provide academic scientists with the information that they require. The library is moving beyond information skills. In future the library will have to support science with the detailed information that is asked for.

Note: This chapter is an extended version of a paper presented at the EUNIS conference in Amsterdam, July 2003 (Kooistra et al., 2003).

References

Kooistra, J. and Hopstaken, C. W .J., (2000) Being@, keep company with electronic evidence! In: Trappl. R. (ed.) *Cybernetics and Systems 2000*, University of Vienna, ASCS, 438–42.

Kooistra, J. and Hopstaken, K. (2002) Ommat: dealing with electronic scientific information. In Brophy, P., Fisher, S. and Clarke, Z. (eds) *Libraries Without Walls 4: the delivery of library services to distant users: Proceedings of an international conference held on 14–18 September 2001, Lesvos, Greece*, London, Facet Publishing, 241–50.

Kooistra, J., Hough R. R. and Hough, T. (2001) Growing Intelligent Agents for the Delivery of Knowledge: a structure, *Systemica*, **13**, 349–58.

Kooistra, J., Hopstaken, K., Ertsen, M. and Lagerweij, N. (2003) Virtual Knowledge Centers: the support of live-long information-based networks in higher education, *EUNIS conference*, Amsterdam, July 2003, www.2ic.uva.nl/eunis2003.

Kooistra, J., Stouffs, R. and Tunçer, B. (2003) Metadata as a Means for Correspondence in Design Analysis. In Tunçer, B., Ozsariyildiz, S. and Sariyilidiz, S. (eds), *E-activities in Design and Design Education*, Europia, Paris, 19–28.

Marcum, J. W. (2002) Rethinking Information Literacy, *Library Quarterly*, **72** (1), 1–26.

Smith, B., Caputi, P. and Rawstorne, P. (2000) Differentiating Computer Experience and Attitudes Toward Computers: an empirical investigation. *Computers in Human Behavior*, **16**, 59–81.

Zhang, D. and Nunamaker, J. F. (2003) Powering E-learning in the New Millennium: an overview of e-learning and enabling technology, *Information Systems Frontiers*, 5 (2), 207–18.

Appendix

SCES scores

Tables 4.3 and 4.4 show the SCES scores.

Table 4.3 SCES scores 1

		Minimum	Maximum	Mean	Standard deviation
Frustration 1	CE	1.60	3.80	2.43	.57
CE n = 20					
Frustration 2	CE	1.40	3.20	2.17	.49
Frustration 1	CA	2.00	4.80	3.30	.74
CA n = 45					
Frustration 2	CA	1.20	5.00	3.25	.87

Continued on next page

Table 4.3 *Continued*

		Minimum	Maximum	Mean	Standard deviation
Autonomy 1	CE	1.83	4.33	3.00	.65
CE n = 20					
Autonomy 2	CE	2.00	4.20	3.00	.52
Autonomy 1	CA	1.83	4.00	2.91	.49
CA n = 47					
Autonomy 2	CA	1.83	4.17	3.01	.49
Training 1	CE	1.33	5.00	2.86	.98
CE n = 20					
Training 2	CE	2.00	5.00	3.25	.75
Training 1	CA	1.33	4.67	3.05	.86
CA n = 41					
Training 2	CA	1.50	5.00	3.28	.69
Enjoyment 1	CE	2.50	4.40	3.48	.50
CE n = 20					
Enjoyment 2	CE	3.00	4.60	3.72	.46
Enjoyment 1	CA	1.00	3.80	2.66	.70
CA n = 47					
Enjoyment 2	CA	1.00	5.00	2.80	.80
Neg. self-efficiency 1	CE	2.83	5.00	3.98	.50
CE n = 20					
Neg. self-efficiency 2	CE	2.83	5.00	4.00	.72
Neg. self-efficiency 1	CA	1.50	4.83	3.23	.76
CA n = 45					
Neg. self-efficiency 2	CA	1.67	5.00	3.25	.87

Notes: CE = Civil Engineering, CA = Anthropology

Table 4.4 SCES scores 2

Cronbach's Alpha SCES	Smith et al.	Average IRBM	Average CA
Frustration	.86	.33	.74
Persistence	.68	.40	.56
Training	.83	.84	.73
Enjoyment	.70	.10	.71
Neg. self-efficiency	.78	.70	.82.

Notes: CA = Anthropology

SEES scores

Tables 4.5 and 4.6 show the SEES scores.

Table 4.5 SEES scores 1

		Minimum	Maximum	Mean	Standard deviation
Confidence 1	CE	2.71	3.94	3.36	.40
CE n = 20					
Confidence 2	CE	2.53	4.29	3.50	.48
Confidence 1	CA	1.60	4.12	2.91	.55
CA n = 47					
Confidence 2	CA	1.71	4.63	3.15	.64
Liking 1	CE	2.35	4.24	3.34	.49
CE n = 20					
Liking 2	CE	2.47	4.24	3.60	.40
Liking 1	CA	1.75	4.56	2.96	.67
CA n = 47					
Liking 2	CA	1.75	4.80	2.99	.62
Worthwhile 1	CE	1.94	4.00	3.19	.59
CE n = 20					
Worthwhile 2	CE	2.65	4.29	3.43	.51
Worthwhile 1	CA	2.12	4.47	3.36	.54
CA n = 47					
Worthwhile 2	CA	1.82	4.76	3.43	.63
Believing 1	CE	1.43	4.18	2.92	.81
CE n = 20					
Believing 2	CE	1.43	4.36	3.38	.80
Believing 1	CA	1.00	4.78	2.90	.80
CA n = 47					
Believing 2	CA	1.00	4.33	2.80	.74

Notes: CE = Civil Engineering, CA = Anthropology

Table 4.6 SEES scores 2

Cronbach's Alpha SEES	Average Alpha CE	Average Alpha CA
Confidence 1 Confidence 2	.74	.86
Liking 1 Liking 2	.86	.89
Worthwhile 1 Worthwhile 2	.81	.90
Believing 1 Believing 2	.90	.90

Notes: CE = Civil Engineering, CA = Anthropology

5

Library services and virtual learning: the DEViL project

Non Scantlebury and Liz Stevenson

Introduction

Many see the recent scale and pace of global e-learning developments as providing one of the biggest challenges to the library profession since its inception. Technological advances constantly pose new challenges to the way that we support the e-learning experience. In the education sector virtual learning environments (VLEs) are now considered to be an essential tool by a growing number of traditional learning providers who until recently concerned themselves purely with face-to-face delivery. The perception is that the VLEs bring a new competitive edge to provision.

Equally, traditional distance learning organizations, which previously monopolized the distance learning market, are having to respond to increasing competition by looking for new ways of engaging e-learners with quality learning experiences that directly result in increased retention and progression. Much of this agenda is driven by political and economic strategy at a national and global level.

It is against this backdrop, and taking account of the competing perspectives of academics, librarians and learning technologists, that the DEViL project sought to identify and address key issues for e-learning stakeholders.

DEViL (Dynamically Enhancing Virtual Learning Environments from within the Library) is a UK Joint Information Systems Committee (JISC) funded project forming part of JISC's 'Linking Digital Libraries with Virtual Learning Environments' Programme (JISC, 2002), and was undertaken in partnership between the University of Edinburgh and the Open University.

Disintermediated approaches to supporting the learner

A key technical part of the project undertook to develop a prototype software tool that would enable the exposure of a range of previously non-interoperable digital repositories to proprietary and non-proprietary virtual learning platforms. The meta-evaluation strand of the project considered the implications for intermediating digital collections at the object or asset level, while disintermediating some of the traditional learner support services that libraries have provided.

The evaluation methodology employed a range of strategies, including developing scenarios from use cases, carrying out face-to-face and telephone interviews, presentations and brief workshops with library staff, and analysis of reflective reports from team members engaged in delivering various parts of the project within their respective institutions.

E-learning stakeholders and behavioural entrenchment

Learning technologists continue to develop appropriate standards, which form the basis of a vision of shareable, repurposed content delivered via global ICT infrastructures. From the work of standards organizations like IMS and CETIS it is evident that there is a range of specifications and methods of wrapping and coding objects, and of content packaging. To enable these systems to interoperate, to provide the reality of a globally shared 'learning object economy', someone has to apply appropriate metadata to these valuable digital assets. These are technical solutions to an ultimately human problem, which will require various skills to guarantee provision of a robust solution to progress development and delivery of e-learning in the 21st century.

Recent research indicates that academics do not yet fully explore or exploit the potential that VLEs could bring to developing entirely new ways of learning (Beaty et al., 2002; Ramsey, 2002; Stiles, 2003).

The DEViL evaluation data controversially revealed that some academics still adopt 'transmissional' pedagogic approaches to teaching with VLEs, or hybrid electronic equivalents, and are mapping traditional behaviours into these environments. In this context there is a danger that librarians could find themselves marginalized, resulting in the library presence within VLEs being confined purely to provision of a search interface to the library catalogue. This may be the preoccupation of some of the learning technologists!

There is evidence within DEViL that librarians have already invested much time producing information literacy materials that attempt to enable learners to understand the digital assets and objects available to them from within internally created and third-party subscription databases. In addition, some learning technologists may be driven by the excitement of the opportunity to provide a technical solution to a particular problem, without taking account of the pedagogy. The diversity of opinion and entrenched perspectives over job roles emerged in the data collated by the project team. There was little evidence of a genuine teamwork approach to developing courseware, or of an approach that could provide the stimulus for the development of creative and innovative e-learning experiences for the future.

In a recent article by Stiles the lack of an all-round appreciation of pedagogy by all those involved in supporting e-learning is seen a critical limiting factor. This evidence of the mapping of traditional transmissional behavioural pedagogy into VLE course creation by academics was mirrored by the lack of engagement in pedagogy on the part of technologists and librarians in the data collated by the DEViL project. 'Failure to recognize the central importance of pedagogy also extends to those involved in supporting learning' (Stiles, 2003, 4). Stiles also notes the INSPIRAL report, which commented that '[pedagogic] issues have a history of being ignored by librarians in particular' (Currier, 2001, 5.2.3.2). There will have to be a considerable cultural shift in perspectives and skill mixes to reach an integrated solution that will provide engaging content and context support for future e-learners. This will require major shifts in behaviour on the part of all, and a need to move away from professional parochialism to true collaboration to meet the challenges of the future.

Mass e-learning by VLE delivery is still in its infancy and there is emergent criticism of VLES being characterized as content-centred. Following a brief piece of desk research, undertaken via an academic mailing list, Stiles presents the issues that underlie the factors that he had identified as responsible for the present limited success in the use of technology in learning:

- failure to engage the learner
- mistaking 'interactivity' for engagement
- focusing on content rather than outcomes
- failure to recognize the social nature of learning
- seeing discourse as the prime collaborative form (Stiles, 2003, 4).

What *is* the library's role?

Traditionally the library has provided an infrastructure and a range of tools to expose data and enable access to a wide range of resources, from 15th-century manuscripts to newspapers on microfilm, to an electronic book hosted on a publisher's server in Boulder, Colorado. The librarian is expert in cataloguing, providing bibliographic detail, information about the location and availability of a resource and its potential use. The explosion of digital publishing has changed the landscape and, while the data has become more complex, the issues of exposing and enabling access to resources remain the same.

The librarian has also had responsibility for the acquisition and management of resources, both print and electronic. Within the academic library context purchasing decisions are generally taken, in consultation with teaching and research staff, to ensure that appropriate resources are acquired. Until the 1990s the majority of the librarian's commercial dealings were with booksellers and journal subscription agents, and most libraries would spread their business across a range of suppliers, avoiding the perceived risk of 'putting all the eggs in one basket'. The growth in consortial purchasing, of both books and journals, has resulted in a reduction in the choice of suppliers used, and has led to an increased need for the librarian to develop negotiating and procurement skills. Within the UK there has been a growth in the choice of nationally negotiated deals, both for software and for digital content. The journal purchasing model has emerged as the most complex, and costly, characterized by the Big Deal (see, for example, Frazier, 2001). Journal inflation costs have always been high, a trend that is further exacerbated by the increased costs of access to electronic journals, and the additional cost of value added tax (VAT). A growing number of non-journal resources are bought on subscription, often with a multi-year commitment to purchase, resulting in a very significant proportion of a library's materials budget being spent on digital content. In the UK the JISC supports and advocates acquisition of these collections, but there are concerns that these rich resources are not being fully exploited or used, so that libraries are not getting the best return on their investment.

Most libraries do not have the resources to measure and monitor the real use of print collections effectively, but the expectation is that this should be achievable with electronic resources. Until now it has not always been possible to obtain consistent and comparable data on use of resources, and this is particularly evident in the case of electronic journals and databases. The work of Project COUNTER (www.projectcounter.org/) addresses this important issue, and should lead to provision of meaningful and useful data. Appropriate information about usage will help to inform purchasing decisions, and should provide detailed data on the actual cost of a resource, down to the cost per use. For full text resources this may result in a shift from subscription-based purchasing to an increase in provision of document-delivery services – acquiring what is actually required, rather than what might be needed.

Ensuring that appropriate and cost-effective content is acquired is one issue, but ensuring that it is then discovered and used is another. Incorporating information about resources into VLEs, with links to full text, is an important development in this area, but needs to take full account of the processes involved. In examining the set-up of one course within the Open University, DEViL has highlighted the problems posed by authentication, and has identified complex barriers to be negotiated before the resource is found. Somewhat ironically, the widening access offered by electronic resources is currently constrained by the terms and conditions of many commercial licence agreements. These require the library to ensure that access to resources is limited to accredited staff and students of the institution – an exception is sometimes made for walk-in users, where external users may consult an electronic resource on library premises. This means that the authentication process is important, not only to enable secure access to the institutional network both on and off campus, but to guarantee that access to costly, licensed resources is protected, and to ensure that the institution is seen to be complying with the licence terms. The librarian's role as gatekeeper and adviser is important, but it can be perceived as blocking rather than enabling use of resources.

Licences may offer a degree of flexibility, permitting the temporary repurposing of content, allowing incorporation of a journal article or book chapter within an electronic course pack. This will not help the user to discover and explore new resources, but it does enhance the service to the user, eliminating some of the barriers to use. The required item is only one click away from the resource list within the VLE, without need for further authentication.

In addition to licensed third-party content, the library is likely to host a range of full text resources within closed repositories. Examples of these are databases of course reserve materials and databases of exam papers. In most instances these are not commercially licensed subscribed resources. In the case of a course reserve repository, there will be a collection of copyright-cleared print and electronic materials, whose use and access are subject to particular terms and conditions. These transactions are usually brokered by the library. In the case of an exam papers database there will be institutional copyright to consider. In both cases there will be access controls in place. These significant resources have already incurred considerable costs to the institution, both in terms of record and resource creation, copyright clearance costs and ongoing service management. For resources that may form part of an institutional archive, such as exam papers, there are preservation and archiving issues and costs to be considered.

The Open University H806 course – 'Learning in the connected economy'

The H806 course developed at the Open University and delivered via the Sun UKeU platform was one of the pilot courses investigated as part of the DEViL project, and is a good example of why librarians should be involved in crafting courses. The issues of access to third-party content and rights management had direct implications for the experience of learners on the course. Not only was the course innovative, in that it was entirely constructed from learning objects, but it was also delivered via a platform external to the organization.

Digital assets from the library were used, in the form of articles provided via third-party subscription databases. In this case the team did not reuse existing externally provided learning objects but created new ones for the course. The team did repurpose (use or convert for use in another format or product) internally owned content. The model for a 'learning object economy' envisages the possibility of being able to repurpose globally and share learning objects. However, under present rights agreements and licence conditions the library-supplied digital assets would have to be decoupled from the object should anyone wish to reuse and repurpose the objects created for H806. In turn, this would have an effect on the coherence of the learning object. The whole is the sum of its parts here!

The course created from these learning objects is delivered via an external platform to the organization and this resulted in difficulties with seamless authentication to library supplied digital articles under strict organizational licensing agreements. At the time of the project DEViL investigation, in order to access the content, students had to take a complex authentication route from the Sun platform into the databases page on the library website, and several clicks later accessed the full text of the article.

This example demonstrates the very admirable attempts of an enthusiastic course team wishing to use available resources fully by adopting an innovative and exciting approach, but crashing directly into the licensing barrier in the outside lane! This course also served to demonstrate pragmatically the actual costs to students and course teams of following a disintermediated approach to library services even though there had been direct use of assets. When students encountered a case of 'link rot', which resulted in the failure to retrieve a required full text article supplied by the library digitally, they had not been supplied with appropriate signposting to the library learner support services for help and assistance should these be required. By disintermediating the library learner support function from the course site, this unintentionally led to increased costs in time and frustration for students on the course when they encountered problems. There were useful lessons learned, however, for the future design and delivery of courses via the UkeU platform and a practical illustration of the need to ensure library support presence in courses even when library presence is perceived not to be a requirement.

In a world of increasing competition for e-learning services it is even more imperative that librarians become fully engaged with the crafting of the content of them and play a key role in supporting learning through greater facilitation. There are strong arguments here to support the case that the agenda should not be driven simply by developing technical systems in the abstract sense to render assets and learning objects from digital collections into VLEs. Disintermediating librarians, who have considerable knowledge and expertise in the acquisition, management, exploitation and development of both print and digital collections, from the engineering and design of the learning process, will not ensure best practice in course design for our present and future e-learners.

The work of DEViL concluded in August 2003 when the project reports were submitted to the JISC. Full details of the project are available from http://srv1.mvm.ed.ac.uk/devilweb/index.asp.

References

Beaty, E., Hodgson, V., Mann, S. and McConnell, D. (2002) Working Towards E-quality in Networked E-learning in Higher Education: a manifesto statement for debate, ESRC, http://csalt.lancs.ac.uk/esrc/manifesto.htm.

Currier, S. (2001) *INSPIRAL: final report*, Strathclyde, Centre for Digital Library Research, www.inspiral.cdlr.strath.ac.uk.

Frazier, K. (2001) The Librarians' Dilemma: contemplating the costs of the 'Big Deal', *D-Lib Magazine*, **7** (3).

Joint Information Systems Committee (2002) Linking Digital Libraries with Virtual Learning Environments, Circular 7/02, JISC, www.jisc.ac.uk/index.cfm?name=circular_07_02.

Ramsey, C. (2002) Using Virtual Learning Environments to Facilitate New Learning Relationships. In *BEST 2002 Annual Conference*, 8–10 April 2002, Edinburgh, www.business.ltsn.ac.uk/events/BEST%202002/Papers/c_ramsey.PDF.

Stiles, M. (2003) Strategic and Pedagogic Requirements for Virtual Learning in the Context of Widening Participation, www.inter-disciplinary.net/Stiles%20Paper.pdf.

6

Virtual learning and teaching resources: the library as a collaborator

A. Anneli Ahtola

Introduction

Learning, teaching and research methods are undergoing rapid and significant changes, which are affecting everybody who reads or writes. Electronic resources are increasingly selected as an information source, and research results are disseminated via information networks. Electronic media also bring about a transformation in how librarians think about their jobs, about information users, and about the whole communication process that they are a part of.

Digital publishing has critical implications for teaching and learning, and calls for a fresh look being taken at instructional strategies and the accessibility of information. Electronic resources and digital libraries have the capacity and promise to affect education significantly, and have an opportunity to create a new environment for teaching and learning (Dowler, 1997). This paper will reflect on environmental changes that affect libraries and identify activities that generate added value for teaching and learning, and which Tampere University library has adopted.

Changes in the work environment

Trends in publishing

Anything that happens in the publishing field affects libraries and there are many changes in scientific information and publishing structures. In some fields electronic publishing has surpassed its printed counterpart, so that many important materials do not exist in conventional formats any longer.

Libraries have an important proactive role in developing and using new publishing channels, and also in assisting faculty and students to make use of those channels. Libraries remain relevant only as long as they supply collections and services that meet the changing needs of their users in the classroom and at the desktop.

Characteristics of university libraries' clientele

The user demographics of university libraries are getting more diverse. Faculty and students are increasingly wide-ranging in their interests, background and skills, and display an increasingly varying set of information needs and expectations. Furthermore, new fields of study and the emergence of virtual universities place additional demands on libraries.

Learning and teaching strategies

New views about learning and teaching with more emphasis on cognition are emerging and the problem-based method is becoming more prevalent. This method emphasizes active learning and expects students to become self-directed learners, assuming more responsibility for information gathering through exploring information resources and networks. Electronic resources offer innovative approaches to teaching, and make virtual, web-based teaching and learning possible (Poikela, 2001). Besides librarians, educators also emphasize that information literacy skills are needed to make effective use of the overwhelming 'cyber space jungle'.

Student learning, faculty teaching and scholarship will suffer without the intellectual wealth and versatility of library resources and services. Very few people or organizations work by themselves to achieve the best results and this is certainly true for university libraries. Strategic alliances and collaborative partnerships are central to the library's mission, and are of paramount importance in advancing libraries' goals, services and programmes (Rockman, 2001).

Activities that generate added value for teaching and learning

Finland as an information society

It is a national goal in Finland that all segments of society should live in an 'information society'. The Ministry of Education aims to raise the level of education and research and to advance every citizen's potential and skills in the effective use of information technology and telecommunications. The national goal naturally presumes libraries will offer appropriate services to meet the challenge.

Tampere University

Tampere University is the third biggest university in Finland. It is multidisciplinary and has six faculties – Economics and Administration, Education, Humanities, Information Sciences, Medicine and Social Sciences. There are more than 14,000 degree-students and approximately 500 foreign students. Around 160,000 students attend courses yearly through Extension Services. Personnel consists of about 1800 people, out of whom half are teaching or research staff (www.uta.fi/english/index.html).

Tampere University library

The library consists of the main library and two branch libraries, one in medicine and the others in humanities and education. The latter also administers a teacher education unit in a nearby town (www.uta.fi//kirjasto/lib/). The library is open to all. In 2002, there were 71 permanent staff positions of which 25 were professional.

At the end of 2002 the online catalogue had bibliographic data for more than 818,000 monographs and periodicals. The electronic periodical collection consisted of 8319 titles, and there were 132 electronic databases. The library belongs to the Finnish National Electronic Library Consortium (FinELib) (www.lib.helsinki.fi/finelib/english/index.html) and the great majority of electronic resources are acquired through this organization.

The library's goal is to take care of new students' needs and to serve researchers at different stages of their work, from when they begin their research to when they publish results. The library strives to function as a hybrid library, integrating printed and digital resources and combining the traditional library space with the virtual space to accommodate the changing scholarly environment of the University. The library strives to become more visible on campus, more involved in teaching, learning and research, and more effective in producing positive learning outcomes.

Collaboration

Collaboration has intrinsic value in library activities and is regarded as an underlying prerequisite for success. Building partnerships and working as strategic partners within and outside the university enable libraries to share their knowledge capital with that of their partners (Iivonen, 2003). When services are made transparent, then the benefits of a partnership will be clear to all parties involved. In a successful partnership everybody has to give something, and then they will also receive something in return. The desire for collaboration is restricted to libraries: research indicates that an important shift in faculty attitudes and expectations has taken place, so that many faculty members are receptive to partnerships with libraries at a higher level than traditionally (Ducas and Michaud-Oystryk, 2003).

There is a natural connection between members of academic faculties and staff in research libraries and it is important that research library staff collaborate with faculty members and other stakeholders at the university. Students form the biggest user group, so it is essential to address their needs. Collaboration with the administration helps integrate libraries into the rest of the university and makes the decision-makers knowledgeable about the information the library provides. At Tampere student government representatives and top university officials are invited to the library a few times a year, concise presentations are prepared on selected current topics, and ideas are exchanged over breakfast or afternoon coffee. The library has permanent representation on several university-wide committees, such as the Teaching Council and the Information and Communications Technology Council.

Liaison programme

The purpose of liaison activity is to overcome the distance, both physical and psychological, between the departments and the library, to integrate the library and its resources more closely into the daily academic work, to acquire a more educated understanding of each others' services and needs, to build interpersonal relationships and to facilitate both informal and formal partnerships with faculty, and, at the same time, to improve the library's status on campus (Seamans and Metz, 2002).

The liaison work is not a new concept at Tampere University library. The programme was rethought and given greater emphasis in 2002 so that every department now has a specified liaison librarian. While some faculty members tend to hold traditional ideas about the role of the library and about the scope of its services, and are uninformed of the spectrum of services available as well as of librarians' skills and capabilities, there is a high degree of confidence in the library and its expertise. The library has been invited to participate in interdepartmental projects, which emphasize the skills that are beneficial for effective teaching and learning, and provide readiness for lifelong learning. In addition to the library, the computer, language and hypermedia centres and the statistics department have been involved. Besides building and improving the services, the projects aim to raise their visibility and awareness among teachers and students.

The library's learning centre

The library's learning centre project supports an open learning environment, which enables web-based services to be integrated and contributes to virtual university education. The project has been a vehicle to develop the library as a modern learning environment by offering working space, workstations and other equipment, and selected software, learning resources and reference services for patrons' use. The project has received sizeable funding from the University's development monies.

The ACRL guidelines (2003) state that the library facilities should be well planned, provide adequate space, be conducive to study and research, and have adequate and functional equipment to support resource-based learning. The learning centre project follows these guidelines. At the start of the project the library was able to accommodate multiform learning and teaching only very modestly. During the project, extensive renovations and remodelling of the premises have taken place. The number of workstations in peaceful settings has increased, several scanners and multiple study-supporting software have been acquired, and group work areas have been established in all library units. Furthermore, a wireless reading room will be set up in the main library in autumn 2003.

Digitization

The library has established a new service entity of acquiring, producing and developing digital course material needed in web-based teaching. Digitization, or digital conversion of material, is a tool to build customized collections tailored to local research interests and teaching programmes. The service covers copyright and digital rights management, and steps from digitization of requested resources, such as articles, book chapters and out of print books, to their online introduction. The process as a whole has turned out to be laborious and time-consuming. Usage rights place restrictions on access so that only some resources are freely accessible on the internet or on university network computers, while others are only accessed within a closed learning environment, such as WebCT. Even though digitization assignments have been fewer than originally expected, it is not feasible, or even possible, to digitize everything. Digitization criteria with a fee structure have been formulated for potential future use.

Electronic books

The Pew Internet & American Life Project (2002) presents data to show that students' use of web-based resources has increased rapidly and that their preference for online resources is becoming predominant. Users naturally go after convenience and easy access. Also, the problem-based method with its analytic approach benefits from digital material more than traditional linear reading. Consequently, the library is investing in digital books. This format is seen as a partial solution to both out of print and heavily used textbooks.

netLibrary

Tampere University library is the first library in Finland to acquire netLibrary (www.netlibrary.com/). From this collection, 94 titles were selected and bought for five years. One-third of selected titles are required course readings. In addition to the acquired titles, patrons have some 3500 books from the public collection at their perusal. The user rights are limited as a result of the traditional print version purchase model, a one-copy-one-user model. Nevertheless, the purchase was considered worthwhile because the selected collection includes many heavily used and expensive books, and because the electronic format adds to the number of available copies also accessible from outside the library building.

Later in autumn 2003 a survey of usage patterns and usability of netLibrary will be carried out. The usage statistics for the first six months of 2003 show that all the selected titles had been used, and the collection had been accessed over 800 times.

Tampere University Press

Libraries have a full role in the information cycle of their learning communities and participate in the creation of knowledge in addition to accessing and archiving knowledge. Academic libraries are increasingly becoming publishing arms of their universities (McMillan, 2000) and Tampere University library is no exception to this trend.

Tampere University Press (TUP) (www.uta.fi//kirjasto/julkaisukeskus/tupengl.html), which is operated and managed in the library, supports innovation in scholarly communication. It publishes printed monographs and their digital conversions. So far, electronic publishing by TUP has meant replication of printed versions. Lynch (2001) has appropriately called this type of publishing 'printed books stored in digital form'. TUP has granted the library unlimited user rights to those digital-format books, which are either required textbooks or else other much used books.

Electronic theses and dissertations

Academic libraries have an important role in making scholarly information public. Tampere University library assists in the processing of electronic materials and helps faculty and students publish and archive electronic documents. The library develops, organizes and maintains the electronic theses and dissertations (ETD) databases of the University.

While 85% of dissertations were published electronically in 2002, only 7.7% of theses were published this way. The library is actively promoting digital publishing through the teaching departments hoping that students realize the benefits of net publishing skills, and understand that having these skills is a marketable asset in their portfolio.

Writing and research help devices

Besides the more traditional materials, such as books and periodicals, the library supports teaching, learning and research by new services linked with writing and publishing.

The library has designed online writing templates for ETDs. The purpose of the templates is to provide formatting standards to achieve uniformity in the document layout, and to facilitate the electronic publication process. The templates allow the author to concentrate on the contents while the layout will be created automatically.

When the library acquired RefWorks (www.refworks.com/), a web-based bibliography and database manager used for a trial period, it was received with enthusiastic welcome by researchers. This is understandable, because the program saves on typing time, decreases the number of potential errors, and allows reorganization and reformatting of references to provide a uniform format for bibliographies.

Information literacy

The fact that students are attracted by the speed and convenience of the web and often use unevaluated and inappropriate resources means that information seeking skills need to be taught (Grimes and Boening, 2001). Information literacy is regarded a fundamental component of the educational process at all levels, and one of the primary outcomes of higher education (Dewald et al., 2000; ACRL, 2003).

Information literacy is not the sole territory of librarians, however. Librarians do not own it, and it is not always described in terms that librarians would use (Oberman, 2002). Joint instructional programmes and course-integrated training are ways to impart lifelong learning skills by combining the expertise of teaching faculty and librarians with professional visions (Herring, 2001).

At Tampere the demand for tailored web-based instruction tutorials has been low. This may be because library education is not included in the official curriculum in all faculties, or because the web has not yet become a commonly used educational method. To speculate further, one is tempted to suspect that the faculty might somehow be sceptical, consciously or unconsciously, of librarians teaching. Perhaps they fear that librarians are stepping on their turf, which traditionally has been the faculty's exclusive domain, and so are stealing something of their expertise. The librarian-as-teacher concept acknowledges that many activities connected with students' research, including learning, takes place in libraries in addition to the classroom, and that librarians are in a good position to facilitate that learning (Wilkinson, 1997).

Survey of service quality

Tampere University library is a service-oriented library and it is of paramount importance to know what the patrons need and which services they consider relevant so that responsive and proactive measures can be taken to build a meaningful future. Accordingly, the library performed a web-based service quality survey in autumn 2002, using a questionnaire consisting of 38 variables, which the respondents were asked to rate in order of importance or degree of satisfaction. The survey showed that having access to collections and other information and the provision of networked services were among the most valued services. Overall, the results produced helpful information for decision-making.

In addition to more traditional library functions the library has adopted many new ones, which require completely new skills or deepening of already existing ones. To cope with new expectations, an extensive staff educational programme has been launched, which concentrates on computer, networking, interpersonal and training skills. A well-qualified body of staff is seen as a prerequisite for its success.

Conclusions

The changing academic environment also calls for new skills in libraries. These are more varied than before, and include strong communication skills, both oral and written, interpersonal skills, and leadership and innovative skills (Huotari, 1999). These new skills go beyond the traditional knowledge base of librarianship (Lynch and Smith, 2001).

Change always brings a range of options, which enable libraries to give their value-added share to teaching and learning. Given their skills, experience, values and philosophical framework, librarians have an essential role in the learning communities that they serve, and should be ready and willing to assume leadership roles. Paradigm shifts in libraries are required if librarians are to control their own future successfully. Libraries need to imagine the future they want, then make it real, and dare to take risks (Stoffle et al., 2000, 894–7).

The change brings opportunities to use the knowledge and ingenuity that is inherent in libraries fully. This knowledge can be used in collaboration with expertise within and outside the university to help attain the institutional mission and goals. Investments do not always have to be large. Academic libraries can no longer afford to be silent partners in their learning communities. They cannot just ask to be trusted, but instead they have to show how they can be integral parts of academic communities, and partners worth trusting (Huotari & Iivonen, 2001). Established relationships provide a steady foundation for ongoing collaboration.

References

ACRL (2003) *Guidelines for Distance Learning Library Services, draft revision*, May 29, www.ala.org/Content/NavigationMenu/ACRL/Standards_and_Guidelines/Guidelines_for_Distance_Learning_library_Services1.htm.

Dewald, N., Scholz-Crane, A., Booth, A. and Levine, C. (2000) Information Literacy at a Distance: instructional design issues, *Journal of Academic Librarianship*, **26** (January), 33–45.

Dowler, L. (ed.) (1997) *Gateways to Knowledge: the role of academic libraries in teaching, learning, and research*, Cambridge, MIT Press, www.netlibrary.com/.

Ducas, A. M. and Michaud-Oystryk, N. (2003) Toward a New Enterprise: capitalizing on the faculty/librarian partnership, *College & Research Libraries*, **64** (1), 55–74.

Grimes, D. J. and Boening, C. H. (2001) Worries with the Web: a look at student use of web resources, *College & Research Libraries*, **62** (1), 11–23.

Herring, S. D. (2001) Faculty Acceptance of the World Wide Web for Student Research, *College & Research Libraries*, **62** (3), 251–8.

Huotari, M. (1999) Informaatioammatit Yhteiskunnan Murroksessa – Muutosko Pysyvää? [Information Professions in the Societal Transition – Constant Change?], *Informaatiotutkimus*, **18** (4), 97–102.

Huotari, M. and Iivonen, M. (2001) University Library – A Strategic Partner in Knowledge and Information Related Processes. In Aversa, E. and Manley, C. (eds), *Information in a Networked World: harnessing the flow; Proceedings of the 64th ASIST Annual Meeting* held on 3–8 November 2001, organized by the American Society for Information Science and Technology (ASIST), Washington DC, Medford, Information Today.

Iivonen, M. (2003) Future Scenarios for Libraries – Finnish Perspective, *Signum*, **36** (4), 96–8.

Lynch, B. P. and Smith, K. R. (2001), The Changing Nature of Work in Academic Libraries, *College & Research Libraries*, **62** (5), 407–20.

Lynch, C. (2001) What do Digital Books Mean for Libraries?, *Journal of Library Administration*, **35** (3), 21–32.

McMillan, G. (2000), Librarians as Publishers: is the digital library an electronic publisher?, *College & Research Libraries News*, **61** (10), 928–31.

Oberman, C. (2002) Introduction. In Grassian, E. and Kaplowitz, J. *Information Literacy Instruction: theory and practice*, New York, Neal-Schuman.

Pew Internet & American Life Project (2002) *The Internet Goes to College: how students are living in the future with today's technology*, www.pewinternet.org

Poikela, E. (2001) Ongelmaperustainen Oppiminen Yliopistossa [Problem-Based Learning at the University]. In Poikela, E. and Oystila, S. (eds) *Tutkiminen on Oppimista – ja Oppiminen Tutkimista* [*Research is Learning – and Learning is Research*], Tampere, Tampere University Press.

Rockman, I. F. (2001) Strategic Alliances: the power of collaborative partnerships, *College & Research Libraries News*, **62** (6), 616–18.

Seamans, N. H. and Metz, P. (2002) Virginia Tech's Innovative College Librarian Program, *College & Research Libraries*, **63** (4), 324–32.

Stoffle, C., Allen, B., Fore, J. and Mobley, E. R. (2000) Predicting the Future: reinventing academic libraries and librarianship, *College & Research Libraries News*, **61** (10), 894–7.

Wilkinson, J. (1997) Homesteading on the Electronic Frontier: technology, libraries, and learning. In Dowler, L. (ed.), *Gateways to Knowledge: the role of academic libraries in teaching, learning, and research*, Cambridge, MIT Press, www.netlibrary.com/.

7

Virtual learning environments and Greek academic libraries

Emmanouel Garoufallou, Rania Siatri and Dick Hartley

Introduction

This paper examines developments in Greek academic libraries using recent research data and the literature and considers whether Greek libraries are ready to support developments in the virtual learning environments (VLEs) of their institutions. To understand the current situation in Greek academic libraries it is necessary to appreciate the Greek higher education system. A description of this is given in the next section of the paper, followed by a summary of the current academic library position. This demonstrates the crucial impact on Greek academic library development of the European Union Second Community Support Framework (SCSF). This discussion leads naturally into the Third Community Support Framework (TCSF), which Greek universities are using to develop VLEs. We describe current developments at the University of Macedonia in Thessaloniki as an example.

Higher education in Greece

Supervision of education in Greece is highly centralized. The Ministry of Education and Religious Affairs controls every level of the educational system through numerous laws and government bodies. Schools, institutions and universities at every level depend financially on the Ministry, which pays all the staff. Furthermore it approves the curricula and controls institutions through a series of centralized bodies.

Higher education in Greece is divided into two levels: the higher education institutions (HEIs), which comprise the universities (anotata ekpaideutika idrimata, AEI, in Greek) and the higher technological educational institutions (anotata technologika ekpaideutika idrimata, ATEI, in Greek), the latter having similarities with the old polytechnics in the UK. AEI concentrate on theoretical and scientific studies and traditional disciplines while ATEI focus on vocational, technological and technical studies. Greece has 34 HEIs (19 AEI, 14 ATEI and the Open University). Education provided by the Greek state is free at all levels and in HE includes free meals for most students and free accommodation for a minority of students.

Educational practices in Greece follow a unique path. The Organization for Publishing Teaching Books (Organismos Ekdoseon Didaktikon Biblion, OEDB, in Greek), under the auspices of the Ministry of Education, publishes one book for each subject or unit for the school sector, and distributes them to schools across Greece. Teachers base their teaching solely on the lectures and exercises in these books. This practice continues at university level. Education is based exclusively on academics' lecture notes, handouts, or a single textbook published either via a commercial publisher or in Simiosis. Simiosis are lecture notes that cover a subject or a unit. The lecturer composes the text that is to be used for teaching and then the department has the responsibility to check its quality. When the department approves it the institution 'publishes' it using reprographic techniques. The vast majority of textbooks in ATEI are Simiosis. Each student gets a textbook for each unit or subject free of charge. Students know that reading a single text per unit is quite enough to pass the unit. This approach to teaching and learning, based as it is on the opinion of a single teacher, and not requiring the exploration of other opinions and ideas, is at best anachronistic and at worst medieval.

Academic libraries in Greece

In this section we summarize the state of Greek academic libraries by the mid-1990s, explain the Second Community Support Framework (SCSF) and consider how libraries have developed through the support it provided.

Greek academic libraries until the mid-1990s

Given the educational environment in which they were operating, it is scarcely surprising that Greek academic libraries played little part in the educational process and until very recently were scarcely viewed as a part of the teaching and learning process. They were more likely to be seen as financial burdens on their parent institutions. A former minister of education, Tritsis (1987, 46), noted that 'the tradition of one basic textbook kills university education'. Furthermore Babiniotis believed that as a result of the one textbook policy 'students stop visiting university libraries . . . [and] today our libraries have the silence of a cemetery' (Babiniotis, 1990, 32).

Our experience and the writings of others (Raptis and Sitas, 1996; Smethurst, Line and Owen, 1997) and a study by the Greek National Documentation Centre (1995), with only a few exceptions, show that before the SCSF academic libraries suffered from:

- limited and uncertain funding
- inadequate staffing both in terms of quality and quantity
- poor buildings and collections with limited opening hours
- university structures and processes that often inhibited the influence of the few professional librarians
- teaching and learning methods that inhibited library development
- lack of strategic planning and management skills
- limited use of international standards
- limited effective use of information technology
- lack of inter-library co-operation
- a very poor image for librarians within the academic community.

The Second Community Support Framework

The support from the EC's regional development plan (RDP) for 1994 to 1999 was the catalyst for the modernization of Greek academic libraries under the Axis No. 4 Development of Human Resources and Employment Promotion. In 1996 academic libraries through SCSF and its special Action of the Operational Programme for Education and Initial Training (EPEAEK in Greek; www.epeaek.gr) started rapidly to change and improve services. This action sought:

- to modernize library services and establish new IT-based services
- to develop the role of the central university libraries and develop a library infrastructure at the institutions with departmental, faculty and central library but no centralized system
- to automate library functions by upgrading existing or acquiring new library management systems (LMS)
- to enrich library collections, create special, multiple copy and short loan collections
- to staff libraries with qualified librarians.

The SCSF programme had two lines of action and a budget of £46.8 million to be shared among Greek institutional libraries. The first line of action (the vertical line) sought the development of each institutional library in order to modernize and develop library services, to implement a library management system, to enrich its collections, to complete its retrospective cataloguing and to provide qualified personnel. The second line of action (the horizontal line) aimed to develop a national infrastructure that would support the future development of libraries and institutions and enable them to be competitive educational bodies in a unified European Community. The horizontal line had four axes: creating a union catalogue of the Greek academic libraries, establishing a serials cost working group, establishing an inter-university digital library system for grey literature and training librarians.

The impact of SCSF

Data collection for another project suggests that there was remarkable development in Greek academic libraries as a result of the SCSF (Garoufallou, 1999, 2003; Garoufallou and Siatri, 1999). This work used a survey of a sample of the staff in all 157 identifiable academic libraries in 32 Greek HEIs. The 129 responses represented a response rate of 53%. Additional data was collected by interviewing librarians, academics and administrators. The data requires several papers to offer a full picture and in the available space we have quoted only a minute selection of quantitative and qualitative data to demonstrate the noticeable changes in Greek academic libraries.

The data shows that at the end of the 20th century 85% of libraries had an LMS and a similar number offered access to electronic information resources, though in 20% of cases this was access for library staff only. In those libraries where end-users had access to OPACs, often only a limited number of terminals were available; in more than 20% of cases only one or two were available. However, it must be recalled that many of the libraries are small departmental libraries.

Around 85% of academic libraries had access to some form of electronic information resource (EIR) such as CD-ROMs and online databases. However, 45% of libraries had no budget for purchasing EIR access and only 3% of libraries had an explicit policy regarding use of EIRs. At the time of data collection, 70% of libraries provided internet access but only 40% had websites. While this may appear to be providing only limited access, it is in fact a transformation in a short space of time. The dramatic changes are borne out by comments from librarians about how their working lives have been changed. The majority now indicate that they could not do their jobs without IT; typical of their comments is the librarian who noted that EIRs 'broaden my horizons as a professional because I learn how to search and retrieve information from EIR. As a result I feel more confident in work and richer in knowledge.'

Further examination of the data from the interviews showed that while these figures indicated considerable progress, they masked considerable problems. The number of PCs is often limited, as is staff awareness to exploit them. While we noted that there was considerable enthusiasm for the use of IT, we also observed that many respondents had a poor understanding of the technology that they use regularly, for example not distinguishing between a browser and a search engine.

A major development has been the transformation of the attitude of the other parts of the university towards library staff. This attitude is usually much more positive, with librarians perceived as agents for change and central to achieving the university mission. Three typical quotations illustrate the improved attitude towards an image of Greek academic librarians. One computer scientist believed that 'librarians fulfil more than 90% of the needs of our academic community' and he illustrated his point by saying that 'without librarians academic staff are like cars without engines'. He was concerned that librarians are not aware that many academics value their work and that they rely on librarians even for the successful delivery of a unit. One of the reasons may be that some academics still hold unconstructive views regarding librarians but 'most academics view librarians as the engine and the car altogether in the institution'. Another believed that 'the university, without admitting it openly, based many hopes on librarians for developing further our library and meeting the demands of a university at the 21st century'. Finally, another academic believed that the SCSF helped librarians 'to establish their profession in the university . . . and showed academics that they are professionals and not workers'. He used an analogy to illustrate the important role that is placed upon librarians:

> If I am able to use an example from the army, I believe librarians are the support or plan forces in an army. Even though they are not getting directly involved in the war, without their help the soldiers [students] and their commanders [academic staff] would not survive or win the war. They provide valuable, up to date information, help the academic community with research, provide access to electronic resources and training to students.

The Third Community Support Framework (TCSF)

Currently, Greek academic libraries are participating in the Third Community Support Framework Programme (second EPEAEK), which runs from 2000 to 2006. The TCSF again has vertical and horizontal action lines. Both lines focus mainly on the further development of SCSF-funded achievements, including the continuity and financial stability of the projects. The main difference of the new programme is that the TCSF programme provides little support to libraries in areas such as employment of new staff, LMS implementation and IT acquisition. So libraries are focusing on improving old and establishing new services in areas such as portals, VLEs, digital libraries and digitization. In the remainder of this paper we concentrate on VLEs and academic libraries in Greece.

VLEs and Greek academic libraries

Like their counterparts in many other countries, Greek academic libraries and their parent institutions are faced with the problems posed by an increasing student population, rapidly expanding electronic information resources and severe budgetary constraints. A further problem in Greece is that, for reasons of political expediency, universities often have campuses in more than one location; these are not simply multiple campuses in the same town or city but campuses in different cities – in the case of the University of the Aegean, campuses on different islands. A consequence of this is further budgetary restrictions and limitations of facilities. Increasingly Greek students are finding it necessary to work to support themselves through their studies. These factors combine to encourage Greek universities to explore the increased use of information technology, including VLEs, to enable a more flexible approach to learning.

The Aristotle University in Thessaloniki, the University of Patras, the University of Thessaly and TEI Thessaloniki have or are undertaking projects that explore the potential use of VLEs in Greek HEIs. As yet unsuccessful attempts have been made to create collaborative efforts among these institutions. In this paper we concentrate on discussing the project at the University of Macedonia, whose experiences in many ways illustrate some of the challenges facing HEIs in Greece.

University of Macedonia case study

The University of Macedonia (Economics and Social Sciences) is one of the newer universities in Greece, created in 1990 from a graduate school, which itself was set up in 1957. It has approximately 140 academic staff and 6000 active students.

One TCSF-funded project at the University of Macedonia is to promote the development of electronic courses. It seeks to create a VLE that will act simultaneously as an online tool and resource for interactive education for students and academics. The objectives are:

- to provide access to teaching material from anywhere irrespective of the university premises
- to allow academics to have a more holistic view of their teaching and provide space for changes and improvements at a more consistent and detailed level
- to allow adaptation of teaching to individual user needs
- to create a discussion forum for each unit
- to digitize the reserve collection and link to the course material.

The University of Macedonia library has started to explore issues concerning the decision to install, develop and maintain a VLE. Seven phases were identified for the implementation of the project:

- market research
- communication with academics
- piloting the system
- evaluation of the pilot
- implementing the system
- user education
- disseminating and marketing the project.

By 'market research' is meant an investigation of the available VLE software. It was rapidly noted that the University had to use either commercially produced or open source software. Indeed the choice between these options was the first and most controversial decision to be made. The library wanted to purchase Blackboard, as it provided a greater coverage of the university's needs as well as being the choice of three other universities in Greece. This could provide opportunities for closer co-operation in areas such as sharing expertise of the software and exchanging course materials. Furthermore there would be the possibility of a stronger negotiating position with the company, considering that this would be their first break into the Greek market. However, the university administration requested that the library should acquire the open source software, E-Class, which has been translated and developed from Claroline to accommodate the needs of Greek universities by the GUNET (Greek University NETwork), which formed part of a project under the SCSF and is supported officially by the Ministry of Education.

According to the initial specifications report, E-Class could not adequately serve the community. However, having decided to use this software, it was necessary to examine its pros and cons. On the negative side it became apparent that it could not support a fully developed distance learning course. However, it does offer an alternative platform and distribution aid for delivering a unit. Another drawback is the lack of a feature that could link library and teaching material. The absence of such a feature raised concerns over the use of convenient information sources by the academics at the expense of library resources. For example, a list of further reading might comprise links to websites, which are much more convenient to create than checking for new print or electronic resources available via the library. These issues are discussed by MacColl (2001) with reference to the ANGEL project, which aims to overcome these difficulties.

On the positive side, E-Class offers a very friendly interface with well-signed and labelled menus and options that makes it easy to use for a first time user.

Given that most of the academics have not used such software before these features may prove to be very important advantages in encouraging academics to experiment with VLEs. Another important issue is that the technical support is based in Greece, unlike the other software we considered. The GUNET team has proved to be easy to approach and has been ready and willing to offer advice and support whenever they have been contacted. Furthermore they are committed to further development and support of the product. So it is hoped that the university has chosen a VLE with a stable and secure future. Finally the absence of any purchase cost is attractive because it enables the money saved to be used in areas such as training.

Having chosen and implemented the software, the next important step was to approach the academics and persuade them to participate in the pilot; we contacted 24 academics (three from each of eight departments). We sent an explanatory letter and three short papers on distance learning, the principles of VLEs and an introduction to E-Class. After one week we telephoned them to determine whether they were willing to have an initial meeting to gain a better understanding of the pilot and their contribution to it.

One difficulty in the meetings with the first three academics was their attitudes towards the librarian present; they were rather distant and reluctant to learn. The librarian was not treated as an equal and they appeared sceptical of the fact that this project was paid for by the library research grant. To overcome this obstacle, in the subsequent initial meetings the librarian introduced herself as being both on the university library staff and a lecturer in the Department of Library and Information Systems at TEI Thessaloniki. This seemed to improve relations and the session was then presented from the academics' perspective with indications of how using E-class could benefit the students in TEI. Consequently the academics seemed interested and more eager to learn about the project. Whereas the first three rejected the idea, the rest were keen to use E-Class, although most of them made clear that it was impossible for them to participate in the pilot owing to time constraints and work overload. However, they confirmed that they would like to use the software in the near future when they would have more time to dedicate to the concept of e-learning and the preparation of teaching material. Academics in two departments (Balkan Studies and Music), while enthusiastic about the project, felt intimidated as they seemed less confident with the use of IT and rather overestimated the knowledge they would need to use this software.

Six academics accepted the invitation and felt confident that they would be able to prepare their teaching material in time for the pilot. For the pilot it was decided to concentrate on academics who were comfortable in their use of IT.

In September 2003 the library is seeking to re-form its group of participants after the summer vacation. It is expected that by the end of October 2003 between 10 and 12 units will be running via E-Class. Introductory demonstrations for students will take place during teaching hours. Additionally the library will seek to rekindle the interest of those academics who initially expressed interest in the E-class experiment.

Summary

We noted earlier that with the crucial support of the EU there have been considerable developments in the level of library services within the last decade. At the beginning of the 1990s few Greek academic libraries would have been recognized as such by librarians visiting from regions such as North America or northern Europe. Interestingly, we have also chronicled a considerable change in the attitudes of both academics and administrators towards the role of libraries and librarians in Greek HE. Although these developments are considerable and exciting, we have reported that the technological infrastructure provides only limited access to PCs and that staff knowledge could be summarized as 'patchy'. Clearly if Greek HEIs are to make significant use of VLEs in teaching and learning then the technological environment requires considerable development. While we reported that there has been a marked increase in the use of IT by librarians, and indeed they are often seen within an institution as experts in its exploitation, we have also noted that in some cases this expertise may be more apparent than real. Responses to the questionnaires and interviews suggest that the level of knowledge librarians have is often limited and although many librarians are well informed about the use of IT, this is not always the case. To their credit, it must be noted that many recognize this through their statements about current and future training needs.

We reported developments at the University of Macedonia, not to suggest that this is either the only or the best example of VLE development in Greek academic libraries but because it is typical of current developments in the country and one of us (RS) is intimately involved with this development.

It would be possible to argue that, given that the current technological infrastructure might not support heavy use of VLEs and that there are gaps in the knowledge of librarians, it is not the time for librarians to be experimenting with the development of VLEs. However, a much more positive argument is that, given the opportunity afforded by the SCSF, Greek academic librarians have already demonstrated a capacity for rapid development of library services. In doing so they have already transformed their role and image within their institutions. Active involvement and even adopting a leadership role in the creation of VLEs can only further enhance the role of librarians in Greek higher education. These are certainly interesting and exciting times to be a librarian in Greek higher education.

References

Babiniotis, G. (1990) H Paidia tou Enos Vivliou (The One Book Education), *To Bima* (Daily Newspaper), (30 September); cited by: Zachos, G. (1994) *Greek University Libraries in the European Context: a comparative evaluation*, PhD thesis, Loughborough University, 49.

Garoufallou, E. (1999) The Impact of Information Technology on Greek Academic Libraries and Librarians: preliminary results. In Digital Libraries: interdisciplinary concepts, challenges and opportunities, *Proceedings of CoLIS3*, Zagreb, 304–9.

Garoufallou, E. (2003) *The Impact of the Electronic Library on Greek Academic Libraries and Librarians*, PhD thesis, Manchester Metropolitan University, Department of Information and Communications.

Garoufallou, E. and Siatri, R. (1999) The Impact of Information Technology on Greek Academic Libraries and Librarians: preliminary results. In Clapsopoulos, G. and Hagiala, N. (eds) *Organization and Collaboration of Academic Libraries in the Digital Age, proceedings of the 7th Greek conference of academic libraries*, Volos, 4–6 November 1998, Volos, University of Thessaly library, 49–67.

Greek National Documentation Centre, *Study on Assessing the Present Situation of the Markets for Electronic Information Services in Greece* (MSSTUDY) (1995) Athens, National Documentation Centre, www.ucy.ac.cy/~ftsimp/msstudygr.pdf.

MacColl, J. (2001) Virtuous Learning Environments: the library and the VLE, *Program* **35** (3), 227–39.

Raptis, P. and Sitas, A. (1996) Academic Libraries in Greece: a new perspective. *Libri*, **46** (2), 100–12.

Smethurst, J. M., Line, M. B. and Owen, P. (1997) *New Strategies for the University Library: a report for the University of the Aegean library*, www.lib.aegean.gr/INFO/New-strategies.pdf.

Tritsis, A. (1987). *Proceedings of the 12th meeting of the Council of Higher Education*, Deltio, 12 (July).

Disclaimer

The views expressed in this paper are those of the authors and do not necessarily reflect or even agree with the official policies of the institutions for which they work.

Theme 2

The relationship between user needs, information skills and information literacies

8

Embedding information skills in the subject-based curriculum

Kay Moore

Introduction

A quick trawl through information skills packages currently being delivered in virtual learning environments (VLEs) will reveal that there are basically two types of package: generic and customized. Generic packages are by far the most common; these are usually created by library staff and are often external to the curriculum. The second type is the customized package, tailored to a particular subject area or student group. Customized skills packages are undeniably more expensive to develop, but are they worth the extra effort and cost? This is a brief overview of our experience of creating and delivering such a package at Sheffield Hallam University in the UK.

To customize or not to customize?

What are the essential criteria of a good information skills programme? Ask any information professional and they will probably respond with a range of factors, but most of them will agree that they should be timely, relevant and engaging. It is quite a challenge to achieve success in all three areas in the traditional, face to face mode of information skills teaching, but even more so when we transfer that teaching to the more impersonal environment of virtual learning. With careful management the 'timely' aspect can be well supported by the use of VLEs. Materials are usually accessible at the point of need and can be revisited as often as required. But how well are we doing in satisfying the other criteria of good information skills teaching? How do we make the material relevant to the students and how do we really hold their attention long enough to encourage the development of effective information skills?

These were the questions we tried to address at Sheffield Hallam University when we first set out to create an information skills tutorial to be delivered in the Blackboard learning environment. The first decision we made was that whatever we designed had to support the pedagogy of sound information skills teaching and not to sacrifice this on the altar of the VLE. So we took time to reflect on what good information skills teaching meant to us.

When delivering a traditional information skills session, what would we normally do? The most important consideration is that it is relevant to the student. So, first we would learn as much as we could about the students in advance. What is their background, skills level, age mix, experience of using IT and so on? Then we would try to determine their specific needs. What is distinctive about their course? What resources will they need to access? What are the assessment criteria for the course? How will the information skills that they develop help them to succeed? If we really wanted to create a good learning experience virtually, then it was clear to us that we had to create a package that would allow us to respond to these issues. That meant that our material should be capable of customization in order to provide relevance to whatever course it was supporting.

Relevance and engagement sit hand in hand when it comes to information skills teaching. A traditional skills session always works best when it captures the student's attention by using interesting, relevant examples and a variety of teaching methods, ensuring that learning is enjoyable. Our experience at Sheffield Hallam of delivering other key skills material taught us that it is far more effective when delivered within the context of a student's own course. So, for us, the decision was clear cut; anything other than a customized package that was tailored to the student's areas of study and course requirements would be selling the student short.

The other benefit of developing customized programmes is that they could eventually replace face to face information skills workshops. This was an important consideration as we began to feel the impact of the growth in student numbers and increased diversity that many other institutions will be familiar with. We simply could not keep up with the level of demand for information skills sessions and knew that we would have to find a truly effective way of filling the gap without sacrificing quality. Students coming to us with little recent experience of education also needed to be able to develop skills at their own pace, but would, more than most, find it harder to grasp the concepts unless they were clearly related to their topic of study. We had to provide a customized package that students could work through at their own pace and return to whenever the need occurred.

Establishing these principles at the outset made it relatively easy for us to determine the membership of our development team. We needed information specialists, experienced in delivering skills teaching and with a good knowledge of resources. We needed academic staff input to help us to create a package that was capable of being closely embedded into the subject curriculum and we needed staff with the skills to create exciting learning objects in virtual environments. Out of these founding principles our information skills package, InfoQuest, was born.

What is InfoQuest?

InfoQuest is an online information skills package, delivered in five modules. It takes students on a structured route through information skills development. Students are introduced to the key concepts of information skills, but set in the broad context of Sheffield Hallam University's resource structure and in the specific context of their own subject discipline. It takes three approaches to learning. The theory is addressed, usually through word documents. Practical skills are developed and applied in live databases (though the use of split screens). Reflection and reinforcement is achieved through use of online formative assessment activities, often supplemented by seminar-based associated tasks. A generic framework was created, designed to be easily customized at specified points to allow for the introduction of subject specific concepts, resources and activities.

InfoQuest is delivered through Blackboard. A tailored, subject specific version is normally embedded within an existing research unit, or other appropriate unit in a particular course. It is currently being used across all schools of study in the university, with approximately 30 customized versions created to date.

Have we achieved our aims?

Our initial aims were that the package should enable information skills to be delivered through the virtual learning environment in a way that was timely, relevant and engaging.

Timely

One of the key strengths of InfoQuest is not so much the content – there are many good information skills packages in existence – but the way that we are building that content to develop academic engagement. As the creation of subject specific versions of InfoQuest requires partnership with academics, we are able, through that partnership, to influence the timing and delivery methods. Often InfoQuest is delivered using a team teaching approach, introduced at the most relevant time for students and phased in a way that supports the rest of the course. For example, some courses prefer to have InfoQuest delivered in one semester, usually the first, while others prefer a phased release of modules to match the delivery of the rest of the course and to tie in with tutorial programmes. Access at the point of need is an important principle of InfoQuest so, after finishing the unit in which InfoQuest is based, students can continue to access InfoQuest when they need to from within the organization area of Blackboard.

Relevant

Customization is the key to relevance. Even fairly small amounts of tailoring can encourage increased ownership of the material by the student group. Doing fictitious searches on topics that they will never have to research for their studies is not the greatest motivator. Developing students' skills, while at the same time getting them to engage in live searches of databases for their subject area, is a far more worthwhile experience. Students are increasingly becoming strategic learners and will only engage with material where they can see the payback. With InfoQuest normally being centred within their course, with clearly expressed learning outcomes and clearly defined assessment criteria, students are more willing to engage with it.

Engaging

InfoQuest was designed to use a variety of teaching methods: thinking, doing and reflecting. Having multimedia designers on our development team was a big bonus, as they could translate our ideas into attractive activities, designed to hold students' attention. Statistics available through Blackboard show a generally high level of interaction with InfoQuest, and evidence of students returning to it as they approach their period of assessment.

If they are engaging with the material in the way that we intended then the outcome would be that we are helping to develop students who can more effectively locate, evaluate and use information to support their study. Have we achieved this aim?

Evaluation of InfoQuest

Ongoing evaluation of InfoQuest suggests that, where the package is embedded into the course and clearly seen by students as an essential element of it, skills development does take place. With some cohorts we have performed pre and post InfoQuest skills analysis and the results have shown a marked improvement in student's confidence in using information. The most notable area of improvement was in their understanding and use of information databases and journals. This was a key area for us as there were increasing concerns that students were ignoring the rich resource of quality academic journals in preference for the quick fix 'Google' approach. Feedback from academics was also positive. In some instances we were able to make direct comparisons between previous cohorts pre-InfoQuest and current InfoQuest-supported students. The latter were generally perceived to perform better, consulting a wider range of sources, and were deemed capable of producing a higher level of academic argument in their written work.

However, there are areas of concern. Observation of student use of InfoQuest and feedback from questionnaires has prompted us to review the level of activities in relation to the amount of text. Students often skip the text part of the unit and head straight to the activities. The challenge for the development team is to redesign the modules to ensure that the context and meaning is incorporated in a more active way into the package, and to provide an opportunity to reinforce this learning through repeated practice, either within or outside InfoQuest.

There is also a tendency for younger students, reared on a diet of computer games and web surfing, to over-rate their own skills when it comes to using the internet for research. It is sometimes difficult to get them to engage with the material if they feel that they already possess adequate skills. While we do not want students to become disaffected through working at a level beneath their ability and experience, we do need to make sure that they have appropriate skills. For each of the modules we will develop a pre-module skills analysis. Students will be asked to estimate their own skill level against the learning outcomes for that module. They will then do a short self test which will indicate how realistic their own assessment was and should highlight those areas that the student needs to engage with in order to come up to the required level.

The downside of taking the customized route

If you are inspired by our experience and are thinking of developing your own customized version, what are the drawbacks of this approach? The obvious, big factor is cost. We have spent nearly two years developing our current product. It has taken time and effort from a team of multimedia developers, information specialists and academics, all of whom have been doing their 'day job' at the same time. We are fortunate at Sheffield Hallam to have a strong pool of multimedia designers to call on and expert advice on learning and teaching from our Learning and Teaching Institute (which is located within the Learning Centre). Design costs are inherent in any VLE package, customized or not, but for customization there needs to be much more attention to detail and structure. Design for reusability becomes more critical.

The other cost is associated with creating new versions for different subject groupings. At Sheffield Hallam, this is managed through Learning Centre subject teams, led by an information specialist and in collaboration with the relevant academics for that subject area. The initial training and development of Learning Centre staff is expensive but, once trained, they can create new versions fairly easily. Another benefit is that staff are developing skills that are necessary for supporting the move to virtual learning, and are thus more effective when it comes to providing advice and support to students or academic staff in this area.

Depending on which VLE you use, file management could also be an issue. It became quite complex for us to manage the files for each of the different versions. We often ran into trouble with VLE administrators for trying to introduce short cuts or new ways of managing versions. Yet what we were trying to do with InfoQuest was groundbreaking and challenged the capacity of our system in many ways. We are now dealing with file management more centrally and recent improvements in Blackboard will make this less onerous in future.

In our experience, customization only works well if you can secure some academic input. Their knowledge of the course and cohort helps you to create a more meaningful learning experience for the student. Yes, it is sometimes painful to pin down academics, but the payback is well worth it. Not only do you have a more valuable resource, but you are establishing dialogue and developing partnership as a result. One word of warning though: beware of the floodgates opening. Word spreads like wildfire around a faculty and you may be overwhelmed with demand. We have found that we need to talk staff down a bit from some of their initial ideas of how much customization they would like.

How much customization is enough?

Surprisingly little. Of the 30 or so versions of InfoQuest currently in use, some of them have fairly extensive customization and some relatively little. All have some. We have found that it is important to use a subject-relevant database when introducing students to the concept of database searching. Students will not bother to engage with resources that they don't see as relevant to their course of study. Other modules can be customized by judicious use of course related topics to practice searching with, leaving the essential core of text or activity unchanged.

As demand for InfoQuest grows we need to adopt a more stringent approach to customization. Modules have been reviewed to determine where customization can be an option and where a generic approach is acceptable. This should make for quicker customization but still retain relevance for users. As different groups of academics adapt the way that they embed InfoQuest into their courses, we are realizing that associated learning activities, delivered through seminar or collaborative activities, can add strength and depth to the learning that takes place within InfoQuest. In order to facilitate this approach we will be introducing teacher notes to signpost opportunities for collaborative learning and for integration into assessment.

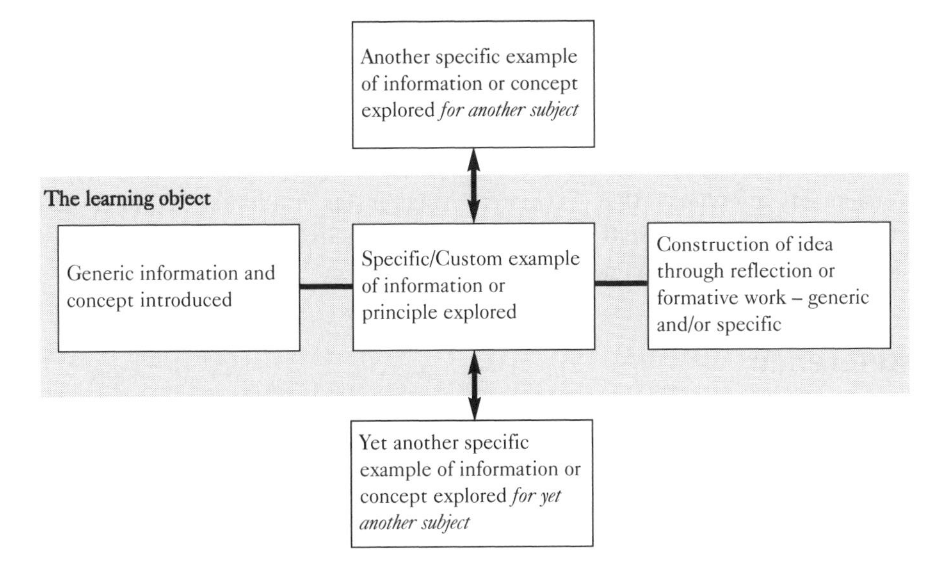

Figure 8.1 Structure of a learning object in InfoQuest (Middleton, 2003)

We will be revisiting each module to reshape the content so that each can work as focused, cohesive learning objects. This will add a new level of flexibility to the material, allowing repackaging to suit the needs of specific cohorts. The approach we are now taking is that customization can more easily be achieved by adding to or deleting from the generic core rather than amending the core of material itself, as illustrated in Figure 8.1. Thus the main strand of learning is generic in its approach, but use of customized examples and customized opportunities for practice will increase engagement and ownership.

Conclusion

Creating and developing a customized information skills package has been a major commitment and has absorbed much staff time. It would certainly have been easier to opt for a generic approach or, easier still, to buy an off-the-shelf package. We have to ask ourselves what would that mean to students and to the way that we support them. InfoQuest now meets students' needs on three levels: it introduces them to the concept of literature searching, it introduces them to the context of information for their own subject of study and it familiarizes them with the learning resource structure at Sheffield Hallam University. Staff support in delivering InfoQuest is minimal and for distance learner students or those with long periods of placement there is a high quality, tailored resource that they can access at point of need.

We have many exciting plans for the continued development of InfoQuest, including the opportunity to create a commercial product for use by other institutions. At the outset we said that we wanted to adhere to the underlying principles of good teaching; a good teacher constantly reflects, evaluates and refines. By the start of the next academic year we hope to have launched a new version of InfoQuest that is more engaging for students, requires less customization work by staff and is even more effective in helping students to become confident and competent users of information.

Reference

Middleton, A. (2003) Created for the development of InfoQuest by Andrew Middleton, Senior Multimedia Developer, Sheffield Hallam University.

9

Ways to engage widening participation students

Lynne Rutter and Penny Dale

Introduction

Widening participation (WP) students are so-called 'non-traditional' students from diverse backgrounds who are being encouraged to consider further and higher education. This paper seeks to show that by identifying the learning issues of two different groups of WP students it is possible to find better ways of responding to their needs. Without this understanding we are relying on 'what the teacher does' rather than 'what the student does' within the learning environment and thus failing to engage the student fully (Biggs, 1999).

In the absence of engagement, information skills work cannot be embedded or integrated, and is thus perceived to be unconnected with study, work or professional practice. It is seen as a means to an end only – encouraging a surface learning approach (Marton and Saljo, 1984). It can also be counter-productive as students who are not engaged can display negative behaviour, be disruptive and spoil the group dynamic. At a surface level there can be little real engagement for the student, no matter how well sessions are planned or how good the content.

The previous and current learning experiences of students affect their perceptions and expectations and can be associated with the three barriers to learning as identified by Cross (1981) and cited by Merrill (2000). Within new situations these perceptions and barriers can have a significant influence on learning approaches and styles (Prosser and Trigwell, 1999). WP students from FE (further education) or a professional background are likely to have more varied learning experiences than traditional students. To understand this relationship and determine how students perceive their situation is a further step towards developing appropriate learning and teaching contexts for successful engagement and deeper learning.

Profiles of the two courses

The Post Qualifying Social Work award

The full Post Qualifying Social Work (PQSW) award (six parts in total) is a professional social work qualification, linked to the requirements of higher education (HE) carrying 120 academic (H level) credits. PQ1 is met through a portfolio of evidence, and PQ2 to 6 through a variety of taught and portfolio routes. It is an award for all qualified social workers who wish to have their post qualifying experience and learning recognized, evaluated and extended, although it will eventually be a professional requirement in many situations (http://ihcs4u.bournemouth.ac.uk/pqsw.asp).

The Sc Equine Studies foundation degree

This is a foundation degree (FD) validated by Bournemouth University (BU). It is run by a partner institution, Kingston Maurward College (KMC), an agricultural college about 25 miles from Bournemouth. The students come from a wide rural area, are mostly working in equine-related occupations and have studied to diploma level (www.bournemouth.ac.uk/library/subjects/equine_studies.html).

Student perspectives

There is a wide diversity in the skills base of the students on both courses, related to their continuing professional development experiences, but the underlying level is usually diploma or lower. All of these students are adult learners with specific needs for experiential and active learning (Knowles, 1990). Adults returning to academic study are likely to lack confidence in themselves as learners and to underestimate their own powers. They tend to be over-anxious and avoid the risk of making mistakes, exaggerating any stress and anxiety lingering from early schooling experiences (Knox, 1977; Cross, 1981; Daines, 1992 cited by Michie et al., 2001). Many also find the complexity of being both a worker and a learner, along with the increased responsibility within a learner-centred process, a struggle, as evidenced by Boud and Soloman (2001).

For some students there can be problems identifying with HE and their role within it. There is understandable loyalty by some students to their local FE college, which has served them well to this point in their learning. For social workers there can be perceptions of themselves as practitioners rather than students, too busy to read or undertake research of any kind (Ennis and Baldwin, 2000; McCrystal, 2000).

Barriers: dependency and anxiety

Merrill (2000) refers to three barriers to learning, identified by Cross (1981) as 'situational' (learner's life and circumstances), 'institutional' (associated with aspects of institutional provision) and 'dispositional' (linked to learner's self-perception and attitude).

These barriers are interesting because they describe issues that are outside the learning experience but which relate directly to that experience. For example, information literacy and the evaluation of resources are a challenge to many students because they require transferable skills and critical thinking. These can be particularly difficult concepts for HE students within the FE context as they adapt to becoming self-directed learners.

Social work practitioners experience feelings of pressure, anxiety and lack of confidence regarding the necessity for the award, their academic ability and use of electronic information. Their expectations showed a general mistrust of the university environment, often perceived as elitist and totally unrelated to the 'real world' of practice. These findings appear in various studies (CEBSS, 1998; McCrystal, 2000; Everitt, 2002). The wide range of evidence and research relevant to social work practitioners in non-bibliographic areas like practice guidance, policy and professional information, is also an issue (Watson et al., 2002).

Responses

To help students overcome these barriers and acquire the skills to engage with information research demands a re-evaluation of the way that students' perception is taken into account when delivering information skills sessions within the FE and professional environment. However, as WP gains momentum some of the methods and interventions described next may be increasingly applicable within the whole HE sector.

The Mexican Hat applied to foundation degree students

The term Mexican Hat (see Figure 9.1), as used by Robinson and Udall (2001), describes a series of interventions at different stages of learning. It resembles the hierarchy of levels of reflection that Brockbank and McGill (1998) use to describe the difficulty experienced by learners to 'reflect-on-action' (Schön, 1987). In this paper it is used to show levels of student engagement, and interventions to enable them to move to deeper learning.

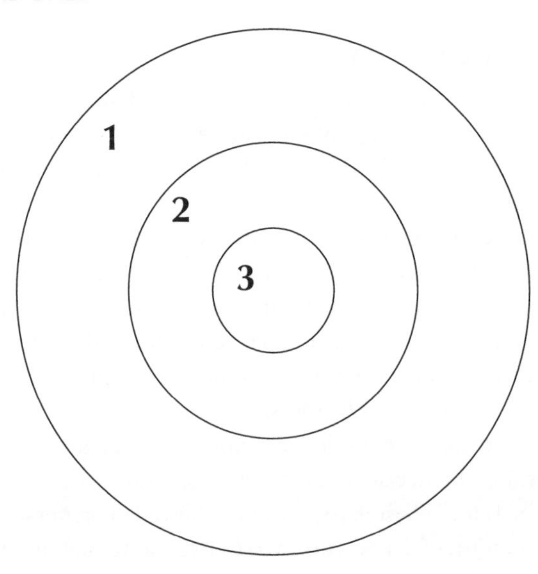

Figure 9.1 The Mexican Hat (Robinson and Udall, 2001)

Zone 3 of the Mexican Hat

At the outer rim of the hat the students are not engaged. They are taking a surface approach to learning and are at best listening and waiting for answers to be fed to them. Ramsden (1992) and Prosser and Trigwell (1999) describe the characteristics of deep and surface learning. The students are passive and almost resentful, reluctant to take any responsibility for their own learning and they exhibit all the signs of surface learning. To overcome these complex barriers between the students and active learning the following interventions were put in place in our study.

1. A workbook was written to take the students through the stages of information handling. The style of this workbook was deliberately relaxed and referred to resources at KMC and BU to help establish and reinforce the identities and complementary roles of the two institutions. The reaction to this workbook was positive and provided a focal point for a subsequent session.
2. Time was spent ensuring that all members of the group had a personal Athens account to enable them to access resources remotely. Most of the group had forgotten their account IDs by the next session, indicating that they had not been used in the intervening period and that the importance of these accounts had not been fully understood.

Zone 2 of the Mexican Hat

In the middle zone of the hat the students are beginning to participate in the learning process. This engagement was achieved through the following interventions.

3. Full text articles were distributed. These articles were all available from the online resources available to the students, and when they were handed out at the start of the session the level of engagement rose noticeably. When the group realized that articles just like these were attainable they began to be much more participative, and understood why the Athens personal accounts were so important.
4. The students were then reminded how to search for articles, and referred back to the workbook that explained searching skills.
5. They were asked to track down the article in front of them from a database with full text content (EBSCO Academic Search Elite), writing down the steps needed to find it and noting any problems they encountered. This enabled individuals to discuss problems as they arose and for the group to work together to solve them
6. Students were then asked to find other articles on the same topic and note down the steps that they took.
7. Finally the students began to look for articles on other topics relevant to their needs. They were not told when to do this but all did so as their confidence grew, and the more confident members helped the others.

By this process the students began to move away from the notion that to complete an assignment they need to have all the resources to hand in their college library. At this stage they are still not fully independent learners because, for example, some found it difficult to ask questions about finding resources. One student whose online search failed to find a full text article on the welfare of horses in transport just looked out of the window. When she was asked why she thought she was having a problem her response was 'There's nothing there, there never is'. It was possible to work with this student to look at her search strategy and the databases she was using and prevent her moving back to Zone 3, while others in the group were moving towards Zone 1. The growing confidence of the group was evidenced as students chose to change databases to find more references and then successfully transferred their search terms to fit the new interface.

The interventions in Zone 2 were underpinned through the following measures.

8. A specially designed web page was introduced linking the full text and bibliographic resources available, as well as providing links to e-journals, newspapers and useful websites.
9. The workbook from the first session was made available in pdf from the web page.

Zone 1 of the Mexican Hat

In the centre of the hat are the fully fledged reflective learners. Interventions at this stage are minimal, as contact with BU is restricted to e-mail. Evaluation is necessary to establish how many of the group reached the middle of the hat, and for how long they stayed there. It would be useful to establish how much movement exists between zones 1 and 2. Movement between these zones is probably inevitable, given the profile and location of the group. Realistically some may retreat to zone 3. Staff at KMC Library with support from BU will guide the progress of this group.

Implications of the Mexican Hat

So what next? As the preceding description shows, this work has not been evaluated at the time of writing. Until the cohort has completed their studies and we hope transferred to BU for their final year it will not be possible to judge how effective this technique is in the long term, but this work is being continued. To enhance the student experience of HE within the FE environment and respond to the needs of WP students studying in partner colleges, Bournemouth University is managing the Dorset, South Somerset and South Wiltshire Higher Education Partnership (DSW), a project funded by the Higher Education Funding Council Executive (HEFCE). Part of the funding for this project has been directed at a post of peripatetic training support librarian, working with several of BU's partner colleges including KMC. Any library or information skills developments with the FD Sc Equine Studies will be undertaken by this person in conjunction with the course team and library staff at KMC. As a secondee from BU library, the peripatetic librarian has been involved with the delivery of services to partner colleges and before appointment was aware of the methods that were being used with the group.

The developmental work is already being used in other ways. A workbook to support a BSc programme at another college has been developed from the KMC model and used with a small group of students to help them acquire independent research skills. Finally, the experience of using the interventions will inform a review of the undergraduate information skills teaching for the School of Conservation Sciences at BU during 2003–4.

A bespoke service: the PQSW award

Candidates on the Bournemouth PQSW programme are provided with an holistic package under the title 'information skills' and have a dedicated student support lecturer. The remit of this post is to engage fully with the candidates and the requirements of the programme, and develop appropriate responses. A taught information skills workshop is offered by the lecturer with supporting handouts and help sheets; a dedicated web portal has been designed; online texts have been made accessible; and opportunities for contact time with the lecturer are available.

One of the primary aims when dealing with PQSW students' perceptions and anxieties has been to treat them with respect while limiting any form of intimidation. A reduction of threat and anxiety were found by Marton and Saljo (1984) to be associated with increased motivation to learn. Belbin and Belbin (1972) illustrate how important it is for adults to have built a sense of confidence first before they can acquire specific skills. The PQSW information skills workshop is therefore relaxed and informal, developing a sense of trust, and encouraging active participation.

More specifically, one of the first activities is designed to respect and use students' practice experiences and knowledge. Rogers (2002, 32) states that the more learners are involved and offer their own experience, 'the more they are likely to learn at speed'. Their experiences of finding and using information at home or work are shared and explored with the whole group. By relating to everyday situations and problems where information is used, students begin to feel less unfamiliar with the idea of 'research' and therefore less anxious about it. As Bigge and Shermis (1999, 248) state, 'understanding is seeing the relation between particulars and generalisations'. They also begin to realize they are not alone with their fears, worries or their perceived lack of knowledge and skills. Students are encouraged to evaluate academic knowledge and research critically against their practical knowledge as well as other literature. This addresses many misconceptions regarding academic elitism.

The dedicated PQSW web portal has also been designed to provide a fully tailored service. Specific information skills web pages within the portal allow non-bibliographic and practice-based information to be made available on an equal footing alongside more academic resources, and reiterate the commitment to an understanding of students' needs.

Portfolio case study exemplars are used as a basis for the taught information skills procedure. Relevant information areas (theory, research, policy and law), listed as marking criteria for the portfolio, are used as starting points in this procedure rather than information type or format. This is important as it allows the workshop to integrate completely into the PQ unit, and shows relevance to the students' information needs, while also reflecting the requirements of evidence-based practice. As Grafstein (2002) explains, emphasis should be placed on the process of locating and retrieving information procedures because these are the skills that students need and they will facilitate students' ability to acquire new information as the need arises – they are transferable.

Active teaching methods (discussion, questioning, use of flip charts and Post-its) are employed when sharing this procedure with the group to allow participation, questioning and interaction. In this way students are not just 'told' how to do it; they can become involved with understanding a case study and its various areas of evidence, identify specific information needs and begin to form their own ideas for relevant sources using the procedure as a framework.

The web pages also reflect the information skills procedure explored within the workshop, using similar structures and language. These pages are used to access electronic sources during the practical part of the workshop. Candidates work at their own pace to develop confidence and skills with plenty of positive reinforcement and encouragement. The workshop therefore provides an holistic approach, able to base its structure, content and resources entirely on the needs and perspectives of the students, unrestricted by the frameworks of more traditional information services.

A unique level of bespoke information skills provision and engagement has been enabled by the appointment of a dedicated student support lecturer within the academic team. Although this position is fairly unique it reinforces the need for, and the ultimate success of, embedding information skills teaching within the curriculum (Dee, 2001; JISC, 2002).

Implications of the bespoke service

The way we have identified and responded to the needs of PQSW students gives an added-value experience to pave the way for more positive and effective interactions with information for evidence-based practice, reflective practice and lifelong learning requirements. There has been a positive response to a survey of candidates attending the workshops. Of the 90 completed forms during March to July 2003, 85% said they will use the information resources they had learned about, and 91% said they found the web pages useful.

This approach can now be followed for further responses to specifically identified learning needs. At present a workbook to support the writing of academic reflective assignments is being produced, adding a further element to the provision for post-qualifying social work education at BU.

Conclusion

In this paper we have described techniques and interventions that in themselves are neither new nor different. What we think is innovative is the way that the Mexican Hat and the bespoke service identify and recognize the relationships between experiences, perceptions and students' learning experiences and use this understanding to develop appropriate methods to engage the students' process of learning information-handling skills.

The perceptions of these groups of WP students in many ways typify the perceptions of the increasingly diverse student body within both FE and HE. We hope that some of our experiences and conclusions will provide food for thought for colleagues in FE and HE who are reinventing their services in response to WP.

References

Belbin, E. and Belbin., R. M. (1972) *Problems in Adult Retraining*, London, Heinemann.

Bigge, M. L. and Shermis, S. S. (1999) *Learning Theories for Teachers*, London, Longman.

Biggs, J. (1999) *Teaching for Quality Learning at University: what the student does*, Buckingham, SRHE and Open University Press.

Boud, D., and Soloman, N. (2001) *Work-based Learning: a new higher education?*, Buckingham, Society for the Research into Higher Education and Open University Press.

Brockbank, A. and McGill. I. (eds) (1998) *Reflective Learning in Higher Education*, Buckingham, SRHE and Open University Press.

Centre for Evidence Based Social Services (1998) Evidence-based Social Care. *Newsletter of the Centre for Evidence Based Social Services*, Issue 2, Summer.

Cross, K. P. (1981) *Adults as Learners*, San Francisco, Jossey-Bass.

Daines, J. (1992) *Adults Learning*, Nottingham, University of Nottingham, Department of Adult Education.

Dee, M. (2001) Who Needs Academic Librarians? Universities do!, *SCONUL Newsletter*, **23** (Aug), 8–11.

Ennis, E. and Baldwin, N. (2000) Lifelong Learning for Care Professionals. In Pierce, R. and Weinstein, J. (eds), *Innovative Education and Training for Social Care Professionals*, London, Jessica Kingsley.

Everitt, A. (2002) Research and Development in Social Work. In Adams, R., Dominelli, L. and Payne, M. (eds), *Social Work: themes, issues, and critical debates*, 2nd edn, London, Palgrave in Association with Open University, 109–19.

Grafstein, A. (2002) A Discipline-based Approach to Information Literacy, *Journal of Academic Librarianship*, **28** (4), 197–204.

Joint Information Systems Committee (2002) Big Blue Project, Final Report, JISC, www.leeds.ac.uk/bigblue/finalreportful.htm.

Knowles, M. S. (1990) *The Adult Learner: a neglected species*, 4th edn, Houston, Gulf Publishing.

Knox, A. (1977) *Adult Development and Learning*, San Francisco, Jossey-Bass.

McCrystal, P. (2000) Developing the Social Work Researcher through a Practitioner Research Training Programme, *Social Work Education*, **19** (4), 359–73.

Marton, F. and Saljo., R. (1984) Approaches to Learning. In Marton, F. et al., (eds) *The Experience of Learning*, Edinburgh, Scottish Academic Press.

Merrill, B. (2000) *The FE College and its Communities*, London, FEDA, www.lsda.org.uk/files/PDF/ISBN1853385336.pdf.

Michie, F., Glachan M. and Bray, D. (2001) An Evaluation of Factors Influencing the Academic Self-concept, Self-esteem, and Academic Stress for Direct and Re-entry Students in Higher Education, *Educational Psychology*, **21** (4), 455–72.

Prosser, M. and Trigwell, K. (1999) *Understanding Learning and Teaching: the experience in higher education*, Buckingham, SRHE and Open University Press.

Ramsden, P. (1992) *Learning to Teach in Higher Education*, London, Routledge.

Robinson, A. G. and Udall, M. D. (2002) *Developing the Independent Learner: the Mexican Hat approach*, On Learning, Teaching and Higher Education, working paper (13) 1, Southampton, Southampton Institute.

Rogers, A. (2002) *Teaching Adults*, 3rd edn, Buckingham, Open University Press.

Schön, D. (1987) *Educating the Reflective Practitioner*, London, Josey-Bass.

Smith, R. M. (1983) *Learning How to Learn: applied theory for adults*, Milton Keynes, Open University Press.

Taylor, I. (1997) *Developing Learning in Professional Education: partnerships for practice*, Buckingham, Open University Press and The Society for Research into Higher Education.

Watson, F., Burrows, H. and Player, C. (2002) *Integrating Theory and Practice in Social Work Education*, London, Jessica Kingsley Publishers.

Websites

Equine Studies,
www.bournemouth.ac.uk/library/subjects/equine_studies.html.

Post Qualifying Social Work,
http://ihcs4u.bournemouth.ac.uk/pqsw.asp.

(guest password required for access – please contact Lynne Rutter at lrutter@bournemouth.ac.uk.)

10
Information literacy and learning

Sirje Virkus

Introduction

The emergence of the knowledge economy has caused a wide debate about what kinds of competencies young people and adults need. While there is a growing agreement on the importance of skills as a key engine for economic growth and the spread of the knowledge economy, there is far less agreement on which competencies and skills make the difference (OECD, 2000). The general move is clearly towards a stronger attention being paid to employment prospects and the acquisition of core or transversal skills. The new qualification frameworks adopted in the UK and Ireland are heavily outcome-based and qualifications are mostly defined in terms of skills and competencies acquired by graduates (CRE and the Confederation of EU Rectors, 2001). However, there is no general agreement what these transferable skills should include (NCIHE, 1997; Stasz and Brewer, 1999; Overtoom, 2000; OECD, 2001a). A number of researchers have identified certain high-level competencies that appear to transcend other competencies (Linstead, 1991; Hyland, 1992; Nordhaug, 1993). These competencies (creativity, analysis, problem solving, communication, self-development and related learning skills) may either enhance other competencies or be important to their acquisition. Linstead (1991), Hyland (1992) and Nordhaug (1993) use for them the term *meta-competencies* (Cheetham and Chivers, 1996; 1998). However, a number of recent and ongoing OECD works seek to develop better definitions as well as an overarching theoretical framework for the identification of relevant skills and competencies and measures of skills: the *International Adult Literacy Survey* (OECD and Statistics Canada, 2000), the *Programme on Definition and Selection of Competencies: theoretical and conceptual foundations* (Gilomen, 2002), the *Adult Literacy and Life Skills (ALL)* survey, and the *Programme for International Student Assessment (PISA)*.

In this context, several reports have emphasized the importance of finding, evaluating and using information in the rapidly changing information and communication technology (ICT) environment (ERTI, 1995; 1997; OECD, 1996; 2000; 2001a; 2001b; 2001c; European Commission, 2000; O'Mahony, 2001; Coimbra Group of Universities, 2002; Virkus, 2003). Having the competence to use information effectively has been suggested also by management gurus as essential to organizational success (Drucker, 1993; 1994; Grainger, 1994; Senge, 1994). It seems that organizations are becoming increasingly aware of the value of information and its management for their competitiveness and success.

Concept of information literacy

Librarians and information professionals name these competencies related to information handling and use as 'information literacy'. They believe that information literacy is absolutely critical literacy for the 21st century (Bruce, 2002) and a prerequisite for participative citizenship, social inclusion, the creation of new knowledge, personal empowerment and learning for life (Bundy, 2003).

There are lots of definitions and models of information literacy. Some authors perceive it as an 'umbrella' term, for example, incorporating tool literacy, resource literacy, social-structural literacy, research literacy, publishing literacy, technology literacy and critical literacy (Shapiro and Hughes, 1996) or computer literacy, library literacy, media literacy, network literacy and visual literacy (Breivik, 2000). Bruce (1997) defines information literacy according to how people perceive or experience it: the information technology experience, the info-sources experience, the info-process experience, the info-control experience, the knowledge construction experience, the knowledge extension experience and the wisdom experience. Webber and Johnston (2002) define information literacy as an efficient and ethical information behaviour. However, among many definitions perhaps the most widely accepted and cited is that provided by the American Library Association (ALA) Presidential Committee on Information Literacy: 'To be information literate, a person must be able to recognize when information is needed and have the ability to locate, evaluate, and use effectively the needed information' (ALA, 1989, 1). However, how people perceive and define information literacy depends on how they perceive and define other related terms: for example, *information*, *literacy*, *competence*, *competency*, *skill*, *learning* and *expertise*. There are numerous definitions about all these concepts and lack of commonly understandable terminology (Virkus, 2003).

It should also be noted that information literacy consciousness, as well as the term, has spread mainly among librarians and information professionals and neither is explicitly and extensively recognized in other circles (Town, 2002; Audunson and Nordlie, 2003; Gómez Hernández and Pasadas Ureña, 2003;

Homann, 2003; Skov and Skáerbak, 2003). Twelve European open and distance learning leaders were interviewed by the author during the annual conference of the European Association of Distance Teaching Universities (EADTU) in Glamorgan, Wales, in 2002, yet only a few of those interviewed had any understanding of what 'information literacy' might be (Virkus, 2003).

Information literacy and learning

Increasing attention to information handling and use in recent years is partly the result of information overload, especially related to the growth of digital information, and partly because of the new focus on student learning in a lifelong learning context. Although there has always been a need to find, evaluate, and effectively use information, the abilities needed to do so have just grown larger, more complex, and more important in the ICT environment. In our modern society students face diverse and abundant information choices; information is available in different forms and places; information comes increasingly in unfiltered forms and in uncertain quality. E-everything and plagiarism is also a concern (Wilson, 2001). It is also believed that new learning approaches and greater emphasis on resource-based and problem-based learning demands a higher degree of information literacy.

In this context, several authors have expressed concern that many students lack the information literacy to transform information into knowledge and wisdom. Bundy (2002) notes that instead of emphasizing issues of digital divide in the ICT context, the real focus should be towards information literacy divide. Breivik (2000) also notes that academic institutions will have failed their graduates if they do not empower them to be independent lifelong learners who can access, evaluate and effectively use information. She also points out that in our rapidly changing society, schools and academic institutions can never directly meet all the learning needs of their graduates throughout their lifetimes, but they can assume significant responsibility for creating generations of independent learners. According to Breivik, information literacy abilities both enhance student performance in formal learning settings and allow students to learn independent of such offerings.

Different approaches have been used to develop information literacy among students. For example, developing a guide for students to use or for resource evaluation, presenting a class session, creating a course website giving students a guided tour for searching the web, developing an assignment where students work on a search strategy appropriate to a problem statement, assisting students in preparation of their literature reviews, developing online tutorials or integrating information literacy into curriculum. It is believed that an integrated curricular approach is a best practice (Wilson, 2001). Many educators have written extensively about the need to promote information literacy as an integral part of the education process (Breivik and Jones, 1993; Lenox and Walker, 1993; Nahl-

Jakobovits and Jakobovits, 1993) beginning in the earliest grades (Brittingham, 1994; Boekhorst, 2003). It is to be expected that an integrated information literacy component in learning would have a positive impact on students' mastering of context, fulfilling research tasks and problem solving, becoming more self-directed, and assuming greater control over their own learning (Todd, 1995), enabling individuals to engage in a variety of learning situations and opportunities in optimal ways (George and Luke, 1995).

Bruce (1997) notes that there have been two competing views in the information literacy discourse: the behavioural and information processing approaches to learning, and the constructivist approaches. The former have successfully dominated thinking about information literacy. Consequently, models of information literacy that are skill-based and 'measurable' have been developed. According to behavioural approach an information user, to be described as information literate, must exhibit certain characteristics and demonstrate certain abilities. Less strongly apparent in the literature are the constructivist and relational approaches. Several researchers refer to the elements of constructivism, but coherent models still do not exist. Their attempts to emphasize inquiry-based, resource-based and problem-based learning are theoretically incompatible with pictures of information literacy that emphasize skills, knowledge, attitudes and linear processes. Bruce suggests a focus on investigating the mental models of experienced information users, as has been done by Borgman, or the ways in which people make sense of information. The relational approach supports the idea that any phenomenon may be described as the sum of the different ways in which it is experienced and Bruce's own research support this approach (Bruce, 1997).

However, despite some progress over the past decade, library and information professionals still report that universal information literacy is a distant, if not a receding, goal (Bruce and Lampson, 2002). Johnston and Webber (2003, 338) note that even in the US, 'whilst much attention has been paid to information literacy by American policy-makers, librarians and academics, the results are still relatively narrow, giving a potentially superficial guide to the nature of a curriculum for information literacy in HE'. And yet while library and information professionals are often cast as primary players in the quest for universal information literacy, many of them still feel they lack the training and expertise for this role (Bruce and Lampson, 2002).

Why information literacy integration has not been easy solution

While an integrated curricular approach to information literacy is described as a best practice, we must realize that the world of teaching and training is also changing dramatically. The faculty have to cope with many other challenges and information literacy is not the only concern. There is a growing impact of economic pressures – the increase in enrolment and operating costs, while funding for teaching and training is decreasing (Treuhaft, 1995; Collis and van der Wende, 2002). Developments in the workplace, changes in student demographics and global competition are exerting pressure on educational institutions as well. There are also new learning concepts, learning approaches, learning goals, knowledge domains and ICTs. Kathy Tiano highlights a change of paradigm and characterizes the old and new paradigms of HE as shown in Figure 10.1.

It is acknowledged that universities all over the world face an imperative to adapt and adjust to a whole series of profound changes that fall into six major categories:

- the increased demand for HE in a lifelong learning context
- the internationalization of education and research
- the need to develop co-operation between universities and industry
- the proliferation of places where knowledge is produced
- the reorganization of knowledge
- the emergence of new expectations (European Commission, 2003).

To respond to these changes many HE institutions have had to rethink their environment in the light of new technologies. Increasing numbers of instructors are

Old paradigm for HE	**New paradigm for HE**
Take what you can get	Courses on demand
Academic calendar	Year-round operations
University as a city	University as idea
Terminal degree	Lifelong learning
University as ivory tower	University as partner in society
Student = 18- to 25-year-old	Cradle to grave
Books are primary medium	Information on demand
Tenure	Market value
Single product	Information reuse/info exhaust
Student as a 'pain'	Student as a customer
Delivery in classroom	Delivery anywhere
Multi-cultural	Global
Bricks and mortar	Bits and bytes
Single discipline	Multi-discipline
Institution-centric	Market-centric
Government funded	Market funded
Technology as an expense	Technology as differentiator

Figure 10.1 Old and new paradigms of HE (after Kathy Tiano, cited in Inglis et al., 2002, 22)

experimenting with student-centred learning approaches and basing their teaching on constructivist models of learning. There has been an attempt to improve and innovate traditional HE as well as to provide new and alternative learning opportunities. In particular, online education and electronic learning environments are perceived as innovations that offer the potential to promote lifelong learning by supporting flexible learning, fostering learner control and stimulating learner engagement. However, it is one of the most complex issues facing HE institutions today. Many educational institutions also open their doors to non-traditional learners, design new programs and courses and experiment with collaborative learning and teaching supported by ITC. However, change in education is a long process. According to an international comparative survey on the current and future use of ICT in HE in the USA, Australia and Europe, the traditional lecture has still remained the 'core medium' for many HE institutions with ICT serving as a complement to already existing instructional tools (Collis and van der Wende, 2002; Virkus and Wood, 2003).

A lot of questions have not received an answer and Koper (2000) highlights the questions that occupy (or should occupy) the politicians, managers, educational scientists, directors of education, teachers and human-resource managers: Which knowledge and competences will be under discussion in the initial phase of HE, and which will come after that? How do you teach people to regularly and efficiently acquire new knowledge and competences themselves? How do you make manifest, in a reliable and valid way, the competencies and knowledge that someone has? How do you accredit competencies? Which educational models can adequately fulfil the current requirements and possibilities? Where is face-to-face instruction advisable, where distance education, where a mixed form and where other approaches such as on-the job help and coaching? When do you-and do not you-use ICT? How do you use ICT adequately in education?

Another problem is the existing gap between different professional and research communities and the lack of common and understandable terminology. One OECD report (2002) highlights the need for creating more bridges between different research communities and developing dialogue between several disciplines and interests. For example, different research communities (information science, education, psychology, cognitive neuroscience, health and policy) speak different languages and such concepts as information, competence, competency, skill, learning, knowledge, expertise and intelligence are defined and perceived differently.

For example, in a learning domain, there have been numerous theories of learning. Merriam and Caffarella (1991, 138) have typified four orientations to learning: *behaviourist*, *cognitive*, *humanist* and *social/situational*. Each of them views the learning process differently: behaviourists see it as a change in behaviour, cognitivists as an internal mental process (including insight, information processing, memory, perception), humanists as a personal act to fulfil potential and representatives of social or situational orientation to learning as an interaction or observation in social contexts and a movement from the periphery to the centre of a community of practice (Smith, 1999).

Greeno, Collins and Resnick (1996) make a distinction between three major streams of instructional theories: empiricist (behaviourist), rationalist (cognitivist and constructivist) and pragmatist–sociohistoric (situationalist). The Educational Technology Expertise Center of the Dutch Open University has also added a fourth type of model: the eclectic model. These are instructional design models using principles from different stances, just for the practical occasion. All stances have different views on knowledge, learning, transfer and motivation (Koper, 2001).

According to the empirical approach all reliable knowledge is based on experience. In the rationalist approach thinking is considered the only reliable source of knowledge. According to the pragmatic and socio-historic approach or educational theory as social constructivism, knowledge is distributed among individuals, tools and communities, such as those of professional practitioners. The assumption is that there is collective as well as individual knowledge (Koper, 2001, 13).

However, according to the OECD study *Understanding the Brain* (2002) the science of learning as a branch of human psychology is still in its infancy. We do not understand sufficiently well how children and adults learn. For example, for more than a century, one in six of young people and adults, reflecting on their childhood, have reported that they 'hated school'; a similar proportion have failed to master the elements of literacy and numeracy successfully enough to be securely employable. The OECD study poses a question: 'Maybe traditional education as we know it inevitably offends one in six pupils? Possibly the classroom model of learning is "brain-unfriendly"?' and adds that the more we learn about the human brain, especially in the early years, the less comfortable we find ourselves with the traditional classroom model and imposed curriculum of formal education (OECD, 2002, 10).

As yet, there is also no coherent theory of learning styles. There appear to be a multitude of learning styles, but we are nowhere near an adequate theory or practical analysis of learning styles as yet (OECD, 2002, 24). Not much is clearly known also about human intelligence. The work of Gardner (1983) with the idea of multiple intelligence and Goleman's (1995) concept of emotional intelligence has further complicated the picture. Science has to say little also about our likes and dislikes and why do people differ in what interests, excites, bores or repels them (OECD, 2002, 14).

It is believed that cognitive neuroscience might in due course offer a sounder basis for the understanding of learning and the practice of teaching and in the future we might be able really understand what exactly happens when learning occurs (OECD, 2002). For instance, new findings about the brain's plasticity to learn anew over the individual's lifecycle have been made, and new technologies of non-invasive brain scanning and imaging are opening up totally new methods of work for research (OECD, 2002, 3). The OECD report concludes that the above-mentioned issues, coupled with the advent of the computer, the growing doubts about the efficiency and effectiveness of state-controlled social provision of services and the emerging findings of cognitive neuroscience call into question some of the fundamental building blocks of traditional education – schools, classrooms, teachers or even the curriculum, and even concepts like intelligence or ability (OECD, 2002, 11).

Conclusions

Several reports have emphasized the importance of finding, evaluating, and using information although the term 'information literacy' is not used. There are many definitions and meanings of information literacy and the nature of information literacy is complex and difficult to capture. There are two competing views in the information literacy discourse: the behavioural and information processing approaches, and constructivist approaches. Information literacy integration is not an easy solution and in designing information literacy instruction, library and information professionals should also know what happens in education and the developments in research.

References

Adult Literacy and Life Skills (ALL) Survey, www.ets.org/all/survey.html.

American Library Association. Presidential Committee on Information Literacy (1989) *Final Report*. Chicago, ALA.

Audunson, R. and Nordlie, R. (2003) Information Literacy: the case or non-case of Norway? *Library Review*, 52 (7), 319–25.

Boekhorst, A. K. (2003) Becoming Information Literate in the Netherlands. *Library Review*, 52 (7), 298–309.

Breivik, P. S. (2000) Information Literacy for the Skeptical Library Director. In *Virtual Libraries: Virtual Communities, Proceedings of the IATUL conference, Queensland University of Technology, Brisbane, Australia, 3rd–7th July 2000*, www.iatul.org/conference/proceedings/vol10/papers/breivik_full.html.

Breivik, P. S. and Jones, D. L. (1993) Information Literacy: liberal education for the information age. *Liberal Education*, **79** (1), 24–9.

Brittingham, B. (1994) Higher Education Processes, www.rrpubs.com/heproc/.

Bruce, C. S. (1997) The Relational Approach: a new model for information literacy, *New Review of Information and Library Research*, 3, 1–22.

Bruce, C. S. (2002) *Information Literacy as a Catalyst for Educational Change: a background paper*. White Paper prepared for UNESCO, the US National Commission on Libraries and Information Science, and the National Forum on Information Literacy, for use at the Information Literacy Meeting of Experts, Prague, The Czech Republic, www.nclis.gov/libinter/infolitconf&meet/papers/bruce-fullpaper.pdf.

Bruce, H. and Lampson, M. (2002) Information Professionals as Agents for Information Literacy, *Education for Information*, **20** (2), 81–107.

Bundy, A. (2002). Growing the Community of the Informed: information literacy – a global issue. Paper presented at the *Standing Conference of East, Central and South Africa Library Associations*, Johannesburg South Africa, April 2002, www.library.unisa.edu.au/papers/growing-community.

Bundy, A. (2003) One Essential Direction: information literacy, information technology fluency. Paper presented at *eLit 2003: second international conference on information and IT literacy* held at Glasgow Caledonian University 11–13 June 2003, www.library.unisa.edu.au/papers/papers.htm.

Cheetham, G. and Chivers, G. (1996) Towards a Holistic Model of Professional Competence, *Journal of European Industrial Training*, **20** (5), 20–30.

Cheetham, G. and Chivers, G. (1998) The Reflective (and Competent) Practitioner: a model of professional competence that seeks to harmonize the reflective practitioner and competence-based approaches. *Journal of European Industrial Training*, **22**, (7), 267–76.

Coimbra Group of Universities (2002) *EU Policies and Strategic Change for Elearning in Universities.* Report of the project 'Higher education consultation in technologies of information and communication' (HECTIC), Brussels, Coimbra Group of Universities.

Collis, B. and van der Wende, M. (2002) *Models of Technology and Change in Higher Education: an international comparative survey on the current and future use of ICT in higher education*. Report, December 2002, Twente, Center for Higher Education Policy Studies (CHEPS).

CRE and the Confederation of EU Rectors (2001) *Towards a European Higher Education Area: survey of change and reforms from Bologna to Prague:* art 2: complement and an update to the report 'Trends in Learning Structures in Higher Education' prepared for the Bologna conference of June 1999 by Guy Haug and Jette Kirstein.

Drucker, P. (1993) *Post-capitalist Society*, New York, Harper Business.

Drucker, P.F. (1994) *Managing in Turbulent Times*, Oxford, Butterworth-Heinemann.

European Commission. (2000) *A Memorandum on Lifelong Learning*, Brussels, European Commission.

European Commission (2003) *The Role of the Universities in the Europe of Knowledge*. Commission of the European Communities, Brussels, Com(2003) 58 Final, http://europa.eu.int/eur-lex/en/com/cnc/2003/com2003_0058en01.pdf.

European Round Table of Industrialists (1995) *Education for Europeans: towards the learning society*, Brussels, ERTI, Education Policy Group.

European Round Table of Industrialists (1997) *Investing in Knowledge: the integration of technology in European education,* Brussels, ERTI.

Gardner, H. (1983) *Frames of Mind.* London, Heinemann.

George, R. and Luke, R. (1995) The Critical Place of Information Literacy in the Trend Towards Flexible Delivery in Higher Education Contexts. Paper delivered at the *Learning for Life Conference*, Adelaide, 30 November–1 December, 1995.

Gilomen, H. (2002) *Definition and Selection of Competencies: theoretical and conceptual foundations (DeSeCo),* Swiss Federal Statistical Office, Society and Education Statistics, www.deseco.admin.ch.

Goleman, D. (1995) *Emotional Intelligence*, New York, Bantam.

Gómez Hernández, J. A. and Pasadas Ureña, C. (2003) Information Literacy Developments and Issues in Spain, *Library Review*, **52** (7), 340–8.

Grainger, P. (1994) *Managing Information: your self-development action plan*, London, Kogan Page.

Greeno, J. G., Collins, A. M. and Resnick, L. B. (1996) Cognition and Learning. In Berliner, D. C. and Calfee, R. C. (eds), *Handbook of Educational Psychology*, New York, Simon & Schuster Macmillan, 15–46.

Homann, B. (2003) German Libraries at the Starting Line for the New Task of Teaching Information Literacy, *Library Review*, **52** (7), 301–18.

Hyland, T. (1992) Meta-competence, Metaphysics and Vocational Expertise. In *Competence and Assessment: the quarterly journal of the Employment Department* **20**, Sheffield, Employment Department, 22–4.

Inglis, A., Ling, P. and Joosten, V. (2002) *Delivering Digitally: managing the transition to the knowledge media*, 2nd edn, London, Kogan Page.

Johnston, B. and Webber, S. (2003) Information Literacy in Higher Education: a review and case study. *Studies in Higher Education,* **28** (3), 335–52.

Koper, R. (2000) *From Change to Renewal: educational technology foundations of electronic learning environments*, Heerlen, Open University of the Netherlands, Educational Technology Expertise Center.

Koper, R. (2001) *Modelling Units of Study from a Pedagogical Perspective: the pedagogical meta-model behind EML*, Heerlen, Open University of the Netherlands, Educational Technology Expertise Center.

Lenox, M. F. and Walker, M. L. (1993) Information Literacy in the Educational Process, *Educational Forum,* **57** (3), 312–24.

Linstead, S. (1991) Developing Management Meta-competence: can learning help? *Journal of European Industrial Training,* **6** (14), 17–27.

Merriam, S. and Caffarella (1991) *Learning in Adulthood: a comprehensive guide*, San Francisco, Jossey-Bass.

Nahl-Jakobovits, D. and Jakobovits, L. A. (1993) *Bibliographic Instructional Design for Information Literacy: integrating affective and cognitive objectives*, Research Strategies, **11** (2), 73–88.

National Committee of Inquiry into Higher Education (1997) *Higher Education in the Learning Society* (Dearing Report), London, HMSO.

Nordhaug, O. (1993) *Human Capital in Organizations*, Stockholm, Scandinavian University Press.

O'Mahony, M. (2001) *EUA Thema: consultation on the EC draft memorandum on lifelong learning*, www.unige.ch/eua/En/Publications/LLLdraft/welcome.html.

Organization for Economic Co-operation and Development (1996) *The Knowledge Based Economy*, Paris, OECD.

Organization for Economic Co-operation and Development (2000) *Learning to Bridge the Digital Divide*, Paris, OECD.

Organization for Economic Co-operation and Development (2001a) *Educational Policy Analysis 2001*, Paris, OECD, Centre for Educational Research and Innovation.

Organization for Economic Co-operation and Development (2001b) *Learning to Change: ICT in schools*, Paris, OECD.

Organization for Economic Co-operation and Development (2001c) *Cities and Regions in the New Learning Economy*, Paris, OECD.

Organization for Economic Co-operation and Development (2002) *Understanding the Brain: towards a new learning science*, Paris, OECD.

Organization for Economic Co-operation and Development and Statistics Canada (2000) *Literacy in the Information Age: final report of the International Adult Literacy Survey*, Paris, OECD and Statistics Canada.

Overtoom, C. (2000) *Employability Skills: an update*, ERIC Digest No. 220, Syracuse, NY, ERIC Clearinghouse, ED445236.

Programme for International Student Assessment (PISA), www.pisa.oecd.org/index.htm.

Senge, P. M. (1994) *The Fifth Discipline: the art and practice of the learning organization*, New York, Currency Doubleday.

Shapiro, J. J. and Hughes, S. K. (1996) Information Literacy as a Liberal Art: enlightenment proposals for a new curriculum, *EDUCOM Review*, **31** (2), March/April, 31–5, www.educause.edu/.

Skov, A. and Skáerbak, H. (2003) Fighting an Uphill Battle: teaching information literacy in Danish institutions of higher education, *Library Review*, **52** (7), 326–32.

Smith, M. K. (1999) Learning Theory. In *The Encyclopedia of Informal Education*, www.infed.org/biblio/b-learn.htm.

Stasz, C. and Brewer, D. J. (1999) *Academic Skills at Work: two perspectives*, MDS-1193, Berkeley, CA, RAND and the National Center for Research in Vocational Education.

Todd, R. (1995) Information Literacy: a sense making approach to learning, In *The Learning Link: information literacy in practice*, Adelaide, Auslib Press, 17–26.

Town, J. S. (2002) Information Literacy and the Information Society. In Hornby, S. and Clarke, Z. (eds) *Challenge and Change in the Information Society*, London, Facet Publishing, 83–103.

Treuhaft, J. (1995) *Changes in Education*, Algonquin College of Applied Arts and Technology, www.algonquinc.on.ca/edtech/change.html.

Virkus, S. (2003) Information Literacy in Europe: a literature review, *Information Research*, **8** (4), http://informationr.net/ir/8-4/paper159.html.

Virkus, S. and Wood, L. (2003) Change and Innovation in European LIS Education, *Proceedings of the EUCLID/ALISE Conference*, July 30–August 1st, 2003, Potsdam, Germany (in press).

Webber, S. and Johnston, B. (2002) Assessment for Information Literacy. Paper presented at the *International Conference on IT and Information Literacy*, 20th–22nd March 2002, Glasgow, Scotland.

Wilson, L. A. (2001) Information Literacy: fluency across and beyond the university. In Dewey, B. I. (ed.) *Library User Education: powerful learning, powerful partnership*, London, Scarecrow Press, 1–17.

11

Information literacy – who needs it?

Gill Needham

Introduction

There is a set of skills and some underpinning knowledge that librarians and an increasing number of other people call information literacy. In the UK, policy in further and higher education is beginning to acknowledge a need for these skills to support the development of lifelong learners, but, in this respect, we lag far behind our colleagues in Australia and North America. While we may never catch up with them, we are extremely fortunate in being able to learn from their experience and be inspired by their success. However, an audit of higher education and further education institutions in the UK in 2002 reported that 57% of participating institutions included information literacy in their learning and teaching strategies, which is most heartening (Big Blue, 2002). In other words, according to librarians and education policy-makers, learners need information literacy.

The last five years in the UK have seen valuable exploratory work carried out by both the Society of College, National and University Libraries (SCONUL) Advisory Committee on Information Literacy and the Joint Information Systems Committee (JISC)-sponsored Big Blue project. Both report that, despite excellent examples of good practice, there is still confusion, patchy provision and a lack of nationally accepted definitions and guidelines. Indeed our professional body, the Chartered Institute of Library and Information Professionals (CILIP), held an expert seminar as recently as June 2003 to try and agree an 'official' definition of information literacy.

Given this background it is hardly surprising that the holy grail of information skills integrated throughout the curriculum in UK further and higher education can appear elusive. Similarly, a study of information literacy in third level undergraduate education in the Republic of Ireland found that 'examples of successful initiatives are comparatively rare (although increasing), and non-existent in some contexts' (McGuiness, 2003, 245).

Experience at the Open University

The Open University (OU) is a large distance teaching university with around 200,000 registered students dispersed around the UK and worldwide. Like many other universities we have a major objective to 'integrate [information literacy] skills into the curriculum' (Open University Library Information Literacy Unit Strategy, 2003) and we are monitoring our progress carefully. Despite some notable successes, we recognize that progress will be slow and in some areas we will encounter major barriers, such as:

- academics who remain unconvinced of the role of generic or key skills in the curriculum
- a reluctance to replace standard course content with information skills activities (despite the university's commitment to encouraging independent learning)
- concerns about increasing student workload where course content is already 'fixed' (time poverty is an important issue for the OU's part-time learners, 75% of whom are in full-time employment)
- the sheer size of the task – requiring library staff to engage with more than 400 courses.

It is therefore reassuring to read that even in North America the goal of full integration is by no means achieved. A recent study of Canadian universities suggests that in the majority of universities information literacy instruction is still optional for students (Julien, 2002).

Do learners themselves think they need information literacy skills?

What, if anything, do we know about the extent to which learners (and potential learners) value and require these skills? We know that provision of information literacy training is universal but that the models vary considerably in scope – from 'library induction' to comprehensive (and assessed) modules or courses – and also in the extent to which learners are required to participate. Martin and Williamson (2003) report on their experience at Edge Hill College of Higher Education where the skills are fully integrated into specific courses via the College's virtual learning environment. Through systematic pre and post testing students report improvements in their skills, which they say are valued and appreciated.

Where students are offered a comprehensive information skills programme as an optional extra, what is the take-up? Hodges and Johnson (2003, 164) report a 50–60% uptake for their impressive ILIAD programme at York University, despite the fact that students pay a small fee of £15.50 for 12 hours of study.

MOSAIC

At the Open University in 2002 we launched a free-standing short course in information literacy called Making Sense of Information in the Connected Age, known as MOSAIC (course code U120). This is a 12 week course (80–100 hours of study), which awards ten points at level one. It forms part of the University's growing portfolio of short courses. These are all advertised within the OU prospectus and can be taken either as elements in a degree programme or as one-off courses. We deliver MOSAIC twice a year – May to July and November to January.

This is an extract from the University's online prospectus, available at www.open.ac.uk:

> This new course provides a practical introduction to making the most of information, whether for your studies or for day-to-day use. Structured interactive activities help you to learn about topics such as the role of information in today's 'information society', searching for information with electronic tools like databases and internet search engines, and evaluating and managing the results of your searches. This will help you to become a confident information user.
>
> The course is designed to help you with practical skills, such as using a range of search tools, selecting appropriate sources of information, and writing a bibliography; and also with more academic skills such as critical evaluation of information, and working in a methodical and systematic way to search for information. The course materials are presented online from the course website, with access for registered students only. We assume that you might be fairly new to computing but are not a complete beginner.
>
> This course will appeal to you if you use information every day and want to make the most of libraries and online resources; or if you intend to continue your studies (perhaps towards a degree) and so will need skills of this kind.

It is perhaps significant that we do not use the phrase 'information literacy' but have chosen instead to describe the course in terms of its intended outcomes. MOSAIC's learning outcomes are heavily influenced by the US and Australian guidelines and the SCONUL Seven Pillars model (SCONUL, 1999). They are presented thus on the course website (http://library.open.ac.uk/help/infolitunit.html):

> The course aims: to help you develop skills and confidence in finding, using and handling information.
>
> By the end of the course we hope you will be:
>
> - familiar with a range of information sources
> - familiar with tools and techniques for searching for and organizing information
> - able to plan and carry out a systematic search for information
> - able to use a systematic approach to judge the quality of information
> - able to organize information and present it in an appropriate way.

MOSAIC is taught entirely online and uses a variety of interactive activities to engage the learner and allow them to practise their developing skills. Many of the activities allow learners to save their responses and then compare these to automated feedback from the course authors. The assessment is via an online reflective portfolio, which is completed and revisited throughout the course and then submitted electronically at the end. Students receive a pass or fail and also a detailed skills profile.

Who are the MOSAIC students?

We identified a potential market for this course through our experience of supporting OU students, many of whom seem to struggle with use of library and e-resources. We were also informed by the exploratory work carried out by the then SCONUL Task Force on Information Skills, which identified a need for a generic course. We did not know what kinds of student might be attracted to the course and what the nature of their motivation might be. When the course was first presented the cost was £75 – this has now risen to £95. While we consider that this represents excellent value for a ten point course, it is still a not insignificant investment for the students and suggests that they place a significant value on the outcomes of the course.

Since May 2002 more than 800 students have studied MOSAIC. The results in this paper are derived from demographic data and questionnaire surveys of the 638 students who sat the first two presentations in May 2002 and November 2002.

Of the 638 students, just under half (300) were new to study with the Open University, while just over half (338) were 'continuing' students. The majority of the students (614) were based in the UK with 24 studying abroad. The course has so far been more popular with women than men (63%–37%). The age range is fairly broad, from under 25 to over 65, but the largest proportion is in the 30–59 range (see Figure 11.1). This corresponds to the average profile of OU students

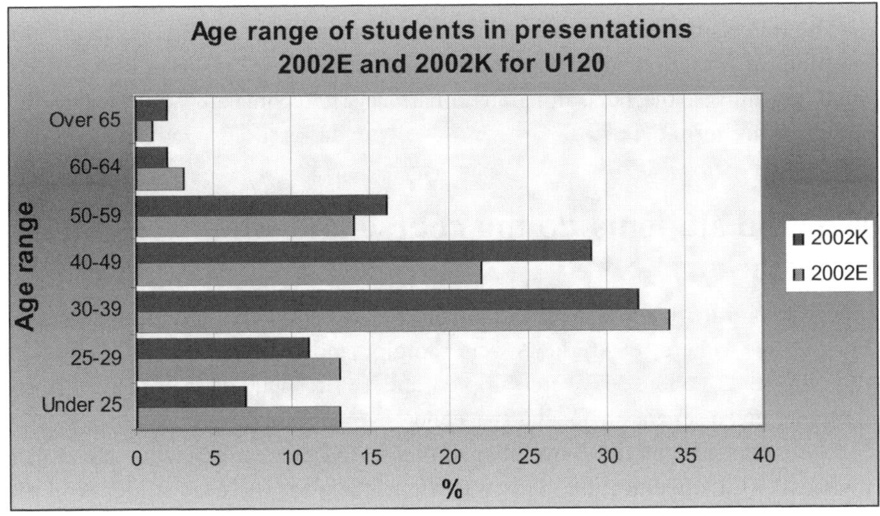

Figure 11.1 Age range of students in the May and November 2002 presentations for U120. Note: 2002E is the May 2002 cohort; 2002K is the November 2002 cohort

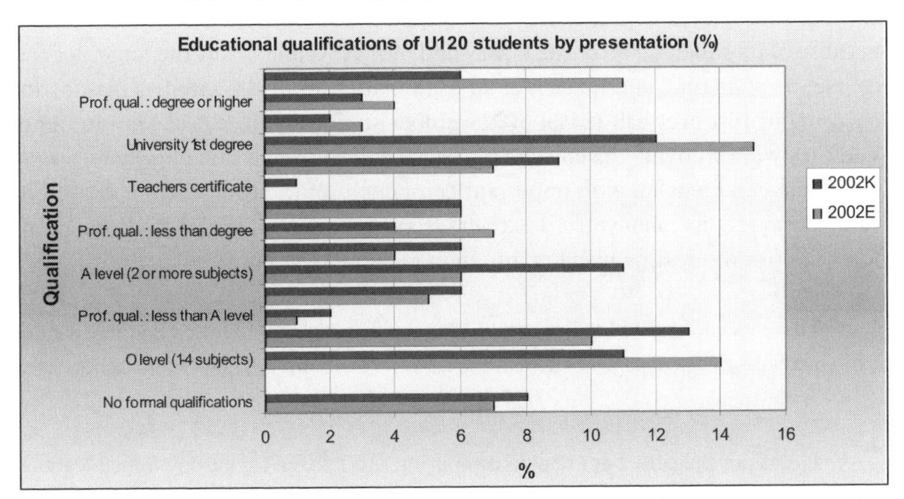

Figure 11.2 Educational qualifications of U120 students by presentation (%)

and might also support a hypothesis that older students are more likely to be concerned about information literacy than younger ones.

Only 5% said they were of non-white ethnic origin, but 150 didn't complete this part of the registration form. 16% of the students qualified for financial assistance from the University. 7% declared a disability.

Students have approached this course with a very broad range of educational qualifications as shown in Figure 11.2, from 8% with no formal qualifications at all to the 19% with university degrees.

The university does not collect information about students' employment. Our anecdotal information suggests our students are in a wide range of occupations, including nurses, teachers, librarians, pharmacists, technicians and bank clerks, and some are retired.

Why did students do the course and what were their expectations?

These results are drawn from questionnaire surveys of the two cohorts of students. For the May cohort 186 students were sampled and 75 responded (40%) and for the November cohort 361 were sampled and 185 responded (51%). Results are therefore given separately for the two cohorts.

More than half of the November students (54%) were studying the course towards an OU qualification. This was slightly less for the May students (43%) while more than half of them (57%) were studying to pursue their subject interest (43% of the November students). A small but important group of students were trying to find out whether distance learning suited them (21% for November and 39% for May). The majority of students said they had chosen the course because of its subject matter (82% May and 69% November) but the length of the course, its start time and its lack of an examination were also cited as reasons for choosing it. Just over half (51%) of November students and 29% of May students said they were studying the course for a balance of vocational and personal reasons.

Online conferencing is an important component of the course and it is used in various ways. Some anonymized extracts from the informal 'coffee and chat' conference offer interesting insights into individual motivation:

> I have recently retired to live here in Crete and am doing U120 because there are not many English language libraries in the area and so I want to know how to access what is out there.

> I am from Bulgaria. I am new to computing and I haven't done any formal learning for a long time. It's very difficult for me but I hope with your help to cope with the material, to enjoy myself and meet some interesting people.

> I started off as an Arts student . . . but have now changed tack and want to complete my degree asap with IT type courses and then go on to do a Masters in Library and Info Science with Uni of Aber.

> I signed up for this course because I felt that it would help me to find online information for my History studies. Since I'm disabled I can't make trips to the local library so the internet could become an invaluable source.

I . . . worked in banking for 19 years until a year ago and am aiming to get a degree in Computing and IT through the OU.

I want be able to help my grandchildren with their homework.

How did students get on and what did they think of the course?

Tables 11.1 and 11.2 show how successfully students felt they had met the stated learning outcomes of the course and their own learning objectives.

Table 11.1 How successfully students felt that they had met the stated learning outcomes of the course

Cohort (2002)	Fairly successfully	Very successfully
May	59%	23%
November	53.3%	25.5%

Table 11.2 How successfully students felt they had been able to meet their learning objectives

Cohort (2002)	Fairly successfully	Very successfully
May	54%	24%
November	48.4%	32.1%

In terms of external measures of success, the pass rate for the course has been high and the general standard of the submitted portfolios has been impressive.

Of particular interest has been the students' assessment of the skills they have gained from the course and their perceived future usefulness (Table 11.3). We asked if the students will be able to use the generic skills they have developed through the course in further study, in their paid employment and in other activities.

Table 11.3 Perceived future use of generic skills which students have developed through the course

Cohort (2002)	In your paid employment	In further study	In other activities (for example voluntary, social or everyday)
May	76%	97%	87%
November	73.9%	96.4%	93.1%

This encouraging picture is further reinforced by numerous comments volunteered by students about the future usefulness of the skills. Many emphasized their further studies (some already in progress), for example:

> It has broadened my scope for accessing information off the internet.

> I am now studying T171 and find what I have learned about plagiarism and referencing very useful.

> Already used the knowledge gained to produce a bibliography on my new course . . .

> Skills such as producing a bibliography and evaluating information are needed in most courses.

> Had I had these skills last year I feel that I could have achieved far better TMA (assignment) results.

Others felt that their paid work would benefit, for example:

> I will use my skills in my job with the information department of my company.

> My work is in health information so the course has been directly useful.

> I embarked on the course to help me in my job as an assistant librarian and although I didn't complete the portfolio I have learnt useful information about searching databases and using search terms which I will be able to utilize when helping students.

> It has already proved useful in my employment.

> I am an OU Arts tutor – hence I shall be using my skills with my own students in the future.

And others focus on personal development and their day-to-day lives:

> It was mainly for personal development, although I hope that in the longer term it may help in career development. The skills I have now will enable me to assist my children with their learning needs.

> It will also provide me with skills to develop IT work further and enhance my personal life as disabled person.

> Helping with village website and newsletter.

> Day to day, generally being more sceptical in the analysis of information presented to me.

While a few students commented directly on the course's relevance to all spheres of their lives:

> I intend to return to social sciences later and expect to use the skills widely then in research for TMAs [assignments]. Also there have been a number of occasions since completing the course where I have wanted information for personal interest and for friends and I have used electronic journals and databases and internet gateways to find it. Before the course I would probably not have thought to use these resources and would not have known where to start looking.

> This course should be a must for anyone who has to find information for study, work or personal purposes. I have copies of the checklists printed out at work and the course has enabled me to find information easily on the web. I am less apprehensive about tackling web searches, libraries and databases. I wish I'd had access to this when I was doing my first degree.

What did the students think about information literacy?

Towards the end of the course students are introduced to the term 'information literacy'. They are given an article by Sheila Webber (2001) in which Sheila argues that information literacy should be given a higher profile and be taken seriously as a subject in its own right. Students are asked to share their comments on the article in an online conference. The thoughtful discussion that emerges is extremely gratifying to those of us involved with developing the course:

> Sheila Webber's article I believe sums up the whole essence of what U120 is trying to teach us and gets across the need to re-examine our way of thinking about how we find out information. The world today is a far cry from yesteryear and the amount of information available to us is immense. If we rely on the old hit and hope routine that we have adopted in the past, we may achieve certain results but better ones are out there, if only we spend a little time learning how to first plan and then execute a well thought out search.

> My own experience – as an undergraduate – of information and literacy skills teaching was limited and superficial. On some courses it was something that seemed to be added on as an afterthought.

> Like Webber I believe that the teaching of information . . . should begin at secondary school.

> I would think it sensible to include these skills as part of all level one courses, like note taking and reading skills, and an optional extra for those starting at level two or three who need to develop the skills. Information literacy is probably a gap in many undergraduates.

> Whilst librarians are ideally placed for assisting with the task, the responsibility surely lies with all educators for future lifelong learning.

> I disagree however that students are unaware of their incompetence. It is more that it is difficult to admit to a lack of what is seen as a basic requirement of the 21st century. Librarians anxious to highlight student ignorance would only make the situation worse.

What are the lessons from MOSAIC?

It is clear from the survey results and comments reported above that MOSAIC has been valuable for these particular students and we hope that this will be the case for subsequent cohorts. The majority have emerged with an acute awareness of the value of information literacy for lifelong learning in its broadest sense, encompassing formal studies and both personal and professional development. For us at the Open University, this is powerful data we can exploit to support the implementation of our Information Literacy Unit's strategy (2003).

It may be, however, that the demographic profile of these students and the range of environments within which they are studying is too atypical to be relevant to other parts of higher and further education. We are testing this to some extent with a project whereby colleagues in three other UK universities are delivering a stripped down version of MOSAIC to groups of their students within their own programmes. It will be very interesting indeed to see whether their students react in a similar fashion.

We are aware of the need to collect more objective data on the effectiveness of the course. We are currently testing a prototype of a diagnostic test for information literacy, based on the detailed learning outcomes of the course, which we hope to be able to use both to identify gaps in knowledge and skills and measure the effectiveness of MOSAIC and other programmes.

Conclusion

We acknowledge that MOSAIC is a very small case study and that more data is required. We are also aware that our students may differ from others and we hope that the pilot study with our three partner universities will help us to test this hypothesis.

The MOSAIC students' stories are interesting in themselves, however, and we believe that our data could be usefully pooled with qualitative and quantitative data from similar initiatives in the UK and elsewhere. Working together in this way and with support from bodies like SCONUL and JISC, we could build up a rich and detailed understanding of learners, their motivation and their attitude to information literacy as well as the impact our programmes have on their formal learning, professional and personal development This way we would stand a far better chance of convincing the education community as a whole that everybody needs it.

References

The Big Blue (2002) *Information Skills for Students: final report*, www.leeds.ac.uk/bigblue/.

Hodges, S. and Johnson, G. J. (2003) One Size Fits All? The Illiad Experience. In Martin, A. and Rader, H. (eds), *Information and IT Literacy: enabling learning in the 21st century*, London, Facet Publishing, 161–8.

Julien, H. (2002) Miles to Go Before We Sleep. Keynote paper presented at *River runs: trends in library instruction, 31st Annual Workshop on Instruction in Library Use (WILU)*, held on May 13–15 2002, in Fredericton, the capital city of New Brunswick, http://flay.hil.unb.ca/WILU/presentations/JulienKeynote_files/frame.htm.

Martin, L. and Williamson, S. (2003) Integrating Information Literacy into Higher Education. In Martin, A. and Rader, H. (eds), *Information and IT Literacy: enabling learning in the 21st century*, London, Facet Publishing, 144–50.

McGuiness, C. (2003) Attitudes of Academics to the Library's Role in Information Literacy Education. In Martin, A. and Rader, H. (eds), *Information and IT Literacy: enabling learning in the 21st century*, London, Facet Publishing, 244–54.

Open University website, courses and qualifications, www.open.ac.uk.

Open University Library Information Literacy Unit (2003) Information Literacy Unit Strategy, http://library.open.ac.uk/help/infolitunit.html.

SCONUL (1999) *Information Skills in Higher Education: a SCONUL position paper*, www.sconul.ac.uk/publications/publications.htm#2.

Webber, S. (2001) Myths and Opportunities, *Library Association Record*, 2001, **103** (9), 548–9.

Theme 3

Usability and accessibility of digital library services

12

An incremental usability and accessibility evaluation framework for digital libraries

Neil King, Terry Hoi-Yan Ma, Panayiotis Zaphiris, Helen Petrie and Fraser Hamilton

Introduction

Information and Communication Technologies (ICTs) are enabling a global audience to share knowledge and ideas with one another by the click of a button. One of the key tools of this revolution is the internet, which is replacing CD-ROMs with online databases, traditional hard copy books and journals with digital libraries and atlases with interactive geo-spatial data. The success of these services is maximized if end-users are well supported to easily accomplish their desired tasks.

The nature of digital libraries

In recent years the information superhighway, the internet, has become a global gateway for information dissemination. With the ability to share worldwide collections of information, digital libraries (DLs) have become one of the common mediums to store and disseminate information by individuals or groups that select, organize and catalogue large numbers of documents.

DLs, generally referred to as 'collections of information that are both digitized and organized' (Lesk, 1997), give us opportunities we never had with traditional libraries or even with the web. Current design of DLs contains complex facilities including text search, functionality relating to hypertext, multimedia, the internet and highly interactive interfaces.

According to Theng (1997), if we have problems producing good websites (as evidenced by much research done in addressing problems on the web), then because DLs are more than just websites, we can expect to have problems creating good DLs too. Also, Dix et al. (1995) suggested that even if the best methodologies and models are adopted in the design of a usable interactive system, it is still necessary to assess the design and test the system to ensure that it behaves as expected and meets the user's requirements. Therefore, there is a need for a usability and accessibility framework that supports the development of effective solutions for DLs in order to produce truly usable and accessible DLs.

A crucial factor for libraries is that the information they preserve and deliver must be effectively organized. With regards to DLs, Arms (2002) notes that a '(d)igital stream of data sent to earth from a satellite is not a library. [However, the] same data, when organized systematically, becomes a digital library collection.' This is one of the key dimensions of a DL. Highly effective cataloguing, organization and structure of information separates DLs from other ad-hoc web services where the information architecture and navigational mechanisms have no particular justification.

Another key dimension is user behaviour. Websites are often designed to support browsing activities, whereas DLs need to support task-orientated navigation. Vora and Helander (1997) define the difference between these two information-seeking behaviours. The main distinction between navigation and browsing is based upon user goals. In browsing, users explore the available hypertext to get a general idea about one or several topics. Whereas, in navigation, users have a specified goal in mind (Vora and Helander, 1997).

Previous evaluations of DLs identified key design flaws that needed improving (Theng et al., 1999). The main issue was to provide better navigation support mechanisms to address the 'lost in hyperspace' problem. Navigation here is used in terms of end-users' confidence in navigating within the DL. From their investigation, navigation of DLs is still not desirable. Users still experienced some degree of 'lostness'.

Soergel (2002) developed a framework for DL research. His research proposed some guiding principles for the development of DLs. The principles that related to usability issues were:

- DLs need linked data structures for powerful navigation and search
- the interface for the DLs should guide users through complex tasks
- innovative DL design should be informed by studies of user requirements and user behaviour.

Usability and accessibility

John and Marks (1997) identify three key factors to assess the usability of an interface:

1. Usability is measured by the extent to which the intended goals of use of the overall system are achieved (effectiveness).

2. The resources that have to be expended to achieve the intended goals (efficiency)
3. The extent to which the user finds the overall system acceptable (satisfaction).

The usability of a system is also related to issues surrounding its accessibility. There is a broad range of users to whom web-based services are directed, and the services provided ought to be accessible to them (this group includes visually, hearing, physically or cognitively impaired people or even those with different experience of and attitudes towards technology).

The Disability Discrimination Act (DDA) in the United Kingdom began to come into effect in December 1996 and brought in measures to prevent discrimination against people on the basis of disability. Part III of the Act (to be enforced in Autumn 2004) aims to ensure that people with disabilities have equal access to products and services. Under Part III of the Act, businesses that provide goods, facilities and services to the general public (whether paid for or free) need to make reasonable adjustments for people with disabilities to ensure they do not discriminate by:

- refusing to provide a service
- providing a service of a lower standard or in a worse manner
- providing a service on less favourable terms than they would to users without the disability.

There is a legal obligation on service providers to ensure that disabled people have equal access to web-based products and services. Section 19(1) (c) of the Act makes it unlawful for a service provider to discriminate against a disabled person 'in the standard of service which it provides to the disabled person or the manner in which it provides it'.

While no websites in the UK have so far been pursued under the Act, it does appear that courts will use the World Wide Web Consortium (W3C) Web Accessibility Initiative (WAI) guidelines as the accepted standard required for compliance with the DDA (Sloan, 2001). Interestingly, in April 2003 the Disabilities Rights Commission launched a formal investigation (to be carried out by the Centre for HCI Design at City University) into the accessibility of public and private websites (for more information refer to www.drc-gb.org/newsroom/newsdetails.asp?id=393§ion=1). Additionally, under the eEurope Initiative launched in December 1999, the European Commission has committed the member states to 'make all public websites and their content accessible to people with disabilities' through the adoption of WAI Guidelines. Although this is a non-legal requirement and only applies to public sector websites, there is also a commitment to review legislation and standards – which could see the initiative extended outside the public sector.

An important proviso here is that education is not covered by the DDA, but by the Special Educational Needs and Disability Act 2001 (SENDA). This Act introduces the right for disabled students not to be discriminated against in education, training and any services provided wholly or mainly for students, and for those enrolled on courses provided by 'responsible bodies', including further and higher education institutions and sixth form colleges. Student services covered by the Act can include a wide range of educational and non-educational services, such as field trips, examinations and assessments, short courses, arrangements for work placements and libraries and learning resources. In a similar wording to the DDA, SENDA requires responsible bodies to make reasonable adjustments so that people with disabilities are not at a substantial disadvantage.

So if digital library services and resources are used by people with disabilities as part of their work or personal development, they will be subject to the DDA (as providers of goods and services to employees of educational or research institutions or members of the public); if they are used by students or prospective students, they will be subject to SENDA.

Interface design should therefore be governed by the requirements of all stakeholders of the system. Thus a variety of issues have to be taken into account throughout by using a highly user-centred design process.

Usability and accessibility iterative framework for digital libraries

Libraries have always tried to remove obstacles to information access. A poorly designed DL is certainly a barrier to the library user; therefore a need exists for a specific usability and accessibility framework for DLs, which if adopted can ensure quality and enhanced usability of a service.

We regard the most important aspect in evaluating a system to be the identification of real user problems; therefore our framework plays specific attention to evaluation techniques that involve current and perspective users. Expert evaluation methodologies are also conducted to supplement user evaluations and address areas that are not covered by previous evaluation techniques. After each stage the findings must be evaluated, enabling appropriate design and modification of the techniques in the next stage of the framework, thus ensuring maximum effectiveness.

The framework shown in Figure 12.1 can be broken down into seven key steps:

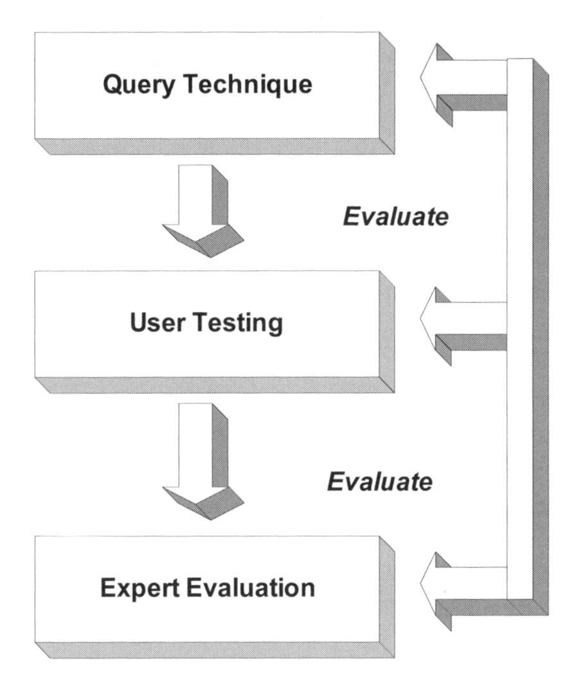

Figure 12.1 Usability/accessibility framework for digital libraries

1. **Conduct query – requirement gathering** Identify satisfaction levels of current users of the system and establish key positive and negative aspects of the interface, what features they would like to see, and so on.
2. **Analysis** Evaluate current findings and identify issues not yet addressed.
3. **Perform empirical (user) evaluations** We regard user testing as the strongest evaluation technique, allowing us to identify real user problems by observing users interacting with the system. Retrospective focus groups or interviews conducted after the evaluations also provide a volume of qualitative data.
4. **Analysis** Establish key problems and assess if any areas of the service have not been covered by user evaluations.
5. **Expert evaluations** Appropriate modification of expert evaluation techniques maybe required so that they supplement previous evaluation findings, and address any areas or issues that have not as yet been covered.
6. **Analysis** Analyse all data identifying key issues that need to be addressed in the redesign of the service. Establish new usability and accessibility goals for the design.
7. **Iterative process** Re-conduct all stages in the iterative framework to evaluate redesign.

Different techniques were used under each of three categories as follows:

- Query techniques (questionnaires, interviews, focus groups)
- User testing (retrospective, concurrent)
- Expert evaluations (heuristic evaluation, cognitive walkthrough).

The evaluation techniques applied to the DL framework also need to address the highly organized and task-based nature of DLs. In our evaluations of four Joint Information Systems Committee (JISC) services (a bibliographic service, a portal, a geo-spatial DL and an Image database) the tasks applied to the user testing evaluations and cognitive walkthroughs were designed with these two dimensions in mind, for example:

- Image Database – User Testing, Task 1
  Retrieve images of London Bridge, ONLY from the collections below:
  Design Council Archive: University of Brighton
  Women's Library: Suffrage Banners Collection
- Portal Service – Cognitive Walkthrough, Persona 3
  Find the education materials – Internet for Education from the SOSIG site.

These examples are both task orientated, and require a high level of content organization by the services.

However, not all usability requirement gathering and evaluation techniques are applicable to all of the services in the same manner. In addition, the goals and actions that users wish to achieve vary according to the nature of the service. Therefore, it is imperative that the specific usability issues that apply to each service are clearly identified, along with the corresponding stakeholder requirements for each resource.

For example, the usability issues surrounding virtual map libraries differ in some aspects from those of other DLs owing to the specific type of information they preserve and display. The technical nature of the information means that the interface must provide visualization tools that all users can operate. Hence the systems usability, especially in terms of interface design, must be strongly correlated with the end-users' productivity. Methodologies that gather user requirements and evaluate usability must also be adapted to suit individual services in some instances. Query techniques like questionnaires need to be designed to specifically extract users' requirements in relation to that service.

The requirements of the different types of users also differ between, and within, a service. Some users require a service to offer an abundance of advanced tools, thus providing greater versatility when interacting with the application. Other users, however, want clearly structured and formulated steps to help them accomplish their tasks, although perhaps at the expense of flexibility.

Conclusion

Our usability and accessibility framework for digital libraries concentrates on establishing a framework that focuses on the main characteristics of digital libraries. This focus is based on the findings we gathered from the extensive research we did of current usability practices adopted by JISC, the requirements of the stakeholders and additional investigation in the area of digital libraries.

According to our findings, the main characteristics of a truly usable and accessible digital library are that they:

- support task-based information-seeking behaviour
- have highly organized information content.

The framework was constructed in a way that specifically addressed these factors, and met the usability and accessibility needs of digital libraries. Therefore ensuring that by adopting the framework, truly usable and accessible digital libraries can be produced.

The evaluations of the four JISC services were conducted using the usability and accessibility framework established for digital libraries. The methodologies adopted in this study were both analytic and empirical. Query techniques were used to establish the requirements and key problems that users currently experienced. User testing was conducted to further identify major usability and accessibility issues with each of the JISC services. This was followed by analytic evaluations such as heuristics evaluations and cognitive walkthroughs with usability and accessibility experts evaluating the JISC services based on their expert knowledge. Each stage in the process was supported and supplemented where needed by the one that followed in order to clarify the findings, identify further usability and accessibility issues and produce an iterative process.

The evaluation framework specified the stages at which designers should employ such methodologies and techniques in the iterative design process – from requirement elicitation, design generation to the evaluation stages. In the usability and accessibility framework, we regarded that the most important aspect in evaluating a system was the identification of real user issues; therefore our framework focused on the evaluation techniques that involved both the current and perspective users. Expert evaluation methodologies were embedded as part of the evaluation stage within the framework. Expert evaluations act as a supplement to the empirical user testing evaluations and address areas that have not been identified by the previous evaluation stages. The findings gathered from the evaluations at each stage are then analysed, enabling appropriate design and modification of the techniques in the next stage of the framework, thus ensuring effectiveness and efficiency when conducting the evaluations, maximizing the benefits resulting from the findings of the evaluations. This workable framework will enable designers and developers of DLs to employ the most suitable methodologies and techniques for each aspect, at each particular stage, in the development of their service.

We believe that by employing the usability and accessibility framework and guidelines established in this study, JISC will be able to produce truly usable and accessible services and resources for the existing and future JISC Information Environment.

Suggestions to practitioners

Practitioners could apply the usability and accessibility evaluation framework into the evaluation of existing or future DLs in order to assess the usability and accessibility issues of these services.

In the meantime, the usability and accessibility guidelines established from the findings of the four JISC services we evaluated, could be adopted into the redesign of other services and resources as well as in the design of future DL services. This would ensure that appropriate usability and accessibility practices are adopted into the design lifecycle.

Suggestions to researchers

Future research directions could be undertaken to investigate how appropriate human-computer interaction (HCI) design principles could best be applied within DL services and resources, and also how to address current developments in HCI design and synthesize these for use within the context of the information environment. In particular, to cover the role of HCI design in the delivery of learning, teaching, research and, most importantly, to further investigate how DLs could be adopting these principles for HCI design within its practices more formally in the future.

At the same time, an investigation of visualization techniques for use by DLs and resources could be conducted, establishing sets of visualization techniques and guidelines for DLs to enhance the delivery of information for learning, teaching and research within the JISC information environment.

Finally, future research could be undertaken into specific digital libraries, such as geo-spatial information services and bibliographic database services. An in-depth investigation into these services specifically would help us to refine our framework and guidelines presented in this project and further cater for the needs of different digital library services.

Acknowledgements

Work reported herein was supported by a grant from the Joint Information Systems Committee (JISC; www.jisc.ac.uk).

References

Arms, W. (2002) *Digital Libraries*, www.cs.cornell.edu/wya/DigLib.

Dix, A., Finlay, J., Abowd, G. and Beale, R. (1995) *Human-Computer Interaction*, London, Prentice-Hall.

John, B. E. and Marks, S. J. (1997) Tracking the Effectiveness of Usability Evaluation Methods, *Behaviour and Information Technology*, **16** (4/5), 188–202.

Lesk, M. (1997) *Practical Digital Libraries: book, bytes and bucks*, San Francisco, CA, Morgan Kaufmann.

Sloan M, (2001) Web Accessibility and the DDA, *Journal of Information, Law and Technology (JILT)*, http://elj.warwick.ac.uk/jilt/01-2/sloan.html .

Soergel, D. (2002) A Framework for Digital Library Research: broadening the vision. *D-Lib Magazine*, **8**, 12, www.dlib.org/.

Theng, Y. L. (1997). *Addressing the 'Lost In Hyperspace' Problem in Hypertext*, PhD Thesis, Middlesex University (London).

Theng, Y. L., Duncker, E., Mohd-Nasir, N., Buchanan, G. and Thimbleby, H. (1999). Design Guidelines and User-Centred Digital Libraries. Lecture notes in computer science: research and advanced technology for digital libraries (*Proceedings of ECDL '99*), 167–83. Heidelberg, Germany, Springer Verlag.

Vora, P. R. and Helander, M. H. (1997) Hypertext and its Implications for Internet. In Helander, M. H., Landauer, T. K. and Prabhu, P. (eds) *Handbook of Human-Computer Interaction*, 2nd edn, Amsterdam, Elsevier Science.

13

Overcoming barriers to library use by Nigerian professionals

Oluwatoyin O. Kolawole

Introduction

Library and Information professionals are agreed that the catalysts that will empower Africa in her quest for development are information and knowledge. The increasing openness and globalization of the world economy has further made it clear that organizations must lever information effectively to achieve their objectives and stay competitive. The response has been a further pressure on professionals to perform and demonstrate their relevance to their organization's bottom line.

Realizing that access to information and flexible learning are what would differentiate them for success, professionals are turning to libraries for support for their personal and professional development, especially with the dearth of support from other quarters. However, as information becomes more rapidly available in non-book sources, which could be accessed electronically using new and emerging technologies, the relevance of a largely traditional Nigerian library to a highly mobile and constrained segment of its clientele is in question.

As in other parts of Africa, low levels of literacy in information and communication technologies (ICTs) in Nigeria are perpetuated by limited access to computers. Yet, over 75% of organizations in Nigeria put emphasis on possession of demonstrable ICT skills as a requirement for employment. Therefore the need for relevance and employability has recently driven professionals to seek ICT skills training where available, especially in libraries that provide it free of charge.

The use and availability of ICTs in Nigeria

Organizations that are major employers of professionals in Nigeria spend about 478 billion naira annually on ICT and will be inclined to spend 1.6 trillion naira in the near future. Although of the over 120 million people in Nigeria, only about 0.6% have access to a PC at home, the pace of ICT uptake is increasingly encouraging. Nigeria is quickly becoming one of the destinations of ICT product providers in Africa, second only to South Africa. In the last seven years, the number of licensed full internet providers has grown from 3 to 160, 40 of which provide access in real time. With more than a quarter of organizations having a web presence, more professionals have access to the internet (NICT, 2003).

Udeji (2003) reports that despite inadequate and even outdated technology, some components of national information infrastructure (NII) are in place, with current research aimed at developing models to support rural communities to establish access to the NII. This is much like the successful and scalable Computers in Our Future project, which closed the technology gap in 11 low-income communities in California (Fowells and Lazarus, 2001). Having achieved an uptake of the global system of mobile communication (GSM) service by two million people in two years and enabled expansion of fixed wireless lines to achieve a teledensity of 2.63 per 100 people, exceeding the International Telecommunications Union's recommendation of 1 per 100 people, the Nigerian Communications Commission continues to implement the National Telecommunications Policy 2000 by offering licences for operators whose focus will be in underserved markets and community telecentre development projects (Aragba-Akpore, 2003a).

As most of these lines use satellite communication, it could enable interaction with customers even in areas physically remote from the library. With the cost of a text message to any part of the country less than the cost of an intra-city postage stamp, the possibilities for information-sharing between libraries and its customers are extending.

This then is the ICT environment within which libraries currently operate in Nigeria. As indigenous companies in strategic partnership with global companies introduce wi-fi hotspots (Aragba-Akpore, 2003b) and state of the art model cyber-cafés (Ebi, 2003), there are a lot of incentives for libraries to innovate products that take advantage of emerging technologies to deliver quality service to professionals even in the face of current limitations.

Peculiar Lagos

Lagos remains the commercial nerve centre of Nigeria and easily the busiest city in Africa. It is an impossibly difficult city to get around in, especially on work days.

With everyone seemingly going and coming in the same direction, the traffic is chaotic. The risk of damage to vehicles and persons is quite high. The business districts where professionals are engaged are jammed, so the office is a haven even during lunch breaks. Other cities where organizations employing Nigerian professionals are clustered mirror the scene in Lagos to a varying but lesser extent.

Effect of the digital divide: the gimme gimme culture

The overarching effect of the digital divide is the over dependence on the librarian to provide readily usable information, further entrenching a low level of information literacy. The relatively low ability to use ICTs has further compounded the inadequate information-handling skills that librarians have sought to help their customers overcome through user education in largely traditional libraries. Many users are abandoning their responsibility to assess the quality of information they get, uncritically accepting whatever is made available. For a country that needs to develop critical and questioning skills to demand good governance of its people and leaders, this is paralysing.

So what do we do with this mixed bag?

Apparently working with Salinas' (2003) definition of the digital divide as the disparity between individuals or communities who can use electronic information and communication tools, such as the internet, to better the quality of their lives and those who cannot, libraries in Nigeria are placing emphasis and holding professional discussions on the need to digitize their libraries with the provision of computers, internet services and electronic collections, and rightly so. Constrained to provide these, however, they fall into a state of immobility, and remain in what Peters (2003) refers to as 'the bookish mould'.

However, this immobility can be overcome when we remember that the digital divide is about people rather than computers (Chabran, 2000), and a digital library is a collection of information to which the traditional library skills of organizing information have been applied and which is now stored for users to access electronically. So we do what we know how to do but in a different way and using probably newly acquired skills. As Lemos (2002) opined at his guest lecture at IFLA 2002, to continue to be relevant to their user communities, librarians ought to give more thought to what ICTs could do for the accessibility of their resources and services to their clientele who have individual, diverse needs.

Hence, as support for Nigerian libraries to help professionals do what they want to do, this study set out to establish the specific constraints to library use by Nigerian professionals and the services they require to overcome them in the context of emerging technologies, with a view to suggesting library services and policies that could encourage them to use the library more.

Methodology

A purposive survey of 250 professionals visiting the British Council Information Centre, Lagos, was conducted using a structured questionnaire, the distribution of which was staggered over three months. The British Council was selected as the major example of a library open to Nigerian professionals irrespective of their affiliations. There was a response rate of 78.8%, with 197 questionnaires returned. Data was analysed using simple descriptive statistics and the findings are presented below.

Findings

Data in Table 13.1 shows that about 60% of respondents were male and 40% female. Most (74.1%) of the respondents were aged between 25 and 44 years.

Table 13.1 Demographic distribution of respondents to questionnaire (n = 197)

			%
Gender			
	Male	116	59.9
	Female	81	41.1
Age group			
	18–24	26	13.2
	25–34	89	45.2
	35–44	57	28.9
	45 and above	25	12.7

Data in Table 13.2 shows that although about 90% of respondents visit the library once every three months, only about 32.5% visit more than twice a month on average. Traditional library services are well used, and all respondents claimed to use the Electronic Information Service.

Also in Table 13.2, respondents reported some of their constraints to using the library as a busy schedule (68%) and traffic congestion (72%). These are constraints that are not within the control of the library. However, over 83% did indicate that the non-provision of some key services that are important to them was a constraint to their using the library. Forty percent of respondents also indicated a major constraint to be limited ICT skills, a factor that the library could overcome through provision of information literacy skill training.

Table 13.2 Characteristics of professionals' use of the library (n = 197)

		%
Frequency of visit*		
Once in the last three months	179	90.4
Three times in the last three months	125	63.5
At least six times in the last three months	64	32.5
Services used*		
Reference and professional books	163	85.7
Videos	48	24.4
Electronic information	197	100.0
Professional journals	136	69.0
Newspapers and leisure magazines	47	23.9
Constraints to use*		
Busy schedules	133	67.5
Traffic congestion	142	72.1
Limited ICT skill	79	40.1
Key service not provided	164	83.3
Others	53	26.9

*Multiple responses

Table 13.3 shows that although all the respondents reported using the internet within the library premises, only about 13.2% of respondents accessed the internet solely from the library. Some also reported using it at their offices (42.6%) and from cybercafés (71.6%).

Table 13.3 Place where respondents accessed the internet (n = 197)

		%
Office	84	42.6
Library	197	100.0
Cybercafé	141	71.6
Home	2	1.0
Library only	26	13.2

Table 13.4 Services demanded by professionals (n = 164)

		%
Remote access to resources	113	68.9
Support for distance learning	105	64.0
On-site networking	103	62.8
Information by text messaging	125	76.2
E-newsletter and online information	99	60.4
ICT skills training	71	43.3
Coffee shop	110	67.1
Video conferencing	81	49.4
Increased local content	69	42.1
Study area	61	37.2
Others	34	20.7

Of the 83.3% indicating 'key service not provided' as a constraint to use in Table 13.2, the services required but not provided include: remote access to resources (68.9%), information by text messaging (76.2%) ,on-site networking (62.8%), coffee shop (67.1%), support for distance learning (64%) and availability of e-newsletter and online information (60.4%) among others (see Table 13.4).

Discussion

The research showed that convenient access to resources, immediate response to needs and the requirement for a controlled environment conducive to lifelong learning drive the use that professionals make of libraries in Nigeria. Considering that most do not have access to PCs and new technologies at home, provision of facilities that support learning in the library will be invaluable. However, the 'I need it and I need it now' culture and environmental constraints in getting to the library make it imperative for libraries to provide users with access to the resources of the library from wherever they choose to use them. This is especially important with libraries situated in busy business districts where traffic congestion brings a considerable constraint to visiting the physical facilities of the library.

Therefore, faced with diverse interests and needs centred on both traditional and virtual library services within a group, the library that would retain its relevance to this group of society will not remain entirely traditional and physical, nor can it become overwhelmingly digital and virtual. In order to take care of users whose preference will be to access the resources and services beyond the library walls, remote access to resources will need to be provided and supported with information literacy skills to guide users to develop skills in evaluating the worth of the information they find. The users who need to use the resources and services within the walls of the library will also need to be accommodated there. In any case, these preferences will not necessarily be static since users' needs change according to their current circumstance and interests.

Blended information service delivery

As with other aspects of life, the presence of choice brings with it a perception of quality. Users must have control over their own learning and the means through which they do it.

Therefore, librarians will need to be more inclined to providing equal access to library facilities and creative in the way they serve professionals in Nigeria. The library will need to become flexible, providing an appropriate mix of quality traditional on-site resources and networking activities enhanced with virtual, remote access to content and services from wherever the client chooses to use it, whether within the library or from the office, home, or even a cybercafé. The act of leaving the choice of access to the customer further empowers the customer with control over their own needs and would keep them happy and coming back. This appropriate mix is what the author refers to as 'blended information service delivery'.

Possible services

With the expanding capabilities of information and communications technologies, a world of opportunity opens up for libraries to demonstrate their relevance to today's society by providing information in real time and beyond library walls. ICTs in general offer great potential in reducing poverty, improving gender equality and providing inroads into good governance, all essential ingredients for development.

Although decades of misrule and neglect have left libraries with the problem of poor facilities and obsolete technology, compounded by the relatively high cost of emerging technologies that would make it meaningful for futuristic libraries to innovate products for their users, libraries may still take advantage of the ICT revolution going on in Nigeria to serve its professional clientele. Existing services like current awareness and SDI can be enhanced using inexpensive mobile text messaging while new services such as enabling the cost-effective sharing of knowledge through video conferencing can be introduced, all reducing the time between when information is processed and when delivered for the benefit of the user.

Physical interaction, lending services in a culture where books are rare and support for distance learning on-site, which requires a few PCs, internet access and relevant software, could also be essential attractions for professionals to use library services more. Libraries can make a difference to professionals' knowledge base by incorporating information literacy skills training into basic ICT use training. This can be provided cost-effectively as a self-access short guide available on the library's website and in print in the library. In spite of constraints faced by Nigerian libraries, interacting with professionals to communicate information for development in real time without barriers is the challenge that faces the Nigerian library today: providing an innovative blended information service could help make this possible.

Critical success factors for blended information service delivery

Given the restrictions of limited access to PCs and other ICTs, and the low level of information literacy, achieving an appropriate mix of physical and virtual service for professionals in Nigeria will not be an easy task. Critical factors for its successful implementation will require that the library team think globally, but take action on what is feasible for them after researching their particular market. A lot of thinking and planning while starting out could avoid a waste of resources later and forming strategic partnerships could lessen the burden on individual libraries in terms of funding and expertise. Particularly important is the need to plan the use of virtual resources. The planning also needs to be flexible for the future to make it easy to effect appropriate changes as required. The success of the programme will undoubtedly depend on the team that implements it, so librarians need to be trained in the relevant skills to help them be comfortable with delivering a blended information service.

References

Aragba-Akpore, S. (2003a) Government Steps up Effort to Boost Rural Telephony, *Guardian* (26 August), 41 and 51.

Aragba-Akpore, S. (2003b) Nigeria Surpasses ITU's Teledensity Prescription, Now has 3 Million Lines, *Guardian*, (29 August), 15 and 19.

Chabran, R. (2000) From Digital Divide to Digital Opportunity, *Hispanic Lifestyle*, **3** (3), 54–5.

Ebi, F. (2003) One World, Diamond Bank Align for Turnkey Internet Projects, *Guardian* (26 August), 55.

Fowells. L and Lazarus W. (2001) *Computers in Our Future: what works in closing the gap? Lessons from a four year demonstration in 11 low income California communities*, 1–19, www.ciof.org/.

Lemos, G. (2002) Flaming diverse, *British Council Infonews*, **46** (January), 10.

NICT (2003) *Nigeria Information and Communications Technology Handbook*, 37–55.

Peters D. (2003) *Developing Digital Libraries in South Africa: breaking out of the bookish mould*, Unpublished.

Salinas, R. (2003) Addressing the Digital Divide Through Collection Development, *Collection Building*, **22** (3), 131–6.

Udeji, P.C. (2003) Development of National Information Infrastructure. In *Nigeria Information and Communications Technology Handbook*, 297–305.

14
Digital library services at the Italian National Health Institute library

Franco Toni

Introduction

The library of the National Health Institute (ISS) is the most important Italian library in the biomedical science field. It is primarily used by researchers, scientific and administrative personnel of the Institute (more than 2000 people) but it is also open to external users.

A brief glance at its structure is useful to explain the duties of our Institute and our researchers' fields of interest. The ISS is currently made up of 20 laboratories – in an already approved reorganization they will soon merge into seven departments and two national centres – embracing several biomedical disciplines, such as cell biology, epidemiology, haematology, pharmacology, physics, environmental hygiene, veterinary medicine, toxicology and virology.

The library holds more than 200,000 volumes and almost 9000 periodicals. Total annual expenditure is €2.2 million, with €1.6 million invested in serials and journal subscriptions. The continual advance of information technology has greatly modified the way scientists and researchers use the libraries. All this has brought about the need to redefine the duties of libraries completely, modifying policies and strategies in order to manage the flow of information better so that we satisfy the new requirements of users.

In 2000 the ISS library began to develop a project to implement an intranet site that could provide access to any area of the Institute, to online services and to electronic resources related to information needs. Our efforts are especially concentrated on databases and electronic journals. For this purpose our library signed an agreement with CIBER/CASPUR, one of the three large Italian consortia for information sharing in electronic format. The initial terms of this agreement provided access to the Science Direct database with a link to more than 600 periodicals published by Elsevier, the most important scientific publisher.

The new intranet site was launched at the beginning of 2001 and, at first, internal users had free access to about 1100 online full-text journals and to a restricted selection of online databases. This scenario rapidly evolved under the pressure of numerous requests from our researchers and after two years we have activated connections with Kluwer, Wiley and Nature Publishing Group databases, as well as the principal scientific journals such as *Science*, *New England Journal of Medicine*, *JAMA* and others. At the moment more than 2700 periodicals are available online, to which must be added 22 bibliographic and specific databases, among these Medline, Chemical Abstract Collective Index, Chem Bank, Embase, EBM and others.

The survey

In March 2002, 15 months after the service had been started, we decided to carry out a survey in order to monitor and audit the level of satisfaction and interest of our users regarding the general services of the library and in particular the remote services.

For this purpose a questionnaire was prepared and distributed. The questionnaire contained a large section specifically dedicated to the evaluation of networked services, to their mode and level of use, to the changes that these new tools brought to the user's habits and in relation to the traditional library. From a potential target of 2400 internal users, including scientific and administrative staff, we received 562 responses. The deadline for returning the questionnaire was one month.

The six questions on the intranet services had a series of three to six multiple choice answers in order for us to have uniform results. Let us consider the questions in detail.

The first question asked users how frequently they used the intranet and there were four possible answers:

- 3–4 times a week or more
- 1–2 times a week
- less than once a week
- not used at all.

Figure 14.1 shows the results.

Results show that the library intranet is very useful for internal users and is rapidly becoming one of the most important and used tools inside the Institute:

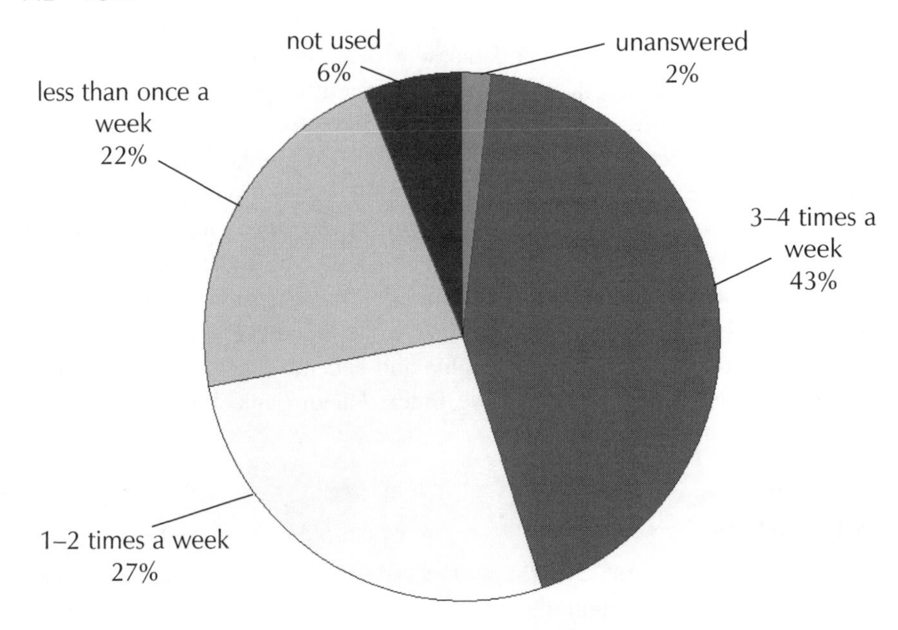

Figure 14.1 Frequency of use of the ISS library intranet

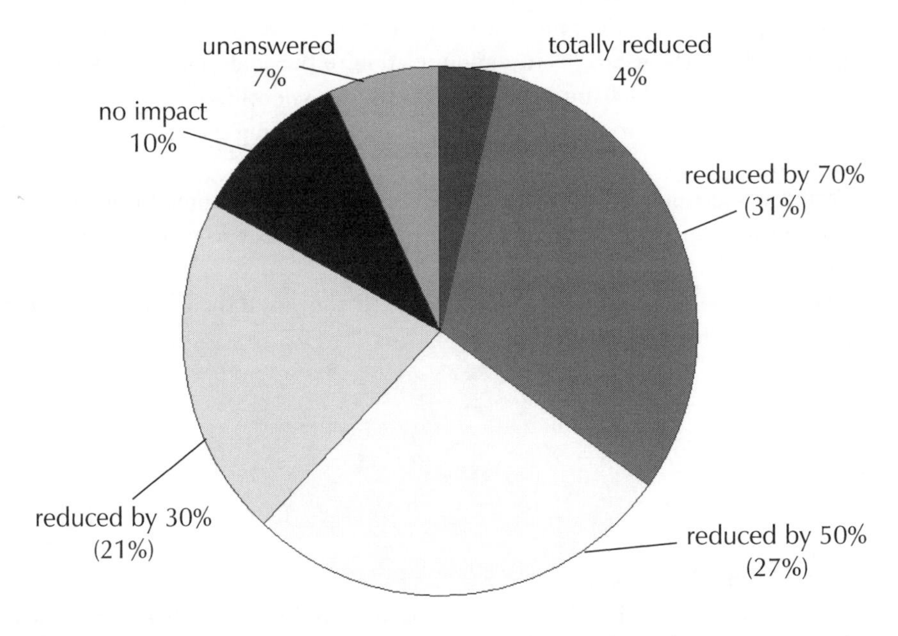

Figure 14.2 Impact of ISS library intranet on the number of visits users made to the library

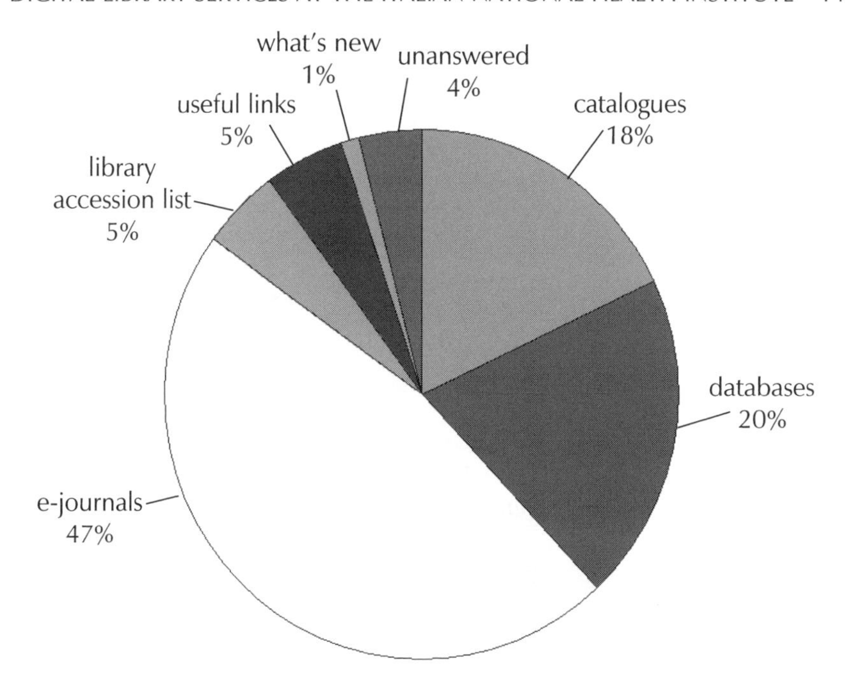

Figure 14.3 Use of services in the library

only 6% do not use it, while 43% use it often, 27% at least once a week and 22% occasionally.

The second question aimed to find out to what degree electronic access had reduced or replaced library visits, since it enables users to satisfy their need for access to information and full-text documents directly at their own desk. Respondents were given five options. Electronic access had:

- totally replaced users' visits to the library
- replaced visits by 70%
- replaced visits by 50%
- replaced visits by 30%
- had no impact on the number of visits users made to the library.

As we can see from Figure 14.2, the introduction of the intranet has replaced one visit out of three in 21% of uses, one visit out of two in 27% of uses, two visits out of three in 31% of uses, and completely in 4% of uses, a total of almost 80% of cases.

The third question aimed to identify which services were used most. Users could choose two out of six options:

- catalogues
- databases
- e-journals
- the library accession list
- useful links
- what's new.

The most heavily used service was e-journals (47%), followed by databases (20%), catalogues (18%), the library accession list and useful links (both with 5%) and finally 'what's new' (only 1%).

The fourth question was directly linked with the previous one: we asked users to state which services they thought it would be most useful to increase. These were only three possibilities because we decided to discard 'catalogues' and to merge the other three options under 'informative pages'. The choices were:

- databases
- e-journals
- informative pages.

The result (see Figure 14.4) was a huge request (55%) to increase the number of e-journals, followed by requests to increase the number of databases (26%) and of informative pages (only 12%).

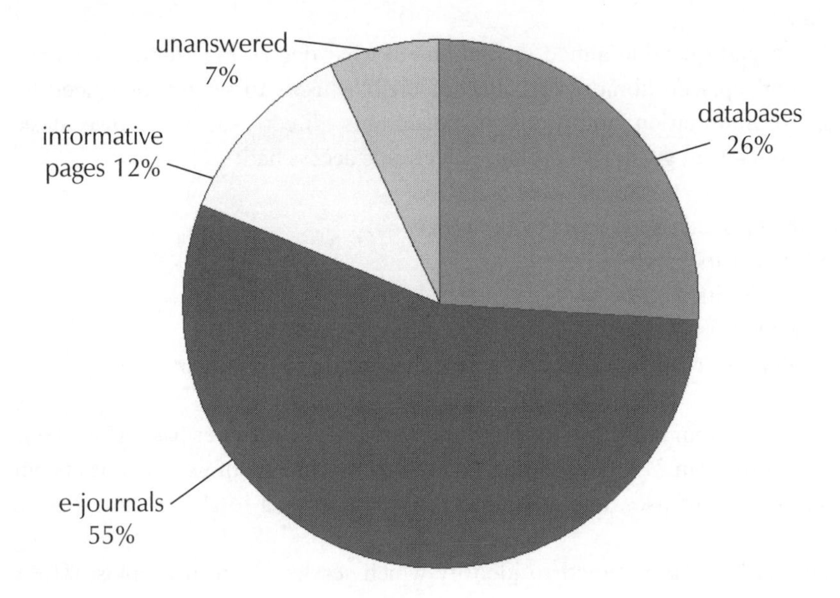

Figure 14.4 Services users thought it would be useful to increase

The purpose of the fifth question was to find out whether researchers found the intranet easy to use; there were four possibilities:

- simple and friendly to use
- fairly simple to use
- fairly difficult to use
- difficult to use.

Figure 14.5 shows the results and it can be seen that one of the principal goals of the project was reached because 86% of our users consider the site simple and friendly or fairly simple to use, while only 5% declare having problems understanding and using it.

The last question intended to evaluate the impact of technical problems – such as availability of a PC or connection time – on users having access to the intranet site. There were three categories:

- strong impact
- slight impact
- no impact.

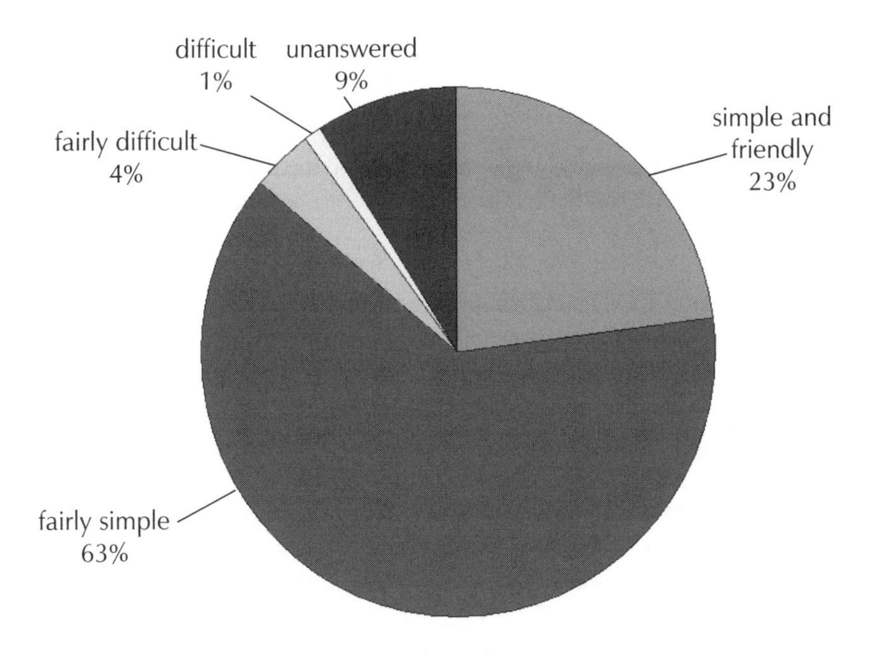

Figure 14.5 Researchers' views on how easy it was to use the intranet

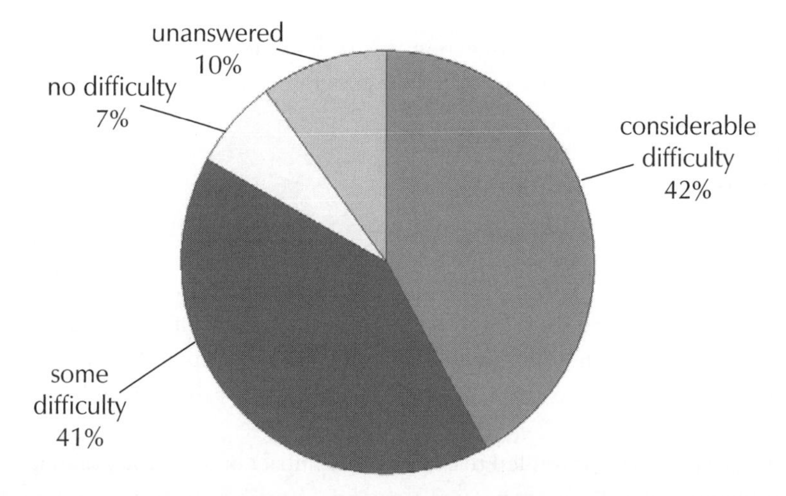

Figure 14.6 Extent to which users experienced problems when accessing the ISS library intranet

Figure 14.6 shows that 42% of users ran into difficulties when accessing the intranet, 41% had experienced some difficulties and only 7% had no difficulty connecting to the network. It should be noted that the problems that were later identified were not directly caused by the library but were connected with the development of the information system and intranet of the whole Institute.

Some observations on the results

First of all some brief comments on the data related to the total number of answers obtained. We think that the 562 returned questionnaires are significant for two important reasons:

- They demonstrate the high level of interest and attention that our Institute has for this kind of survey and in particular in the running of the library.
- They provide a wide and reliable sample of users' trends and needs.

The analysis of data according to the type of user is also important: in the scientific and research area we had 537 answers from a potential of 2185 (a ratio of about 1 in 4), while in the administrative area we had 19 answers from a potential of 243 (a ratio of less than 1 in 10). As one would expect in a research institute, the level of interest in the survey shown by scientific staff is considerably higher than that shown by administrative staff.

The analysis of data concerning frequency of network service use and the reduction of regular attendance shows that a great change in library use has begun, with a gradual shift towards the use of remote services. The percentage of those who use these services as a replacement for traditional use of the library and for reference use inside the building exceeds 80% and, even if only a small number to date (4%), we are already seeing some users withdraw from using the library altogether, in favour of consulting documents electronically.

This trend is confirmed also by the usage statistics for access to documents contained in the most important source of online articles: the Web of Science database of Elsevier's e-journals.

At the moment the library subscribes to 262 titles in paper format but, as member of CASPUR/CIBER consortium, we have access to the full set of electronic journals published by Elsevier (more than 1400). In 2001 our researchers downloaded 30,425 articles, 6685 from non-subscribed titles (21.9%) and 23,740 from subscribed journals (78.1%). In 2002 the total was 42,991 articles, split up into 10,277 unsubscribed (23.9%) and 32,714 (76.1%) subscribed. So it's possible to see that in only one year there was a growth of about 41% of downloaded articles and 2% difference between use of subscribed and unsubscribed journals. Moreover, if we consider the amount that Elsevier journals were consulted in paper format during 2000–2002 we see that in 2001 there is a decrease in use of 8% and in 2002 a decrease in use of 42%. Thus this is evidently a trend towards more widespread use of electronic format. Furthermore, more than half of researchers wanted there to be an increase in the number of electronic journals available and another 25% an increase in the number of databases.

Finally, a brief reflection on the impact of technical problems that can occur when accessing the intranet, which can be critical and risk becoming a bottleneck for the efficiency of the whole system. Users' dissatisfaction is usually brought about because of unavailability of a personal workstation or slow response times of terminals. These problems affect not only library services but the whole intranet of our Institute. Nevertheless, starting from 2003, these issues are being addressed, bringing a marked improvement in terms of speed and performance.

Future development strategies

This survey clearly shows that the trend of our users to replace personal visits to the library by accessing services remotely is growing. It follows the need to define new strategies in management policy and the acquisition and distribution of information resources. In summary, the main patterns of these changes can be identified and we can see how it is possible to manage change and what kind of problems are entailed.

The increase in electronic information sources

The number of electronic information resources available on the market is unlimited and access to it is possible from the technical point of view. The main difficulties relate to costs, to the overlapping of resources within different products (the same journals being accessible through several databases or leading provider sites and consequently paid for twice) and to there being a wide range of interfaces, which could confuse the final user. Our decision to join a national consortium brought some benefits but also some drawbacks. The advantages are higher bargaining power, sharing resources and the potential to co-ordinate an acquisition policy. The disadvantages are the rigidity of terms fixed by publishers through long-term contracts, without the possibility of subscription cuts except for a negligible amount.

Currently, contracts with the most important publishers fix the electronic format fee on the basis of a percentage of costs of paper materials; for example with Elsevier and Kluwer the amount is 6% for having access to subscribed titles and 8% for having access to the full set of journals. A possible solution to reduce costs could be to buy all subscriptions in electronic format and only some titles also in paper format. But this solution, because of the high cost of electronic journals and the effect of VAT (20% in Italy), is reasonable only if the library completely abandons paper journals, and this is still not an easy choice to make at the moment.

A way to reduce costs is to resort to the use of information resources with free access. In the scientific field we now have several projects of this type, such as the Public Library of Science and the Budapest Open Access Initiative. But it is through the Open Archives Initiative that the academic world is trying to break the information monopoly held by publishers. The creation of institutional repositories in many important universities and academic institutions, and the growth of new standards for the interoperability and the exchange of data among these archives, are important steps for the creation of an alternative editorial circuit at low cost. It is very important that libraries encourage this kind of venture, bringing them to the notice of as many researchers and students as possible.

The new relationship between library and user

It is quite probable that in ten years' time scientific information will be communicated exclusively in electronic format and therefore scientific libraries will no longer be specific places and buildings where users can find all they need for their research. Libraries and librarians will be compelled to redefine their roles, becoming more and more selective of the resources that exist on the market. Libraries will become centres of remote distribution, emphasizing their active and purposeful role towards users and their function of orientation within the wide universe of information and documentation. The librarian in particular must undertake the role of expert surfer, thus preventing users from losing themselves in the surplus of information offered. This will involve a new working administration and making the best use of all technological tools.

New tools for new tasks

Signing agreements with publishers and using the web for access to information are not sufficient factors to guarantee an appropriate use of resources available on the internet. Too often the user is confused by too many resources and too many interfaces. The first step that the library must take is to put at the researchers' disposal software that allows a generalized access to various sources through the same interface. There are many products already available on the market – such as OVID for biomedical researches (we adopted it a few years ago), SFX, TDNet and others – that guarantee these functions and also the opportunity of establishing personalized research profiles with automatic periodic updates. Users must also have the opportunity to start their research in a catalogue or a bibliographic database and, once documents of interest have been located, to access directly the full-text articles.

In this context the library must then develop tools to help students in their research: our new website, which is logical and user-friendly, using advanced tools such as a new OPAC and direct access to databases and e-journals through internet portal addresses, became available two months ago. Moreover we are developing a program to strengthen direct contact with researchers. For this purpose we used two basic tools: the creation of a virtual reference desk for research support and solving problems in real time and the improvement of document delivery service by e-mail for articles without direct access.

Finally, we believe it is an essential requirement to monitor the efficiency and effectiveness of electronic services and the level of user satisfaction by the use of specific performance indicators. The revised versions of ISO 2789 and 11620 address this topic and, together with results and suggestions of projects such as EQUINOX, help to supply valid evaluation tools of our achievements.

Bibliography

Brophy, P. and Clarke, Z. (2001) *EQUINOX Library Performance Measurement and Quality Management System*, Manchester, CERLIM, http://equinox.dcu.ie/reports/d2_5.html.

Luce, R.E. (2001) The Open Archives Initiative: interoperable, interdisciplinary author self-archiving comes of age, *Serials Librarian*, **40** (1/2), 173–81.

McKnight, C. (2000) Librarians in the Delivery of Electronic Journals: roles revisited, *Journal of Librarianship and Information Science*, **32** (3), 117–34.

Obst, O. (2003) Patterns and Costs of Printed and Online Journal Usage, *Health Information and Libraries Journal*, **20** (1), 22–32.

Suber, P. (2003) Removing the Barriers to Research: an introduction to open access for librarians, *College & Research Libraries News*, **64**, 92–4, 113, www.earlham.edu/~peters/writing/acrl.htm.

15

The information-deprived continent: can we do something?

Marié Botha

> The only true wisdom is in knowing you know nothing
>
> (Socrates)

Background

For a long time Africa was the centre stage for communication activities. Hieroglyphics, clay tablets, paintings on cave walls and drum messages were a few methods known to, and used by, the African inhabitants to convey messages over great distances. Then came Gutenberg, the invention of the printing press and printing, and eventually the birth of e-books – the rise of the First World and the fall of the Third World?

Libraries in Africa

African culture was, and still is, communicated orally and a large number of Africans are still influenced by oral tradition. Africa also has little to no reading culture. It was even reported that African academics did not show much interest in material published in Africa, and in some instances did not even bother to visit the library. For example, Kenyan University Library reported that 50% of its academics never enter the library (Rosenberg, 1997).

Most libraries in Africa were established as post World War 2 institutions. At the time of their establishment, university libraries in Africa were the best-equipped libraries on the African continent. The economic situation of libraries led to a considerable deterioration of services offered, and forced libraries to rely on donor funding from Book Aid International and the World Bank Book Project to build and sustain their individual library collections. It is still a concern that the collections of Africa's academic institutions did not really grow as they should have, owing to the small budgets that the libraries received from their parent institutions, ranging from 3 to 8% of the total university budgets (Alemna, 1994, 15–17). From 1995 onwards library growth showed a sharp decline or became non-existent in a number of African countries. It became evident that library budgets were mainly spent on salaries and not on stock (Rosenberg, 1997).

African libraries face a variety of other difficulties. For example, the University of Sierra Leone reported that its library's roof was leaking and that there were no electrical lights available for studying. Sierra Leone and University of Kenyatta reported that they managed to acquire generators to generate electricity to bind and to run the computers. Also in Sierra Leone, the library needs to close at 1700 hours daily, because of the political instability.

Africa's telecommunication scenario

Telecommunications diffusion in Africa is the weakest in the world, with the least teledensity. Africa has approximately 816 million inhabitants, representing 14% of the global population, of which 70–80% of the reported population are living in rural areas. There is a general absence of modern telecommunication equipment in Africa, and a lack of skilled people to use and introduce these technologies. Most information channels in Africa are either partially blocked or underdeveloped. Africa suffers from poor quality telephone lines (if any), unreliable power supplies, outdated equipment and a lack of training and knowledge to use the equipment even if it could be found.

Africa has the least number of telephone lines per capita – a total share of only 2% of world telephone lines. There are more telephone lines in Manhattan (USA) and in Tokyo than on the entire African continent. If northern Africa and South Africa are not counted, there are only 3 million lines to be shared among the remaining 600 million people concentrated in the urban areas, an average of one telephone to every 200 people.

Internet connectivity in Africa

Although Africa's connectivity to internet services and increased use of telephone lines is rising, it is still low as a result of the cost of these services and the relatively small income generated by the users of them. However, it is very positive to take note of Jensen's report (2002) that all of Africa's 54 countries now have some form of internet access. In this report he mentioned that most of the internet facilities are situated in and around capital and major cities. The latest NUA report (www.nua.com/) stated that Africa had approximately 6.31 million internet users, which represents 1.04% of the world's online population.

What is the digital divide?

The digital divide can roughly be defined as the gap that exists between those who have access to technology and those who do not. Technology in this sense includes telephone connections, computer and internet connections.

The digital divide occurs when there is unequal access to information technology resources either within a particular country or between neighbouring countries. Other factors that have an impact on the digital divide are social and economic conditions, telecommunication infrastructures and education.

Language differences

The predominant use of English in literature and study aids reinforces the digital divide even further. There is no 'primary' language of Africa. There are over 800 ethnic groups of native black Africans. Each group has its own very distinctive language and the languages are further enriched with an array of dialects or regional languages. Africa accommodates more than 1000 languages that are actively spoken on the continent (see http://ex.matrix.msu.edu/africa/).

Political instability

Africa is well known for its continuing wars that bring devastation to socio-economic development opportunities. There have been more than 100 coups d'état in Africa since 1950.

Telecommunication factors

Africa's infrastructure development is mainly concentrated in and around the capital cities of the African countries. The African population in general has poor or very little access to telecommunication infrastructures and communication technology. Africa has an impossible state of networks of any kind (electronic or electric) on the continent and suffers from highly regulated telecommunications services because of state ownership or monopolies in these areas.

Educational problems

The African continent's educational problems are varied and include high incidences of the 'brain drain' and illiteracy. Africa lost approximately 60,000 professionals (doctors, university lecturers, engineers, nurses and teachers) between 1985 and 1990 to countries abroad. It is alarming that Africa had been losing an average of 20,000 professionals annually ever since (World Markets Research Centre, 2002).

UNESCO designates Africa the continent of illiteracy, with an illiteracy rate among people over 15 years of age of 41%. In Africa 40 million children have no access to education. Only 3% of 18–25 year olds in Africa enrol for further education in colleges and universities. A good example of this is to be found in Ethiopia, where only 30% of all children are enrolled for primary school. Of these children, approximately half make it to the second year of primary schooling, while the other half have to leave school to tend to family matters and daily chores. It is estimated that more than 60% of Africa's illiterates are women in rural areas.

Bridging the digital divide . . . is it possible?

Mutula (2000) felt that initiatives such as New Partnership for Africa's Development (NEPAD) could contribute to bridging the divide. NEPAD aims to eradicate poverty in Africa to ensure that Africa be placed on the path of sustainability and development.

Another initiative, according to Mutula, is the quest to return the skilled people who left the continent to help with the development of their individual countries. It is also planned to instal computers in shops, community centres and schools, and to establish phone shops and cybercafés (already a success in Eritrea, Kenya, Mozambique and Tanzania). Other successes are the Mobile Telecentre and Library Services for Rural Communities project of the Fantsuam Foundation, Nigeria (described on www.fantsuam.com/), and the 'Zimbabwean Donkey-Drawn Electro-Communication Library Carts'.

With these projects, information technology skills and access to the internet and library material is brought to communities in Nigeria and Zimbabwe where there is no electricity, phone lines or internet connectivity.

Internet use

In Mike Jensen's African internet use report (2002) he mentioned that there are approximately 1.5–2.5 million internet users excluding northern Africa and South Africa, representing about one user to 250–400 people. The world average for people using the internet is one in 15. The figure for North America and Europe is one in every two people.

Each computer with an internet or e-mail connection in Africa supports between three and five African users; it is estimated that around 5–8 million people in Africa access and use the internet, of whom approximately 2.5 million are in sub-Saharan Africa. There are three computers per 1000 people in eastern Africa and internet access is available to 1.3 people per 1000 in the same region.

Donations of computers to villages and schools are valuable; the Computers for Africa and PCs for Africa organizations gave a number of rebuilt computers to community centres and are still actively finding more donations for Africa.

The possibilities for establishing a digital library in Africa: a viable option?

Although the picture of Africa's readiness to become part of the global information village has generally been gloomy, there have been notable electronic, electrical and communication improvements in some countries over the last few years, which give us hope to introduce a virtual library.

The potential internet market could be penetrated by a digital library and hopefully would bring some relief to a continent that is one of the most underdeveloped in the world due to the fact that its people do not have access to development-oriented information.

Why e-books?

E-books (very roughly defined as electronic versions of books in print – already published or to be published – that can be downloaded for reading on a portable device, using proprietary software) were chosen for the African Digital Library because they:

- serve as a new 'channel' for the distribution of information
- reduce costs by eliminating paper, printing and physical space to store the books
- provide more search capabilities, which allows for easier and quicker information retrieval
- are accessible any time of day or night anywhere the user had access to the digital library.

The challenge for librarians using or promoting e-books is to make sure that information access, which is a global common good, reaches the poorest of the poor as well as the experienced researcher.

The African Digital Library

The African Digital Library (ADL; http://Africandl.org.za) was created for Africa, in the spirit of the African Renaissance, to address Africa's other famine – the severe shortage of textbooks and information resources as described and touched on by Akst and Jensen (2001).

The ADL is a collection of electronic books (e-books) that can be used free of charge by any person living on the African continent, for either academic research or business purposes. More information can be found at the ADL website (africandl.org.za/).

The aim of the ADL is to provide a digitized full-text resource to learners in Africa via the internet, thereby contributing to the revitalization of education and lifelong learning on the continent and the alleviation of the digital divide that exists between First and Third World countries. By using the ADL and its information we hope to contribute to human development in education, social services and also some commercial activities.

The ADL strives to provide a wide range of materials in support of existing facilities and works in co-operation with OCLC/NetLibrary (www.OCLC.org/), and in southern Africa, SABINET (www.SABINET.co.za/) to provide the technical and other services that are required to establish and build on this initiative.

Overview of the ADL

The ADL is a developmental project aimed at assisting a less developed continent, where basic access to books is limited. It is envisaged that the library should comprise a collection of e-books and other e-resources, made accessible via the internet to all the inhabitants of Africa. The ADL was opened on 1 November 1999 with approximately 3000 e-book titles. The partners in establishing the ADL were Technikon Southern Africa (TSA) (www.tsa.ac.za/), the Association of African Universities (AAU) (www.aau.org/), NetLibrary (www.netLibrary.com) and the World Bank (www.WorldBank.org/).

The library was initially developed with seed funding received from the TSA. Donations were sought and an application was made to the World Bank's Development Marketplace in February 2000 for funding. The ADL managed to secure a $90,000 grant, which enabled the ADL to acquire 2800 e-book titles. At the end of 2000 the collection grew to approximately 7800 e-book titles representing a wide variety of subjects. It consists of approximately 3800 titles, from the ADL collection and 4000 publicly accessible e-book titles that netLibrary provided.

NetLibrary contributed to the project by providing discounted storage fees and programming. The collection is housed at Boulder, Colorado, and is maintained by netLibrary. Access to the ADL is provided through an internet connection on the African continent. Volunteer library staff of TSA currently administer the ADL accounts and registrations.

The ADL could reduce essential costs of obtaining much needed e-library collections or copies of e-books for its users by accessing the ADL. It also provides a medium for virtually expanding every institution's own collections, by making use of the ADL, thereby allowing its user base to access a recent collection of research material needed by its potentially huge clientele – the people of Africa.

The use and impact of the library was not as good as was initially envisaged. This could be because Africa, as was explained earlier, finds itself on the wrong side of the digital divide and is so impoverished that focus on a library is the very last priority of any government that has to deal with health, famine and poverty.

Another factor is the extremely poorly developed and maintained communication infrastructures that exist in Africa. However, use of the ADL shows a slow but steady growth. It is a good source with a huge potential to bridge a part of the existing digital divide – the need for up-to-date information, education and research.

Benefits of using e-books

The ADL provides:

- users with the facility to take notes by copying and pasting directly from the text of the e-book into assignments
- an additional library, free of charge, that is available to all residents of Africa who have access to the internet
- a library that is available 24 hours a day, seven days a week, 365 days a year
- a collection of books that is searchable by key words
- the opportunity to all existing libraries in Africa to add the ADL to their existing collections by providing access to the collection via the internet; if integrated into the traditional library, the ADL would strengthen the base of local information and improve the delivery of information services in these libraries
- a collection of books, none of which can ever be lost, stolen or damaged
- short loan periods (two hours), to ensure that more users can access the same title
- automatically regulated protection against copyright abuse.

User authentication

The ADL is a digital library that is not restricted to one institution, but offers access to people residing all over the continent of Africa.

The normal procedure for libraries with a netLibrary account is to give access to their users by means of an Internet Protocol (IP) authenticated connection or referring to the URL, combined with a user ID and login password. Providing the African continent with access to the ADL presented the proposed ADL and netLibrary with certain challenges. It was not possible to give a range of IP addresses to cover the continent as a whole because the IP addresses in Africa are not contiguous.

Authentication was initially taken care of by domain filtering that would have prevented other regions in the world from accessing the library. At the point of registration the filter would determine in which country the new user was located. This was done by converting the last numerals of the user's IP address back to alpha and comparing these to the 50 top-level domain names of Africa; this either enabled the user to register or would not allow access. The filter was not always correct as many of Africa's domains are '.com', '.org', and so on, and these appear to come from other parts of the world.

It happens that the internet service providers in Africa buy IP addresses from their counterparts in America. The result of this is that an IP address in Ghana might look as if it is situated in the middle of, for example, Boston, USA. Individual users also might not have fixed IP addresses. This resulted in netLibrary having to identify a user coming from Africa by another means.

We now refer individuals who show interest in the ADL to the ADL website to register. Checks are run against country indicators, contact numbers and institutions these individuals are affiliated with, to determine whether they in fact are resident in Africa. Institutions that show interest in joining the ADL, for example, Senegal's National Library, are referred directly to netLIbrary to handle IP registrations and domain filtering by themselves.

The loan period for an e-book is two hours. The e-book is automatically returned to the ADL at the end of the two-hour loan period. If the user still needs to access the book, it can be renewed. Lack of equipment could be a barrier to prospective students as e-books can only be accessed via available computers and the internet.

The establishment and use of the ADL could eventually enable Africa to identify herself with the global information society by:

- providing initiatives to start publishing indigenous knowledge
- linking communities through the web
- publishing research findings with African content
- helping to develop unique African information databases.

These initiatives and unique items can enhance the ADL content in future.

Challenges for the administrator of the ADL

The administrator of the ADL provides informative articles and a CD-ROM containing information about the ADL to all visitors to TSA. Articles are written and published in in-house magazines and library-related publications. Business cards are provided and distributed during conferences in southern Africa and attendees are invited to register as users.

We marketed the ADL on the Africa Library list-serve and were contacted by a representative of the African Virtual University (AVU) (www.avu.org/) expressing her wish to add a link to the ADL collection to the AVU website. We made contact with the librarian of the International Virtual University, which was established as a pilot project in Harare, Zimbabwe. We joined the AFLIB list-serve (aflib-l@mailman.nlsa.ac.za) in 2002 and distributed a letter of introduction to the ADL to all subscribers via the list-serve. This gave impetus to a substantial number of librarians in Africa, who subscribed to the list to register as users of the ADL.

Obstacles

The TSA library was not involved in the establishment of the ADL. After the person who established the ADL left TSA, the ADL went into a state of limbo for more than a year. This inevitably lead to the World Bank giving the ADL a null classification based on the assumption that the library stagnated, because no new content was added to it.

The cost of e-books is extremely high, taking the weak rand–dollar exchange rate into consideration. To the amount paid for every e-Book, 55% must be added to the initial cost to allow for its use in perpetuity. We need to budget carefully to allow optimal development of the collection.

The current collection is in English with American content dominating the initial acquisitions that were made between 1999 and 2000.

Africa is a huge continent – bandwidth is low and slow, and access to the internet concentrated around major cities. Sub-Saharan Africa is still technologically challenged owing to the slow pace at which technological advancement is established and exploited.

Conclusion

It should be noted that the broadest segment of the African population needs access to basic communication infrastructure and enabling services – in short, services like reliable electric power and education. Setting up an electronic library in Africa is a daunting challenge. The needs are real . . . the opportunities are there . . . we have the abilities, but do we, African librarians, have the courage and the conviction to do what is being expected of us as information brokers for this continent? Africa is used to sharing information resources – a newspaper might be read by more that ten people, and an internet dial-up account could carry up to three users at a time.

Is it possible to establish a digital library in Africa? Yes – but it is a journey – *a very long journey*.

Bibliography

Akst, D and Jensen, M. (2001) Africa Goes Online, http://digitaldividenetwork.org/content/stories/index.cfm?key=158.

Alemna, A. (1994) Alternative Approaches to Funding University Libraries in Africa, *New Library World*, **95** (2), 15–17.

Chisenga, J. (2000) Global Information and Libraries in Sub-Saharan Africa, *Library Management*, **21** (4), 178–87.

Jensen, M. (2002) The African Internet: a status report, www3.sn.apc.org/africa/afstat.htm

Mutula, S.M. (2000) IT Developments in Eastern and Southern Africa: implications for university libraries, *Library Hi Tech*, **18** (4), 220–34.

Mutula, S.M. (2001) Internet Access in East Africa: a future outlook, *Library Review*, **50** (1) 28–34.

Odini, C. (1998) An Overview of Recent Library and Information Developments in East Africa, *Library Management*, **19** (1), 12–14.

Rosenberg, D. (1997) *University Libraries in Africa: a review of their current state and future potential*, 2 vols, London, International African Institute.

Thapisa, A. P. N. (2000) The Impact of Globalisation of Africa, *Library Management*, **21** (4), 170–8.

World Markets Research Centre (2002) www.worldmarketsanalysis.com/InFocus2002/articles/africa_braindrain.html.

16

Optimizing resource discovery service interfaces: the Library of Texas challenge

William E. Moen, Kathleen R. Murray and Irene Lopatovska

Introduction

State library agencies in the US are expanding their traditional services by building statewide virtual libraries offering resource discovery services that take advantage of the intersection of metasearch technology and user demand for access to networked resources. Understanding the information behaviours of various user groups and optimizing resource discovery interfaces for users are critical to the success of statewide virtual libraries.

The Texas Center for Digital Knowledge at the University of North Texas began a multiphase applied research project in 2001 in support of the Library of Texas, a statewide virtual library (www.tsl.state.tx.us/lot/index.html). Working under contract for the Texas State Library and Archives Commission, we addressed the design, configuration and system implementation of the Library of Texas Resource Discovery Service. This work became known as the ZLOT Project (www.unt.edu/zlot). The resource discovery service is one component of the broader Library of Texas initiative.

This paper provides an overview of the Library of Texas Resource Discovery Service, its development and current status. More importantly, we identify usability issues of such resource discovery services and suggest possible approaches for improving and optimizing user and search interfaces of these applications through usability assessment.

The context: resources, services and users

The 21st-century library, sometimes referred to as a digital or virtual library, involves the deployment of technologies to enhance access to a wide variety of analogue and digital information resources. Available technologies and applications have the potential to extend the reach and range of users to information resources while reducing the barriers to information access. Libraries have tried various approaches to improve information access in the networked environment. Concepts for these approaches include virtual libraries, resource discovery services, metasearch applications and portals.

There is a wealth of networked information resources available to library users including:

- online catalogues
- licensed databases from commercial vendors
- locally developed databases
- digital repositories
- web resources.

Until recently these resources were typically offered through separate interfaces. The result was a plethora of resources with the attendant challenges of training users on multiple interfaces. While extending the reach and range of users to networked information resources, the multiple interfaces can be viewed as barriers to effective and efficient information access.

State library agencies have been actively involved in making the resources of their public and academic libraries available to citizens. This effort often involved creating a state library portal. Technology now enables the building of virtual library services that respond to users' needs to access resources more effectively and efficiently regardless of the geographic location of users or resources

A resource discovery service offered by a virtual library is another innovation to help users connect with information. Resource discovery services can take the form of metasearch applications; users can search multiple targets concurrently through a single search interface. Improving resource discovery tools can directly affect the capability of users to find information from an array of digital and analogue resources. The first generation of commercially available resource discovery applications has been implemented by single libraries to provide integrated access to local and remote resources, by consortia to leverage access to consortium members' resources and by statewide virtual library initiatives (for example the Library of Texas, the Colorado Virtual Library and the Illinois Find It! application).

With several virtual libraries now in place, there is an opportunity to assess their use and usability by citizens and to understand changing patterns of information need, use and information-seeking behaviours supported by these initiatives. One of the first challenges is to identify and characterize potential users of resource discovery services. While it may be assumed that current library users will use the resource discovery service, there may be an untapped market of users who rely on networked information for resolving information needs but who currently do not visit libraries and use their resources. With a clearer understanding of potential users of a resource discovery service, it may be possible to expand the current constituent and service base of bricks and mortar libraries through the virtual library.

Diversity in users' information-seeking behaviours and needs requires developers to design effective and efficient interfaces for resource discovery services. Both user selection of resource collections to search, and user selection of specific resources from search results, are critical tasks that engage users of the virtual library. The usability of the resource discovery service has a direct impact on the successful fulfilment of user information needs and, by extension, the overall success of a virtual library.

Given a resource discovery service as an entry point to networked information, new usability issues emerge. Users may be comfortable with searching a single database or single library catalogue or other single system. They may have an understanding of the authority, coverage, quality and other important facets of the single resource. The metasearch environment, however, potentially requires users to develop a new mental model for interacting with multiple distributed resources through a metasearch interface.

We are entering a new era of information access that takes as its starting point access to distributed resources. There is a need for a better understanding of user information needs and information-seeking behaviours in the context of distributed search and retrieval. Much as we might transfer many of the services of a physical library environment to a virtual library, the interfaces to virtual library services are quite different from physical library access of the past. Our initial conception both of the services and the interfaces to the virtual library are based largely on our collective experience in the traditional library. We can expect that as more citizens have access to the virtual library in their homes, current and potential users will define new requirements. Now is an ideal time in the maturation cycle of the statewide virtual library concept to identify the characteristics of effective interfaces for virtual libraries and their resource discovery services.

The Library of Texas

The Library of Texas (LOT) is envisioned as a service-based virtual library. It is a project of the Texas State Library and Archives Commission (TSLAC) and the Texas Telecommunications Infrastructure Fund Board and was conceived both as a mechanism for extending the reach and range of Texans to the resources of Texas libraries and for expanding library services through the development and integration of new technologies. Although in its formative stages, the LOT enables Texans access to an extensive array of resources including Texas library catalogues and electronic databases licensed by the TSLAC for statewide use. The LOT initiative includes four basic components:

- providing a statewide resource discovery service
- offering a wide selection of commercial databases licensed for Texas academic and public library users
- indexing and preserving electronic government documents
- training librarians on electronic resources.

This paper focuses on the LOT Resource Discovery Service.

The LOT Resource Discovery Service

A virtual library can extend the reach and range of users across organizational, collection and format boundaries. Yet users face the same challenge as they do with web search engines in identifying relevant materials. A resource discovery service provides users with a variety of tools and approaches for discovering the existence of appropriate resources. Typically, a user will search one or more targets to find, identify, select and access or acquire resources. Two categories of searching can be identified:

- *single database searching*: users search a single target through a common interface
- *broadcast searching*: users concurrently search two or more targets; these targets can be very similar or quite diverse.

A primary goal of a resource discovery service is to provide users with a coherent view of disparate resources. Resource discovery approaches will likely require new levels of technology integration and enhanced interoperability among systems. The Library of Texas Resource Discovery Service (LOT RDS) corresponds with the foregoing description.

Requirements for the LOT RDS

To support the design of the LOT RDS, ZLOT project staff conducted a series of focus groups in Spring 2002. Focus group participants were selected from stakeholder groups representing a spectrum of potential users of the LOT. All participants were library and information professionals from Texas, including reference librarians in small public libraries, library directors in large academic libraries, interlibrary loan service specialists and an executive director of a medical research library.

The needs and expectations discussed in the focus groups informed draft requirements for the LOT RDS. A ZLOT Project Advisory Group reviewed and discussed the draft requirements, and ZLOT staff refined the functional requirements. The result was a list of 53 functional requirements for the resource discovery service prioritized subsequently by the Advisory Group into three levels: must meet requirements, should meet requirements, desirable that systems meet requirements. The process of defining the requirements was of equal importance to the specific requirements themselves. The iterative process used to identify, clarify and prioritize the requirements enabled a wide range of librarians to be involved and to help shape the emerging resource discovery service.

A full description of the 53 functional requirements is available in Moen and Murray (2002). Functional requirements fell into two main categories:

- requirements for Texas library catalogues for interoperable searching
- requirements for the resource discovery service's search and retrieval interface.

Multiple online catalogues may be searched using the resource discovery service. To improve the effectiveness of searches and the utility of results, there is a need to provide common search capabilities across library catalogues and to use technical standards to improve interoperability. The LOT uses standards as a basis for interoperability among systems.

Another important aspect to the resource discovery service is the creation of a common user interface to search and retrieve across different online catalogues and other databases. A common interface to these resources minimizes user training as users will learn to use only one interface rather than separate interfaces for different online resources. An intuitive, web-based, simple-to-use interface was imperative.

Current status of the LOT RDS

In January 2003 TSLAC issued a request for proposal (RFP) for the LOT RDS application. In late Spring 2003 TSLAC awarded a contract for the application to Index Data (http://indexdata.dk/). By August 2003 the first version of the LOT RDS was completed. TSLAC will begin deployment of the LOT RDS in Fall 2003. Table 16.1 provides a summary of key features and functionality of the service.

Table 16.1 Summary of LOT RDS key features and functionality

Search targets available 20+ academic library catalogues. 50+ public library catalogues. 40+ licensed databases. Other special collections.	**Search target selections options** By type of library. By subject area. By strength of collection in subject area. By geographic proximity.
	Search capabilities Simple Google-like keyword searching. Advanced, fielded searching. Date of publication qualifying search.
Retrieval display capabilities Brief record hit list grouped by: • search target • all records sorted by title • all records sorted by date. Full record display. MARC display option.	**Accessing and obtaining actual object** If free online resource, direct connection to object. If licensed online resource, authenticated connection to the object. If non-digital (e.g. printed book), connection to online bookstores to order. If non-digital (e.g. printed book), initiation of an interlibrary loan request.
Persistent authorization Single login for session: • IP authorization • username/password authorization.	**Personalization** Persistent user-defined sets of search targets. Search history.

Usability framework for resource discovery services

The purpose of this section is to propose a framework for addressing the multiple aspects of usability for the LOT RDS. The authors assert that a range of factors will impinge on the user's assessment of the usability of the service. The goal of usability assessment must be to: contribute to the improvement of resource discovery tools and applications that will ultimately provide users with more efficient and effective access to information resources in the distributed search environment. Three key areas comprise the framework:

- users
- the application and its interacting components
- usability criteria and measures.

Users and user groups

The first area that needs attention is the individual users or user groups. The LOT RDS focus groups indicated that different user communities exist within the state, that the needs of these communities may differ radically and that an individual user could belong to more than one group. Additionally, we anticipate that both existing library users and people who do not currently use libraries may interact with the LOT RDS. This expectation predicates the following questions:

- Who are the users of resource discovery services?
- In addition to existing library users, what new market segments can be reached?
- How do the resource discovery patterns and information needs of various user groups differ?
- Are there user group differences based on information literacy variables, demographic variables, or technology adoption variables?
- What design characteristics will optimize use of a resource discovery service across a wide range of citizenry?

Answering these questions can result in a categorization of potential user groups for the LOT RDS. Sample users from among these groups could be subjects for usability assessment, bringing to bear their information needs, problems, resulting information behaviours and expectations for the LOT RDS.

The application and its components

The second area that needs attention is the application and the user interface. A focus on the user interface must acknowledge separate and interacting components that power the LOT RDS. The following provides a preliminary listing of the elements:

- *technical components*: includes underlying hardware and software providing functionality
- *interoperability components*: includes the use of standards and customized scripts to present the user with seamless search and retrieval from multiple resources
- *user interface components*: includes all aspects of user interfaces that assist users in making sense of and using the service
- *collection selection components*: includes the features that assist users in selecting appropriate search targets
- *searching components*: includes the availability of appropriate search functionalities
- *retrieval components*: includes presentation of results and their manipulation
- *task components*: includes functionality that supports users to find, identify, select and access or acquire resources
- *personalization components*: includes features that enable the user to customize the service.

Users may or may not understand how each of the above affects their experience with the service. For various user groups, or for specific information needs, one or more of these components may be more critical than others. What is at issue is the extent to which each of these components needs to be optimized for specific user groups. Usability assessment will require methods to identify potential problems from the perspective of users for any and all of these components and to suggest improvement to provide users with the optimal experience with the service.

Usability criteria and measures

The third area of attention is the development of usability criteria, measures, and methods of assessment. Various writers have identified usability criteria (for example Nielsen, 1993). Quesenbery's (2002) five Es of usability provide a useful point of departure for thinking about usability criteria. Usability criteria must be:

- *effective*: how completely and accurately the work or experience is completed or goals reached
- *efficient*: how quickly this work can be completed
- *engaging*: how well the interface draws the user into the interaction and how pleasant and satisfying it is to use
- *error tolerant*: how well the product prevents errors and can help the user recover from mistakes that do occur
- *easy to learn*: how well the product supports both the initial orientation and continued learning throughout the complete lifetime of use.

Each of these usability criteria needs to be operationally defined and measures specific to the service need to be developed. The relative importance of the criteria for the same service will vary among different user groups, and this may require customization of usability measures for specific user groups.

Figure 16.1 presents the framework for usability assessment that incorporates the multiple user groups, a set of usability criteria and the application and its components. The complexity for usability assessment will revolve around the intersection of the usability criteria and the application's components. The criteria may be used to assess the overall user experience with the service, but addressing the criteria to the separate components may yield more benefits for informing improvements in the service. Although this framework is geared to the LOT RDS, it could easily be adapted to other virtual library services (for example, virtual reference services) or other metasearch and portal environments.

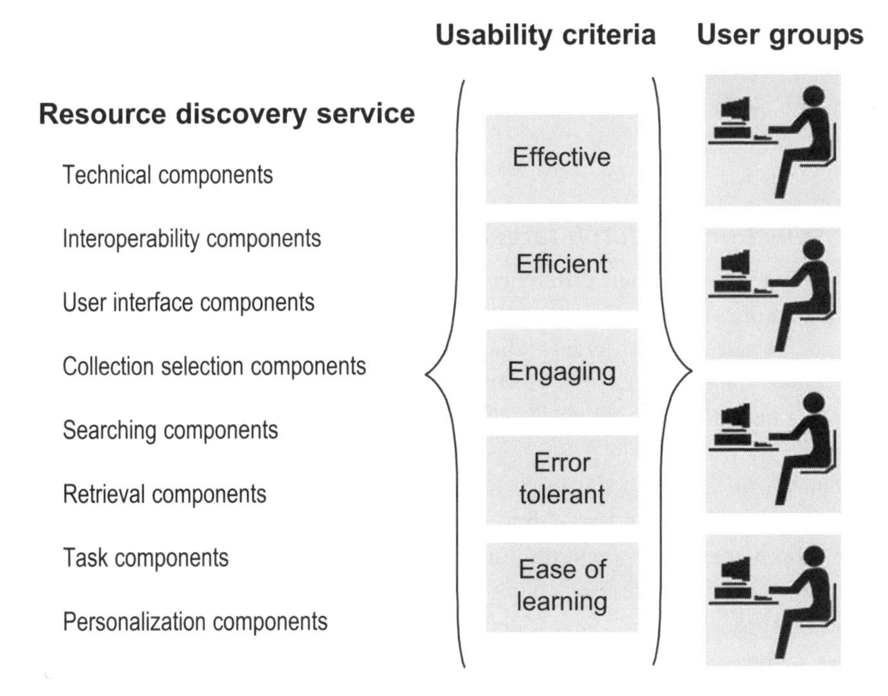

Figure 16.1 Framework for usability assessment of the resource discovery service

Key usability issues for the LOT RDS

The authors suggest that the following three aspects of the LOT RDS are priorities for usability assessment:

- user understanding of the service
- user selection of search targets
- system performance.

User understanding of the service

The initial interface for the LOT RDS offers the user the immediacy of searching. The design is simple and uncluttered. The design goal for the interface was to enable the user to begin searching without having to make many initial decisions. Yet a first-time user may experience uncertainty since there is little to orient the user to the service. Help pages will be available to assist users. Usability assessment can assist the developers in refining the interface to support first-time users while not cluttering the screen with instructions for seasoned users. Another issue relates to the various user groups whom this service may serve. Usability assessment of the existing interface by representatives of different users groups could inform the customization of the features and functionality to better serve these groups.

User selection of search targets

One of the most important differences between a resource discovery service and other portal or gateway websites or web search engines is the availability of multiple and diverse search targets that can be made available. In the initial deployment, the LOT RDS will provide access to over 100 separate search targets. These can be searched individually, all at once, or in groupings defined by the system or the user.

When a user logs into the LOT RDS, the system presents a selected set of search targets (public and academic library catalogues and licensed databases). Target library catalogues are determined by the system based on the proximity of those catalogues with the user's home library and the strength of the general collection of those libraries. The system also presents a selected set of licensed databases chosen by their strength of subject coverage. Users can also select to 'Search by Subject' and when the user chooses one of the ten pre-defined subject areas, the system presents a set of subject-appropriate search targets. Users can also define their own sets of search targets. They simply check the targets they want to search and save that set of favourites persistently across sessions.

Probably the key challenge in optimizing users' engagement with the resource discovery service is to assist them in searching targets that have potentially relevant information. Usability assessment of the initial interface and its collection selection features will be vital to ensure that users will be presented with appropriate search targets that they can successfully search. As more, and different, types of search targets become available through the LOT RDS (for example databases of archival material and digital image libraries), helping users to select search targets will be critical.

System performance

The third area that will affect LOT RDS users' perception of its usability relates to performance. In a metasearch environment, where searches are sent to multiple and diverse search targets, a number of factors affect the success of searches. Some factors can be minimized by adherence to national and international standards such as the ISO 23950/ANSI Z39.50 standard protocol for information retrieval. Not all search targets are accessible via Z39.50 server; this requires specialized scripts to send queries to those individual search targets, and these scripts can be rendered dysfunctional because of changes at the search targets. All searches are sent over the internet; network congestion can reduce response time. It is more problematic when a particular search target is consistently not available or not responding properly. Quality of service from each of the search targets as well as the LOT RDS is important.

Users who have become used to nearly instantaneous responses from web search engines may find the response time from multiple search targets problematic. Helping users construct an appropriate mental model of the metasearch environment could ameliorate negative reactions to system performance.

Conclusion

This paper has described the LOT RDS, a new and exciting approach to helping users find, identify, select, and access or acquire information through a statewide virtual library. The LOT RDS is an innovative metasearch application that was informed by user requirements and built on a basis of national and international standards. Due to the constrained timeline for its development, user-centred activities were limited to focus groups and discussions about requirements. As the LOT RDS is deployed in its first version, we have an opportunity to refine and inform future development through usability assessment. The paper presented a preliminary framework for usability assessment that acknowledges the several components of the LOT RDS that will affect users' experience of the system. In addition, three key areas for usability assessment were discussed to indicate priorities for assessment. Finally, metasearch applications such as the LOT RDS may require new mental models on the part of users to contextualize the resources, capabilities and performance of metasearch applications.

References

Moen, W. and Murray, K (2002) *Functional Requirements for the Library of Texas Resource Discovery Service*, Denton, Texas, Texas Center for Digital Knowledge, www.unt.edu/zlot/phase1/del_c_functional_requirements_krm_30jun2002.pdf.

Nielsen, J. (1993) *Usability Engineering*, Boston, Academic Press.

Quesenbery, W. (2002) *Getting Started: using the 5Es to understand user*, www.wqusability.com/articles/getting-started.html.

Theme 4
Designing the information environment: national and institutional perspectives

17

Supporting learning, teaching and research at Manchester Metropolitan University

Caroline Williams

Introduction

The UK higher education (HE) information environment is amorphous. It is difficult to define and is constantly changing shape. The language that describes it can feel abstract and be difficult to grasp. The information environment is changing in form and nature. The government provides the canvas or frame that dictates the Higher Education Funding Council for England's (HEFCE) funding agenda, which in turn shapes the strategic plans and modus operandi of HE institutions. The objects within this, including the information environment, then take their shape, size and direction.

None of us know what the future holds, but we are all effectively aiming for a one stop shop at the press of a button to academic information relevant and accessible to a wide variety of users within the HE sector. This paper will not present a big new idea or grandiose vision. It will not try to predict the future, or shoehorn the evolving information environment into a rigid framework. Instead it will take four key themes of HE in the UK and look at how a university library, Manchester Metropolitan University (MMU) Library, is playing its part in supporting the objectives of its parent institution. I will paint a picture of a changing environment; describe what we are trying to do and how we are doing it. Many of the areas covered will be familiar to you, your own institutions may be doing similar work, but it will give a full case study of how a fairly typical large UK university library is moving towards the future. The four key themes are: learning and teaching, research, widening participation and reaching out to business and local communities. First some brief background about MMU, its Library and electronic development.

Background

Manchester Metropolitan University (www.mmu.ac.uk/) is widely recognized for its diversity and flexible approaches to learning. It offers 1628 study programmes (part-time, sandwich, graduate apprenticeship, distance, online, foundation to PhD) and is constantly building in new modes of learning to widen access to quality education. It has seven campuses, five in the Manchester area and two at Alsager and Crewe in Cheshire. It is one of the largest universities in the UK with over 30,000 students. A third of its students are over 24; more than 30% study part-time. Many come to the University from non-traditional and under-represented groups. MMU is currently working towards a new estates strategy that aims over the next ten years to consolidate the Manchester sites and merge the Crewe and Alsager sites in Cheshire.

Our virtual learning environment (VLE) is WebCT and, in addition, different faculties have developed their own staff or student intranets hosting PowerPoint slides of lectures, notices, timetables, and so on. We have a small Learning and Teaching Unit, which leads developments in learning and teaching technologies, devolved faculty information systems teams and a central Information Systems Unit managing the networks. These services are not converged, which now makes us atypical.

MMU Library (www.mmu.ac.uk/library/) is a large multi-site operation (including the North West Film Archive (www.nwfa.ac.uk/)), which provides flexible relevant services to our users. Library expenditure totals almost £5 million per annum. A high quality refurbishment programme has been undertaken in recent years to provide flexible library space, accommodating rich information technology (IT) facilities. The Library is part of the North West Academic Libraries (NoWAL) consortium (www.nowal.ac.uk/) and the Consortium of Academic Libraries in Manchester (CALIM). MMU Library is leading the JISC funded Artifact project (www.artifact.ac.uk/). There are almost 200 staff members, deployed across the sites. Our Library Management System (LMS) is Talis.

We aim to support the University in its four key areas of work (learning and teaching, research, widening participation and reaching out to business and local communities) and provide a modern, high-quality library service. Inevitably this means there is a substantial emphasis on technology including electronic content, access, organizational tools, VLEs and the development of students' information skills. In 2001 the librarian identified a need to provide a focus for the development and implementation of electronic library strategy. I was appointed to the newly created position of Library Service Manager (Electronic Services Development) and a small IT team was reinvented to become the Electronic Services Development Team (ESDT). The objectives of the team were articulated but, despite this, I grappled to find a linear diagram that showed our environment and clearly defined our areas of work. Things did not fit into different categories or projects; they merged, evolved, impinged on different parts of our existing service, structures and working practices. I found my solution in the abstract world of blob-like shapes illustrated in Figure 17.1.

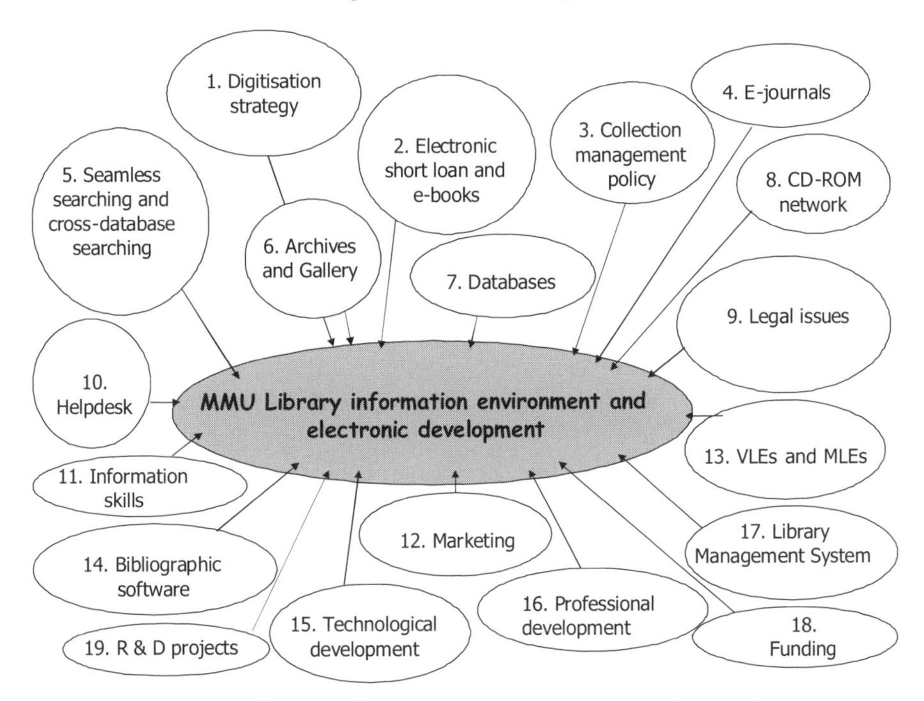

Figure 17.1 MMU library information environment and electronic development

By contrast, the Joint Information Systems Committee (JISC) diagrams of the information environment are structured, complex and technical. A graphical representation of how some services, projects and software applications fit within the JISC Information Environment can be found in Powell (2003). The JISC definition of the information environment reflects this technical approach:

> The development of a robust and appropriate platform to provide access for educational content for learning, teaching and research purposes is a key component of the JISC 5 year strategy to: 'build an online information environment providing secure and convenient access to a comprehensive collection of scholarly and educational material' (JISC, 2003).

Despite this, the amorphous nature of the information environment is apparent to the JISC. In a previous manifestation it was known as the Distributed National

Electronic Resource (DNER), which was described in a paper at the Libraries Without Walls 4 conference (Ingram and Grout, 2002).

Within these complex environments, MMU Library is working to facilitate round-the-clock access to information on- and off-campus for students who are learning in different ways. The challenge for us is to accommodate everything from access to reading list resources, to giving students the information skills they need to find their way through the information environment. We are responding to this challenge, like many other university libraries, in a number of ways.

Learning and teaching

Learning and teaching is the core business at MMU. The University is developing new ways of learning and teaching, revisiting pedagogy, adopting a constructivist approach, accommodating different learning styles, making the practice of learning and teaching inclusive and developing transformative models of learning. E-learning is growing, with some faculties setting targets on the number of courses or modules delivered online. In response to this the Library has begun to engage with academic staff on issues around pedagogy, how students learn, how we can best support them and how best to mould our information environment.

MMU Library has extensive special collections including the book design collection, artists' books, archives and a gallery. We are in the process of digitizing illustrations from these collections, a follow up to the Bookhad Project (www.bookhad.ac.uk/). The digitization project aims to deliver a searchable website of images from these collections. So far we have digitized a sample collection of 280 images, cleared copyright, created metadata and produced a prototype image catalogue (using Invisage software). We have climbed a steep learning curve in order to make this happen. We have learnt about metadata, file sizes for images, copyright clearance and digital image software. It has been incredibly time-consuming and not without setbacks. Undeterred, we are about to rise to the challenge of digitizing 3D objects. We are talking to colleagues in the School of Art and Design about how these images can be used in learning and teaching, and intend to seek funding to undertake a project to embed electronic content in art and design courses.

The Library has an established print short-loan collection of popular, in-demand undergraduate material. In order to make this material easily accessible off-campus to large numbers of students we are embarking upon a project to create an electronic short-loan collection. We intend to use the HERON copyright clearance service (www.heron.ingenta.com/). Another opportunity to make available key material off-campus is presented by e-books. Garrett (2002) gives a full picture of e-book development in MMU Library. More recently, we have been investigating consortial purchase of a significant and relevant collection of e-books. The challenge here has been to find content appropriate to UK HE.

The MMU Library Information Skills Project started in December last year. It builds on current good practice within the Library, and incorporates the research from the JISC funded Big Blue project (www.leeds.ac.uk/bigblue/). It aims to give MMU a high level consistent strategic approach to information skills delivery. Two senior assistant librarians work on the project, which will do two things. Firstly, it will develop library staff knowledge and skills in designing and delivering training, and improve the format and content of all training materials (both print and electronic), ensuring there is adequate assisted take-up in relation to the new materials. In this way both library staff and training resources will have been developed to a consistently high level. Secondly, it will pilot an information literacy programme to selected cohorts of students, working closely with academic colleagues. This will include delivering taught sessions and WebCT tutorials, embedded within the curriculum. The pilot will be used as a marketing tool to raise the profile of information literacy within the University and encourage academic colleagues to appreciate the potential of working in close partnership with the Library and integrating information literacy skills into their syllabi. We are currently undertaking another project for JISC Big Blue Connect (www.mmu.ac.uk/services/library/info/specialproj.html), which will investigate the information skills sets of staff working in the HE and further education (FE) sectors.

Information literacy engendering independent learning and the use of reading lists are complementary. Reading lists provide directed learning from information resources through out a student's course of study. A new product from Talis has allowed us to create an online reading list facility in early 2002. Linked to the LMS, the online lists provide links to books, journals and internet resources, as recommended to students by their tutors. Direct web links are provided for electronic resources such as websites and e-journals. The volume of work required to input the reading lists into the system was significant. We currently have over 5000 reading lists online. Our academic colleagues have welcomed the potential of this facility for encouraging students to find and use a range of resources to support their learning. The Business School links from course information on their intranet to relevant TalisLists. The next stage is to link TalisList to WebCT courses.

Ideas and initiatives around marketing are evolving in the Library. We are formulating our response to the diverse nature of our student population and research that tells us that electronic resources (MMU has 6500 e-journal titles and over 100 databases) are not being used as much as we would like (Currier, 2001; Griffiths and Brophy, 2002; Rowley, 2002). MMU thinking is in line with the SCONUL vision (Corrall, 2001), which anticipates a focus on user needs, characterized by increasing diversity and choice. Knowledge and understanding of our users is key to providing relevant services and resources. We conduct a biannual user satisfaction survey, solicit feedback at course committee and other faculty meetings and have undertaken small-scale user needs analysis. We believe that we could do more and are exploring new ways of developing relationships with our users.

In terms of the MMU VLE, within the Information Skills Project we are using WebCT and have already had some success in creating VLE materials. The law librarian pioneered development in this area, working closely with the Law School to develop two WebCT courses focusing on using law resources. Around 600 students use these each year, and the success of the project was to a large extent due to the degree of collaboration between library and academic staff. Another development is LibWeb, which was conceived as a tool for academic WebCT course developers, to make it easy for them to link their courses to library resources.

Technological developments have made possible other initiatives. We are in the process of installing a wireless network and high specification notebook computers into the restrictive lecture theatre environment in the main library. It will become a more flexible interactive space for information skills teaching. There are issues around staff training and development in particular in this area; many staff (though IT literate) are finding it difficult to keep up with the rapid pace of development; they become uncertain when faced with new systems in rapid succession.

Research

MMU is committed to research. Its results in the last national research assessment exercise exceeded earlier performance along with the rest of the sector. In spite of the threat felt by new universities by the *post hoc* introduction of the 6 star grade, it looks as though one of our departments will be getting a 6 star. The Library's role is to do what we can to make research more efficient and facilitate achievement of quality at MMU. However, the Library has had its research allocation cut by 17% this year. We will have to make difficult decisions about sustaining the current model of library research support and maintaining the subject breadth of our research collections.

Currently, the research support librarian teaches on the Research Students Generic Training Programme, provides Endnote training and support for research staff and students, and compiles the Researchers Weekly Bulletin, a weekly e-mail highlighting new publications, websites, funding sources, and so on. This librarian has developed WebCiTe, a WebCT package designed to teach the basics of bibliographic citation and is about to embark on a University-wide project to develop a research methods course in WebCT. Harrison and Hughes (2001) give a detailed overview of research support at MMU Library.

Library support for research more generally was the subject of a report by the Research Support Libraries Group earlier this year. The recommendation to create a 'Research Libraries Network' (RLN) has yet to be fleshed out and implemented, but reflects the need in the UK for an arrangement to provide access to research information that would serve UK universities as well as world-class universities in other countries. It is expected that this RLN would have a large electronic component and it is our hope that less research-intensive universities will not be excluded as either users or contributors. For the report and a series of reactions to it from different perspectives, see Harris (2002).

Widening participation

The UK Government agenda of widening participation and increasing student numbers is controversial and easier for some universities to deal with than others. MMU has been in the business of recruiting students from non-traditional backgrounds for many years. We have a dedicated head of widening participation and lifelong learning, a foundation year development officer, and a strategic approach to create an 'access' culture in the institution. MMU has more students from areas of social disadvantage than any other university in the UK. We meet or exceed our HEFCE benchmarks on widening participation. We have increasing numbers of students who have differing needs. Students can be inexperienced, have polarized levels of IT and information literacy and they may be required to work in ways with which they are unfamiliar.

Library support in this area is challenging. Our learning and teaching initiatives are underpinned by awareness of accessibility issues and the need to provide different levels and mechanisms to make effective use of resources and services. Library services have be responsive, user orientated and flexible. The Library is involved in the University-wide Transition Induction and Progressions Strategies (TIPS) programme, which recognizes that people new to universities may find the large space and IT-rich facilities of a library intimidating. Library induction can now be accessed in a number of formats and contexts: traditional face-to-face induction sessions, a series of web pages, web-based online lecture (using Boxmind software) and by video streamed over the internet.

We are re-examining the Library helpdesk service, that currently consists of physical helpdesks located within each site library and accessible in person, by telephone or by e-mail. Although phone messages may be left and e-mails received, these helpdesks in fact function only during the library opening hours. Given the large and growing numbers of distance learners, part-time learners and placement students at MMU, there is a need to improve the existing service and to explore new services that would increase the hours of availability and the level of service provided. We are therefore investigating increasing helpdesk hours, consolidating helpdesks, a WebCT library help area, virtual helpdesks, shared helpdesks and 'Follow the sun' initiatives.

Reaching out to business and local communities

Reaching out to business and the community is getting more emphasis in the government's agenda for HEFCE funding. If new universities cease to get funding for research, then the implication of the White Paper (Great Britain. Department for Education and Skills, 2003) is that we should shift our emphasis to the external and regional agenda. MMU has traditional strengths in applied research, work placements and regional specialisms such as food, textiles and the creative industries, which are increasingly being exploited by the business community. More than £8.5 million has been awarded to the University to stimulate projects in the north west, which in turn levers in more private and public monies to drive regeneration, create jobs and improve quality of life of the region.

This is an area that is difficult for the Library especially in the electronic environment. There are problems with database and electronic journal licences and opening hours where courses are taught in vacations and at weekends. How we are going to deliver services and resources to meet this agenda is still uncertain and it presents a major challenge for the future.

Conclusion

I have taken the four key themes of HE in the UK (learning and teaching, research, widening participation and reaching out to business and local communities) and looked at how MMU Library is playing its part in supporting the University to achieving its objectives. I have described what we are trying to do and how and mentioned some of the things that stop or delay us. The main challenges for the future for MMU Library that overarch all this are:

- supporting the aims and objectives of the University
- developing library resources and services in a complex changing information environment
- serving a growing and increasingly diverse user population
- understanding the needs and wants of our users
- moulding the information environment to meet these needs.

> Whether we have lost those users forever or not is unknown. To head off that possibility, we must succeed in figuring out ways to be more central to their information lives. It's not enough to be available and accessible, as we have done yeoman work and spent a lot of money to become. We must be in their minds when important questions or problems arise, so they will think of turning to 'the library' first or second, not fifth or tenth or never at all (Janes, 2003).

References

Corrall, S. (2001) *The SCONUL Vision: academic information services in the year 2005*, London, SCONUL, www.sconul.ac.uk/pubs_stats/pubs/pubs/vision2005.html.

Currier, S. (2001) *INSPIRAL: INveStigating Portal for Information Resources and Learning*, http://inspiral.cdlr.strath.ac.uk/.

Garrett, R. (2002) *E-libraries: adoption and business models, The Observatory: on borderless higher education, briefing note*, www.obhe.ac.uk/products/briefings/pdfs/E-Libraries.pdf.

Great Britain. Department for Education and Skills (2003) *The Future of Higher Education*, London, HMSO, www.dfes.gov.uk/highereducation/hestrategy/pdfs/DfES-HigherEducation.pdf.

Griffiths, J. R. and Brophy, P. (2002) Student Searching Behaviour in the JISC Information Environment, *Ariadne*, (33), www.ariadne.ac.uk/issue33/edner/intro.html.

Harris, C. (ed) (2002) *The New Review of Academic Librarianship*, **8** (whole issue).

Harrison, M. K. and Hughes, F. (2001) Supporting Researchers' Information Needs: the experience of the Manchester Metropolitan University Library, *The New Review of Academic Librarianship*, **7**, 67–86.

Ingram, C. and Grout, C. (2002) A Distributed National Electronic Resource for Learning and Teaching. In Brophy, P., Fisher, S. and Clarke, Z. (eds) *Libraries Without Walls 4: the delivery of library services to distance users: proceedings of an international conference* held on 14–18 September 2001, organized by the Centre for Research in Library and Information Management (CERLIM), Manchester Metropolitan University, London, Facet Publishing.

Janes, J. (2003) Internet Librarian: the centrality or centrality, *American Libraries*, **34** (6), 102.

Joint Information Systems Committee (2003) *Information Environment: Development Strategy 2001–2005 (Draft 2)*, www.jisc.ac.uk/index.cfm?name=strat_ieds0105_draft2/.

Powell, A. (2003) Mapping the JISC IE Service Landscape, *Ariadne* (36), www.ariadne.ac.uk /issue36/powell/intro.html.

Rowley, J. (2002) JISC User Behaviour Monitoring and Evaluation Framework, *Ariadne* (30), www.ariadne.ac.uk/issue30/jisc/.

18

Disintermediation via web services in Portuguese public libraries

Maria Carla Proença and José Miguel Baptista Nunes

Introduction

Libraries are changing through the implementation and use of information technology. The world wide web has transformed the processes of disseminating information and is being increasingly used as a delivery vehicle for information services (Brophy, Fisher and Clarke, 2002). Library online services have been implemented throughout the world to meet the needs of a growing community of users. As a consequence, library users are reaping the benefits of being able to use library services independently at libraries, at home or at work.

In this context, an evaluation study was undertaken in the Department of Information Studies of the University of Sheffield aimed at investigating the use of internet services by Portuguese public libraries that are members of the Portuguese National Network of Public Libraries (NNPL; www.iplb.pt). This evaluation study was based on the emerging concept of disintermediation of information, which has triggered the change in the nature of work in public libraries using the internet (Hooper, 2001). This paper presents the results and findings of this study, by presenting and identifying the current state of the web presence and services of Portuguese public libraries and reporting on the impact of disintermediation. Furthermore, the paper also presents a critical review of how these libraries are meeting the challenges presented by the information society and aims to contribute to development of this field in Portugal while taking part in the expanding research into disintermediation.

Background and context

The information society and its main challenges

Portugal is a southern European country which, for historical reasons, has long been characterized by significantly low levels of literacy and access to information technology when compared with other European Union (EU) countries. This situation was clearly addressed in the Portuguese *Green Book for the Information Society*:

> in the majority of homes, and even in many schools, books are scarce and the computer is not yet an easily accessible tool. Public libraries must be and should be the open door to the new world of digital and multimedia information, the access point to cyberspace for those who, due to socio-economic and cultural reasons, have not, in principle, ways of doing it at home (Ministério da Ciência e Tecnologia, 1997, 28).

This scenario has been one of the major concerns of the Portuguese governments over recent years. As a result, some important steps forward have been taken and considerable investment has been made in technology, teaching and training. At the same time, there has been some concern regarding the creation of adequate legislation and the constitution of working groups able to produce guidelines for the implementation and management of information technology.

A project with a very positive outcome has been the Internet Initiative, which has been developed by the Portuguese Council of Ministers. Its aim is to develop a strong and modernized e-government presence on the internet providing access to public affairs and both direct and indirect administration of the country (Observatório das Ciências e Tecnologias, 2001). Following on from this, successive Portuguese governments have been strongly committed to the creation of instruments regarding the construction and evaluation of the websites of governmental bodies of interest to public libraries.

Overview of public libraries in Portugal

The low levels of literacy in Portugal are closely linked with a poor tradition of public library use. Despite the efforts of the Calouste Gulbenkian Foundation (www.gulbenkian.pt/), which over decades supported a national network of fixed and mobile libraries, public libraries in Portugal were few in number, ageing and very far behind both the needs of users and the standards of other European countries. This began to change when, in 1987, the Portuguese Institute for Book and Libraries (PIBL), a public organization controlled by the Ministry of Culture, started a programme aimed at building a public library in every municipality of Portugal. By the end of 2003, and as a result of this programme, all local authorities will be equipped with a public library of capable of meeting the needs of their citizens.

A set of common standards has been established providing clear rules for the construction and adaptation of buildings, for their organization, human resources, materials, functioning and services (Ochôa, 1998). Consequently, all public libraries are currently providing a series of core common services with the aim of promoting information, education and cultural activity by placing documents and services at the disposal of the public, in line with the UNESCO Public Library Manifesto (1994). At this time and as we are writing this paper, the National Network of Public Libraries (NNPL) is nearly completed. Furthermore, despite the initial low standards, Portuguese public libraries are undergoing rapid improvements both in terms of their general infrastructure and in IT support. As a consequence, these libraries are being looked upon as modern and pleasant places where people actually like to spend their time. These efforts are bringing Portugal closer to the best practice of other European Union countries. Indeed, public libraries are effectively taking advantage of the opportunity to play a very determinant role in helping bridge the digital divide. (Proença and Nunes, 2002).

Situational aspects

As reported above, the public library sector has greatly benefited from central and local government funding of the implementation of ICT (information and communications technology). Investments have been made in the setting up of the network infrastructure, the acquisition of hardware and training of library staff. Also, standards have been established through the Informatics Network of Public Libraries (INPL) regarding infrastructure, number of computers and internet access.

However, there are no specific guidelines regarding the design, development and maintenance of the services to be provided online, styles to be adopted, security and ethical guidelines for online services and the support to be given to libraries both in resources and the training of librarians. This has resulted in a very heterogeneous scenario, with sites ranging from very high quality to others that have been developed following ad hoc principles. Despite these gaps in quality, all the libraries making up the NNPL are providing free access points to the internet, which have been widely used. However, less than half of them offer web-based services, a fundamental component in meeting the requirements of the UNESCO Public Library Manifesto (1994) regarding the accessibility of library services to their users, with reference to outreach services for those unable to attend the library.

Methodological considerations and research findings

The results presented arise from a triangulation of research methods aimed at collecting both quantitative and qualitative data between September and October 2002.

Evaluation of websites

Virtually, all the libraries involved in the NNPL provide internet access. However, 44 (out of 106), that is less than 50%, offered web-based services (data from February 2002). In addition to the online services, this evaluation also took into account other points considered complementary, such as previous consideration of general information about the libraries to which the websites refer, the nature and purpose of public library web presence and the general functional aspects of these sites.

General information about the library websites

Overall, the websites provided insufficient information about their respective libraries. In fact, the evaluation soon exposed the absence of a written mission statement explaining the nature of public libraries represented on the web and their purpose and objectives. In fact, only 20% of the websites presented one. Moreover, nearly the same rate, 16%, was found for regulations and codes of conduct. It is presumed, despite the absence of references, that this information was copied from printed documentation available at the libraries.

Some of the websites were developed by outsourced professionals while others were designed by library or city council staff. Consequently their styles ranged from the very professional to the amateurish. Unsurprisingly, this has led to an enormous asymmetry in the type and number of web services provided, especially in terms of overall quality, information and services, user interface and communication style. None of the websites presented a clear rationale for their web services. In effect, the majority (59%) of the websites did not even contain library contacts (e-mail address, phone, fax, and so on) in a coherent manner. Furthermore, surprisingly, only 18% of these explicitly made public the name of the contact librarian.

In addition, one of the most fundamental pieces of information about such systems, a library plan able to provide useful information to prospective users about library buildings, location of services and facilities, was available in only 23% of the sites. Instead, some libraries provided online information and explanations about different areas available at the libraries and their respective functions.

Nature and purpose of public libraries websites

There were 27% of Portuguese public libraries represented on the web by websites as opposed to 59% that were represented by web pages. These pages were usually delivered through the websites of the municipalities or the Scientific Computation National Foundation. However, for practical reasons it was decided for the purpose of this research to consider both under the designation of website. With this in mind, none of the websites presented a clear rationale for their creation. In effect, none of them provided a mission statement or objectives able to justify their existence.

Some sites were updated very often, others less so. Indeed, only 9% of the sites showed the date of their latest revision. In one case, the information was two years out of date. Moreover, there were only a few sites where the date of the last revision was less than a month before the evaluation period began. There was also an absence of site maps for libraries and even most of the municipalities' websites did not provide the necessary site maps and links for users easily to reach the sites of the libraries. To complete the picture, 25% of the sites were only partially operational.

General functionality of websites

The Portuguese population is made up of a wide range of linguistic communities. However, only 5% of the sites provided language facilities for non-Portuguese speakers. Similarly, none of the sites provided facilities for disabled people or information concerning their access and use of library facilities. This is all the more surprising as it is known that some of these libraries are especially well equipped to provide services to such users. None of the websites provided a virtual tour in the real sense, able to attract prospective users. However, there were two cases where the information available was comparable to a virtual tour, in the form of a combination of library maps.

Online services

Online services were weakly represented in library web provision. In fact the websites offered a large amount of information about the services provided physically in the library, but very little was offered in terms of online service provision (18%). Figure 18.1 shows what services were provided on the websites of the public libraries.

The 'what's new' section was represented on 11% of the sites. These reported on events held at libraries, such as exhibitions, art exhibitions and seminars. In some cases, this section was quite out of date, as referred to previously. Even poorer

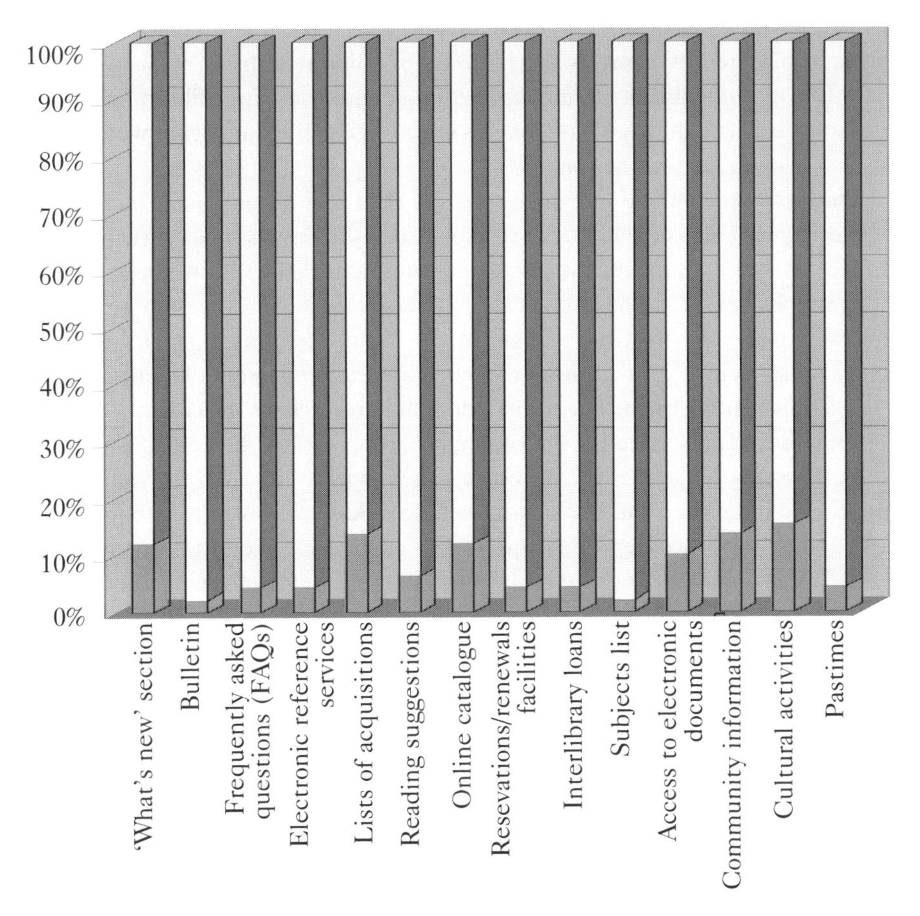

Figure 18.1 Online services provided by public libraries in Portugal

results were recorded as the evaluation continued: the Oliveira do Bairro Library (www.bib-oliveira-bairro.rcts.pt) was the only library that provided access to an online version of a bulletin and only 4% of the libraries provided a frequently asked questions service. Furthermore, the libraries represented on the web did not really provide an electronic reference service but a few (4%) of these possessed e-mail addresses. This research did not test these services and nowadays these facilities are in any case becoming an insufficient medium for meeting the needs of users.

Only 12% of the sites presented a list of documents acquired by the libraries. The Vila Franca de Xira library (www.bib-municipal-vila-franca-xira.rcts.pt) presented the most appealing list, with the digitization of newly acquired covers, which are very interesting as the books presented were children's books.

'Reading suggestions' was another facility available only on a few library websites – 6% of the total. Once again, the Vila Franca de Xira library had one of the most interesting lists, with a brief comment on each document. The online catalogue, considered by many as the lifeblood of a library website, was available at only 10% of the libraries. Online reservation, renewal and inter-library loan facilities were available in only 4% of libraries – the few existing catalogues were mostly available for online searches only.

Only 8% of the libraries provided access to electronic documents. The Abrantes library (www.bmab.cm-abrantes.pt) provided a facility named virtual library, which consisted of providing access to websites classified with the support of the Universal Decimal Classification. This service was created for the purpose of helping users to search for information on the web. This library, in its entirety, provided an archive with a considerable historical collection of online documents, such as a large assortment of current maps, and provided a subject list.

An information service for the community was provided by 12% of the library sites. The knowledge that the web is an increasingly useful source of information must have influenced the decision to include indexes with useful information in some sites; they included newspapers, data about local chemists, weather forecasts, TV programmes, lottery results, official publications and so on. Once again, the Abrantes library had the most developed of such directories. Also important was the information available related to the European Union. One of the library sites had an adviser on European affairs.

Portuguese public libraries are involved in a variety of cultural activities, and at the time of the study they were mainly occupied with exhibitions. However, they ranged from animated tales to meetings with writers. This apparent lack of variety might be explained by the time of year in which the evaluation was carried out (September). This information facility was available on 14% of the sites. In addition, 4% of the sites included a small assortment of pastimes for use by children, such as games, short stories, puzzles and riddles. The Mangualde (www.bib-mangualde.rcts.pt), Palmela (www.bib-palmela.rcts.pt) and Vale de Cambra (www.cm-vale-cambra.pt)libraries provided good examples of this service.

Links to other information systems

Figure 18.2 shows that the majority of public library websites in Portugal did not provide any links to other library resources or information systems. Thus public libraries were not usually offering added value regarding the provision of search tools. None of the websites provided links to other Portuguese public libraries, but to public libraries abroad. This situation is bizarre since, theoretically, all these systems are electronically networked. However, interestingly, it was noted that 9% of the online catalogues allowed access to the catalogues of specialized and academic libraries abroad and 9% provided access to the catalogue of the national library. Special attention was paid to the links with services from the respective

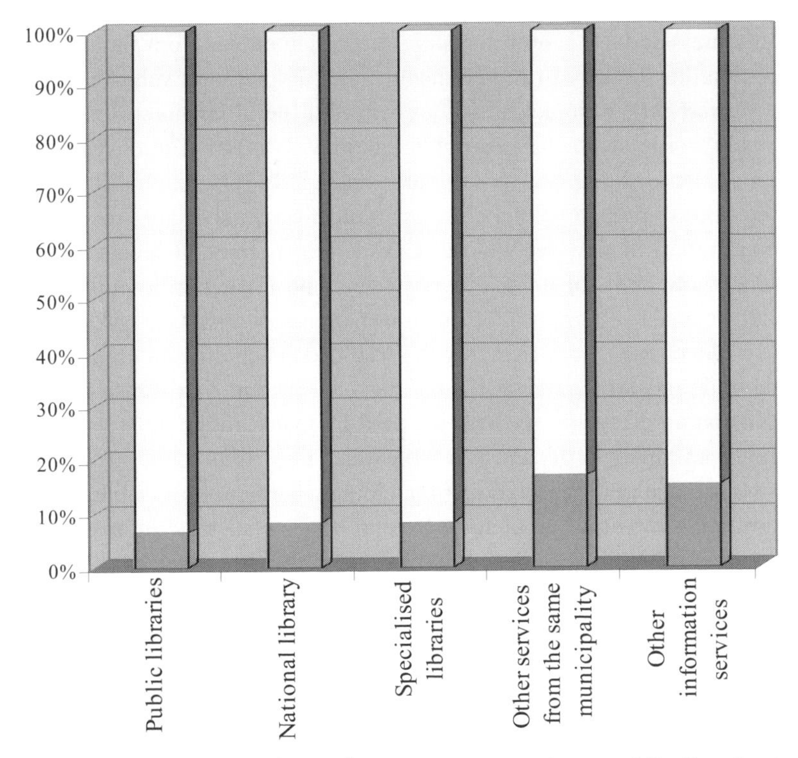

Figure 18.2 Links to other information systems from public libraries in Portugal

municipalities, which were present on 16% of the sites. Finally, there were links to other information services in 14% of the cases, including to systems such as school and academic libraries, and governmental bodies.

Overall, the majority of the libraries do not take advantage of the information technology infrastructure available as a vehicle for providing services to the public. Clearly the provision of online services in Portuguese public libraries is still in its initial stages.

Findings of the interviews

The findings from the evaluation of websites were reinforced through the details gathered from the interviews. Six interviews were held with six librarians who had managerial responsibilities in some of the libraries of the NNPL. This sample was taken from the National Network of Public Libraries directory.

Their responses showed that there were important differences in the levels of motivation, sensibility, knowledge and experience of the different librarians interviewed. Awareness and usage of web disintermediation ranged from the provision of elaborate online services to merely using them as publicity vehicles for the library on the respective municipalities' website. All the librarians were aware of the weak web profile of Portuguese public libraries. No user studies have been undertaken at these libraries to determine users' needs. The librarians were all aware of the need to prepare public libraries for organizational change arising from the implementation of new technology. Consequently, they all recognized the need to adopt new forms of producing, managing and broadcasting information, contents and services, as required for the information society.

However, two of them admitted that the web had yet to offer an original challenge to their libraries, since they had not built a site by that time. Once again, all the librarians pointed out the difficulties faced by many public libraries in conceiving and maintaining a presence on the web. The time spent maintaining websites varied considerably, according to the four respondents with a library website. In addition, some other problems were emphasized, such as the need for an increase in the number of specialized human and technical resources able to set up and run web services as well as more realistic budgets.

From the responses it was possible to conclude that the support given by the PIBL is not being delivered homogeneously across the NNPL. However, all the respondents believed that guidelines to support the creation and maintenance of a web presence at these libraries would be helpful and all agreed that the PIBL would be the most suitable body to co-ordinate these tasks.

Surprisingly, none of the respondents had knowledge of the documentation produced by the central government related to web service provision. As a consequence, websites were produced by consulting and analysing other sites, and consulting books and articles on the subject. The respondents recognized the need for a co-relationship between the libraries benefiting from the support provided by some European Union Projects such as ILIERS and the more developed websites. There are currently serious impediments over the way Portuguese public libraries offer disintermediated services.

Discussion and future work

Public libraries are required to provide increasingly better services. They have the special responsibility of satisfying the information needs of users through a variety of services, supported by information technology. Researchers in the field agree that users increasingly prefer the web as their medium of interaction with information in general and libraries in particular (Lakos and Gray, 2000). This means that these web-based systems will act as disintermediated intermediaries (Brophy, 2001, 92).

Thus, for the foreseeable future, online services should lead to an improvement in public library provision but the above results raised some concern about disintermediation via web services in Portuguese public libraries. Overall, these websites have poor information content and are still over-reliant on physical services. The websites do not provide the links and transparency that might be expected from them (Moore, 2000). Generally, the few online services provided still reproduce traditional library services and online services are still inadequate. This might be explained by the fact that library web provision has been implemented following ad hoc principles, without a clear rationale, mostly according to the subjective interests of local staff. Consequently, the majority of these libraries are still at a primary stage of disintermediation.

This research suggests that in future these libraries should provide a range of minimum services that should include, at least, the provision of OPACs and digital reference services as a basic resource for giving access to a wider range of information and content. It will also be important to ensure the quality of online services for people with special needs and to support initiatives that contribute to overcoming barriers for linguistic minorities, promoting resource sharing and linking the information chain.

The disintermediation of services has been evaluated. However, the degree to which that disintermediation has been useful to library users has yet to be studied. If these dynamics are analysed they can help to bring about better online public library services. This would suggest that additional and more extensive work is required to understand more fully the value and impact of online services in Portuguese public libraries.

Despite the present weaknesses there is room for optimism in that, at least in the authors' opinion, this situation is unlikely to endure for long and that the future of Portuguese public libraries will be linked effectively with the design, development and formulation of web service provision, namely for services that are likely to be disintermediated.

In conclusion, the authors propose that clear and precise guidelines should be created that would assist public libraries to implement disintermediated online library services and make them standard throughout Portugal. It is also suggested that these guidelines should address the needs of IT professionals in web design and content management, to assist them in developing the online services of Portuguese public library websites so that they respond to increasing user demand. Finally, this research suggests that the procedures should be implemented nationally in the expectation that this will result in an improvement in the quality of public library services throughout Portugal.

References

Brophy, P. (2001) *The Library in the Twenty-first Century: new services for the information age*, London, Library Association Publishing.

Brophy, P., Fisher, S. and Clarke, Z. (2002) *Libraries Without Walls 4: the delivery of library services to distant users*, London, Facet Publishing.

Hooper, T. (2001) Management Issues for the Virtual Library, *Electronic Library*, **19** (2), 71–8, http://fernando.emeraldinsight.com.

Lakos, A. and Gray, C. (2000) Personalized Library Portals as an Organizational Culture Change Agent, *Information Technology and Libraries,* **19** (4), www.lita.org/ital/1904lakos.html.

Ministério da Ciência e Tecnologia (1997) *Livro Verde para a Sociedade da Informação em Portugal*, Lisbon, Ministério da Ciência e Tecnologia Official Publications, www.acesso.umic.pcm.gov.pt/docs/lverde.htm.

Moore, N. (2000). The Internet and the Library, *Library Review*, **49** (9), 422–8.

Observatório das Ciências e das Tecnologias (2001) *Sociedade da Informação: principais indicadores estatísticos: 1995–2001,* Portugal, Observatório das Ciências e das Tecnologias.

Ochôa, P. (1998) Las Bibliotecas Publicas y la Sociedad de la Informacíon: Portugal, *Métodos de Información*, **5** (25), www.uv.es/cdde/mei/mei25/pag50.html.

Proença, M. C. and Nunes, J. M. B. (2002) An Evaluation of Internet Services in Portuguese Public Libraries. In Isaías, P. (ed.), *WWW/Internet 2002: proceedings of the IADIS International Conference 2002*, Lisbon, 13–15 November 2002. Lisbon, IADIS, 532–6.

UNESCO (1994) *UNESCO Public Library Manifesto*, www.ifla.org/documents/libraries/policies/unesco.htm.

19

Denmark's electronic research library: from national project to permanent activity

Bo Öhrström

Introduction

During 1998 to 2002, Denmark's Electronic Research Library (DEF – Danmarks Elektroniske Forskningsbibliotek) was a large government-funded project that aimed to build a national virtual research library in Denmark. The project had a vision of a single virtual research library focused on the need to provide easy access to scientific information for researchers and students in Denmark.

In spring 2002 the Ministry of Finance, the Ministry of Culture and the Ministry of Science, Technology and Innovation evaluated the project. The project's results proved to be so successful that DEF was placed as a permanent activity on the government's budget proposal. In December 2002 the budget was approved, and the continuation of DEF became a reality. This paper describes the development of the project. A new organization has been set up and a framework for future activities has been designed.

The budget for the permanent DEF was reduced significantly compared with the budget allocated to it in the project period. However, it was a major achievement to get any funding – the initial planning was to give no money at all – and the resulting budget allows important activities to continue and new ones to start. The reduced budget stresses the need for there to be even closer co-operation in the library sector, and the existing co-operation has to be carefully maintained and developed.

With the same reasoning the existing international co-operation should be strengthened. International co-operation is crucial in order to get more fair terms and prices for the libraries, especially for licences for electronic resources. Other international activities such as SPARC (www.sparceurope.org/) and the Budapest

Open Access Initiative should support these efforts in order to create change and to achieve some competition in the market.

Background to DEF

The national project – Denmark's Electronic Research Library – aimed to move the Danish libraries from being automated, conventional, co-operating individual libraries to the state of one large, coherent, electronic library structure providing integrated information services.

The project was defined in a project description of September 1996 by the three ministries involved: the Ministry of Culture, the Ministry of Research and the Ministry of Education. A governmental agency, UNI-C, and the management consulting firm, Ernst & Young, then conducted a study, and published a report (Denmark, Ministry of Culture, 1997), which described a vision for the development of the research libraries in Denmark.

On the basis of this work the three ministries decided to develop the Danish research libraries over a five-year period (1998–2002) in order to get them to function as one integrated research library: Denmark's Electronic Research Library. The ministries made 200 million Danish kroner (27 million euro) funding available for the project. The project was part of the government's initiative for research and IT in those years, and it is still part of the present political planning for the IT and knowledge society in Denmark.

From project to permanent activity

The national project was scheduled to end on 31 December 2002, and no more funding was expected for DEF activities. The reasoning behind this was that after the five-year project period ended the library sector had moved to a higher technical and organizational level, and the normal budgets would keep the libraries at this level or even lift them higher. During 2000 the steering committee realized that ending the project in 2002 would probably result in decreasing co-operation and therefore a substantial loss of the investment in the project. In 2001 the steering committee tried to influence the politicians and the ministries; it was hoped that more funding would be available from 2003 with an allocated portion of the Danish Budget, but this disappeared when a new government was elected. A new government meant new policies and priorities, and substantial budget cuts were introduced for the public sector.

DEF succeeded in getting attention from the new ministries, however, and in spring 2002 a budget analysis of DEF was carried out. The new ministries involved were the Ministry of Finance, the Ministry of Culture and the Ministry of Science, Technology and Innovation. In this analysis DEF proved that a co-ordinating body was necessary for increased development and efficiency in the research library sector. The framework and key issues for a permanent DEF from 2003 were:

- co-operation, consolidation and extension
- continuation of successful activities
- start up of promising new activities.

DEF was subsequently put into the government's budget proposal for 2003 onwards, and at the end of 2002 this was approved in Parliament. This was a major achievement in general times of budget cutting. As a result of this late decision, no formal extensive evaluation of DEF was carried out, and the careful use of funding in 2002 resulted in a considerable amount of project funding being transferred to the permanent funding in 2003.

Budget

DEF became a permanent feature on the Danish budget from 2003, with an average funding of 13 million Danish kroner (€1.7 million). The budget in the previous years was on average 40 million Danish kroner (€5.3 million) with yearly variations (see Table 19.1).

Table 19.1 Budget of DEF from 2001 to 2006

Year	Danish kroner (m)	Euro (m)
2001	65.2	8.7
2002	38.2	5.1
2003	11.6	1.5
2004	14.4	1.9
2005	13.0	1.7
2006	13.0	1.7

Organization and activities of DEF

The Ministry of Science, Technology and Innovation and the Ministry of Culture have established the permanent DEF and representatives from these two ministries make up the liaison group, which has the overall responsibility for the activities. The liaison group has appointed a steering committee and established a secretariat, which services both the steering committee and the liaison group, see Figure 19.1.

The steering committee consists of six members with the Director of IBM Denmark, Kim Østrup, as chairman. It has formulated a number of programme

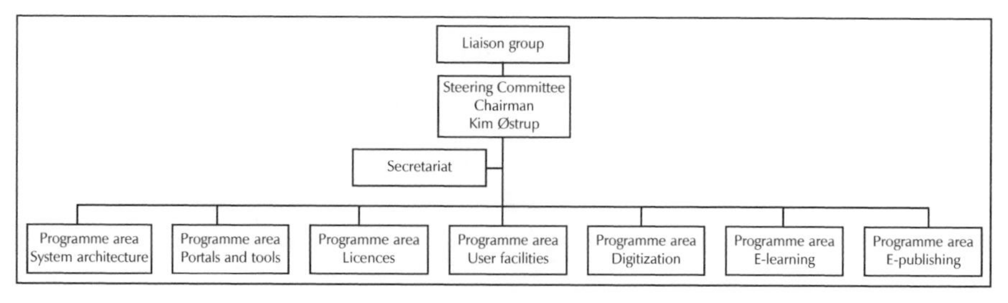

Figure 19.1 DEF organization 2003

areas, which function as a framework for co-operation, the role of DEF. These programme areas are:

- system architecture
- portals and tools
- licences
- user facilities
- digitization
- e-learning
- e-publishing.

Programme areas

Having access to relevant research information is a prerequisite for the continuous development of Danish research and education. As a consequence of the growth in volume of information and the increase in commercial research publishing it will be crucial for research libraries and DEF to ensure there is access to relevant information. Therefore DEF has made it a priority that there should be extended co-operation about the content that can be delivered by the research libraries. The programme areas are licensing, digitization and e-publishing.

The research libraries have an important role in ensuring that the traditional IT systems used to search and present information are user-friendly. Furthermore there will be an increasing demand for new IT systems that can support work with information, such as reference managers, tools for annotation, tutorials and tools for publishing. An important task will be to ensure that the user can get access to relevant information in a preferred, well-known web-environment. The co-operation around the technical framework concerning content is organized in the programme areas system architecture, portals and e-learning.

The traditional information competencies of the research libraries are also used in a digital environment, and guidance in information searching and use of IT systems will still be an important task, just as the research libraries can have an important role in developing the information skills of researchers and students.

DEF wishes to support co-operation concerning the development of user information competencies and development of tools for working with information resources through the programme area user facilities.

The activities in DEF have to be carried out with reduced funding compared with what was available during the project period. This means that financial support will be given to projects that are most likely to give increased value to most users or libraries. These projects are organized under the relevant programme area together with other related activities.

The chairpersons from the specific programme areas refer to the steering committee in biannual meetings. In addition the chairpersons and other participants can be asked to participate when relevant matters are discussed by the steering committee. The chairpersons prepare short plans of action and after approval by the steering committee these plans of actions are implemented as part of the strategy for individual programme areas. They are later incorporated into the total plan of action for DEF and form the basis for the budget made by the steering committee.

The programme areas can start up initiatives and projects with support from DEF by submitting an application, which will be dealt with and approved by the steering committee. Projects in DEF are carried out according to the guidelines made by DEF, which prioritizes requests so that the projects fit in with the vision of DEF and are in accordance with its mission. DEF gives priority to projects that are carried out with the involvement of end-users or user panels. In addition DEF wants to ensure that there is a continuing dialogue with end-users and other stakeholders through one or two open meetings per year, where users and stakeholders can discuss the ongoing development of DEF.

The role of DEF

The steering committee has formulated a draft framework for the permanent DEF activity, the role, vision and mission of DEF. The role is quite simply that *DEF is an organization for co-operation between the Danish research libraries.*

The vision of DEF

DEF is established as a network of Danish research libraries in order to support Danish education and research. This implies that one primary target group for DEF is students at the Danish universities and researchers at public research institutions. Since DEF is a network of research libraries it has a central task to provide services to researchers and students through the universities and public research institutions. Therefore the research libraries are the other primary target group. Ultimately, the results of DEF will be measured by the effect that the network has on Danish researchers and students. Therefore DEF's vision is formulated with the end-user as the starting point:

> Danish researchers and students have access to all relevant research information through user-friendly IT-systems, which in all respects supports the work with information. By virtue of guidance of high professional quality and substantial information competencies Danish researchers and students usage of the information resources is on the highest international level.

The mission of DEF

DEF strives to realize its vision through its mission statement, which prioritizes the development of co-operation between research libraries. The co-operation applies to the organizational and technological network between the research libraries. Organizational co-operation is implemented through a number of programme areas. The framework for the technological co-operation is an IT infrastructure, which has a three-layer architecture as starting point.

The starting point for the organizational network is that co-operation, co-ordination and exchange of experiences can help the individual research library to solve its tasks. Furthermore it is the opinion of DEF that co-operation and integration of resources can create added value for the users of the individual library and in that way add to the realization of the vision of DEF. On the basis of this opinion and the experiences from the project period DEF will use the following mission statement for its work:

> Denmark's Electronic Research Library will develop as a technological and organizational network of Danish Research libraries which provide their information resources for the users through their own or common websites and portals in a simple and coherent way under the existing judicial and economic framework.

DEF gives priority to individual research libraries providing a single entrance to the network and in that way to the participating research libraries' information resources and services. This means, for example, that the user can search and order material from other research libraries through the preferred interface of the user's local research library or learning environment. In the same way portals and other services developed by the research libraries in co-operation can be integrated in local web environments.

In addition it is appropriate for the local research library's information resources and services to be elements in digital leaning environments – both in connection with the mother institution and commercially outside the institution.

In many cases the smaller research libraries will not have the resources to participate in all development initiatives or to implement the results locally. The group of smaller research libraries is a very important target group for DEF, particularly because they service a large number of the Danish researchers. DEF will still maintain a portal (www.deff.dk), which among other things ensures that users of a small library have access to the systems and information resources that library can not offer locally.

Co-operation is crucial

In the national project the philosophy of project development reflected the importance of national co-operation and consensus. No lasting solutions could be implemented without participation from and acceptance by the libraries. Therefore the key words for all activities were co-operation, co-operation and co-operation. Another word could be added: patience, patience and patience. The same philosophy will apply to DEF in its work in future and as a result of it receiving less central funding the emphasis on co-operation will be even stronger.

As in the national project, DEF managers will aim to get quick results. Therefore activities that quickly lead to improved conditions for libraries and their users will be chosen. Similarly, those that meet with little resistance will be carried out but it is inevitable that there will be confrontation; however, confrontation usually results in a peaceful and lasting consensus.

Finally co-operation and effort from the largest libraries is still of great importance. These libraries control most of the financial resources and material, they have managers who can deal with common issues, and they want to make changes.

Successful co-operation projects

DEF co-operation has fostered many successful projects and activities, which will be extended in future. Examples of such projects and activities are:

- common licensing
- a common access system
- a common portal toolkit.

Common licensing

Acquisition of electronic journals and databases in consortia has been particularly valuable for libraries and their users. For several years, an organization consisting of those responsible for acquisitions in libraries and the DEF Secretariat has coordinated the acquisition of electronic information resources at a yearly value of more than 60 million Danish kroner (8 million euro). This is by far the largest of the library sector's acquisitions in this area.

Libraries provide the expertise of information specialists and the DEF Secretariat provides the commercial, legal and negotiating skills. Usually the financing of individual acquisitions has come from major payments from the participating libraries' budgets, combined with a smaller payment from the central funding controlled by the DEF Secretariat. The result of this successful co-operation has been a better exploitation of the existing acquisitions budgets and extended access to information resources for all researchers and students.

In order to accelerate changes in the business model in this market, initiatives like the Budapest Open Access Initiative and SPARC have been born. DEF will support these initiatives together with many other organizations to get more content at a smaller price and with better conditions for the users.

Common access system

A major request from the users is to have access to research information anytime from anywhere. This request is difficult to fulfil, since services providing licensed information have built-in access control restricting access to certain user groups. This access control is often based on Internet Protocol address control and the result of this is normally that the user has to be present at the university campus to get access to licensed information. This obstacle can be overcome by using a proxy service at the university, where the user can log in from anywhere and behave like a physical user at the campus. This solution gets more complicated if institutions are not all able to operate a proxy service, so a common portal will allow access to all users.

Like many other co-operating institutions, DEF has worked with this problem based on the philosophy that a common infrastructure should be established. In this infrastructure, service and data providers could operate under common rules with protection of both service and user data. This general approach appeared to be too ambitious, and DEF decided to build an infrastructure aimed solely at providing access to electronic journals and databases. Therefore a system solving this problem using the above mentioned proxy technique has been built, and all Danish licence users can have access through this system. The number of possible users is now more than 100,000.

In the coming year this system will be developed further along the lines of the Shibboleth architecture (http://shibboleth.internet2.edu/). In this way security will be improved, standards will be implemented, and the Open Source approach will be continued. If the publishers move in this direction DEF will be ready to follow quickly.

Common portal toolkit

A final example of a successful co-operative project is the development of a toolkit for building subject portals. The idea was that a common toolkit would free the libraries from lots of parallel technical work and allow them to spend time on content for the users. Furthermore a common toolkit would simplify exchange of data in the DEF and the international environment. The toolkit was developed in Open Source in order to allow libraries to enhance solutions locally and to allow any improvement of the toolkit made by one library to be delivered easily to the other libraries. The initial target for the toolkit was a simple subject portal based on link collections, but demands for other functions have risen. Today the basic toolkit has been extended with interfaces from the Open Archives Initiatives and now the portals can act as service and data providers in this architecture. Also Z39.50 functionality has been added, giving portals capabilities for searching databases with Z39.50 interface. In this way a portal operates as a Z3.50 client.

Summary

The decision to launch the national project, DEF, and the fulfilment of the project, have been successful. The initial funding and lots of hard work have upgraded Danish research libraries to a modern technological level. Now funding for the permanent DEF has secured continued national co-operation and new development for the years to come. The overall effort could be summarized in the following three statements:

- The national project DEF has provided a remarkable improvement in levels of service for the users of the Danish research libraries.
- The permanent DEF will continue to deliver new services and improve cost-effectiveness as co-ordinator of the co-operation between the Danish research libraries.
- The management and staff of DEF will continue to deliver significant effort to ensure success for libraries and their users in the future.

Reference

Denmark, Ministry of Culture (1997) *Danmarks elektroniske forskningsbibliotek*, www.kum.dk/sw1871.asp.

20

Research resources and the academic researcher

Margaret Wallis and Julie Carpenter

Introduction

The provision of high-quality research information delivered to researchers in a timely fashion is a prerequisite of internationally recognized research. But what information do researchers require? Has their use of library and information sources changed in recent years and do they envisage further changes in the future?

The Research Support Libraries Group (RSLG) was established in 2001 with a remit to make proposals for a national strategy to ensure that all UK researchers continue to have access to world class information sources. The final report was published in Spring 2003 (RSLG, 2003) with the recommendation to establish the Research Libraries Network to develop, prioritize and lead a UK-wide strategy for research information provision.

The report drew strongly on a national survey carried out by the Social Informatics Research Unit at the University of Brighton, Education for Change and the Research Partnership (Education for Change, Social Informatics Research Unit and Research Partnership, 2002). The aim of the study was to provide a picture of how researchers use libraries and other information sources in practice and how they predicted that this use would change over the next five years, especially as more material becomes available online (www.rslg.ac.uk/research). This paper presents key findings from the study, outlining the information needs and user patterns of the UK academic research community, and considers the implications for librarians seeking to provide services that meet the future needs of academic researchers.

Research methodology

The study was carried out between September 2001 and June 2002. The methodology included a literature review, a questionnaire survey of individual researchers and focus groups of researchers drawn from a range of institutions, disciplines and levels of seniority.

The evidence of the research survey, supported by the literature and focus group views, is the principal source for this paper. The survey questionnaire was designed to gather evidence relating to the following broad issues:

- the nature, range and volume of material researchers required in different disciplines
- the nature of access required and how they currently use the material in their research
- the implications for the research process of where materials are located and what achievable patterns of location and accessibility of information sources are optimal
- the extent to which researchers currently access research materials on line, and the perceived advantages and shortcomings of accessing materials in this way
- the relative significance of the internet as a research tool
- potential future changes in how researchers will access and use research materials
- differences in needs and practice between identifiable subgroups of researchers, related to research discipline or other factors.

A sample survey of 3390 researchers in UK higher education institutions (HEIs) was drawn from the 2001 Research Assessment Exercise (RAE) census. A final total of 1440 completed questionnaires was received – a response rate of 45%.

Analysis

The survey responses were analysed by discipline, based on the five broad RAE subject groups: medical and biological sciences, physical sciences and engineering, social sciences, area studies and languages, arts and humanities. This provided the opportunity to compare and contrast any differences in patterns of use and behaviour between these disciplines. The survey respondents were also divided into other sub-groups, such as age, percentage of time spent in research, working methods and RAE rating to identify any relevant differences.

Nature and range of material required by researchers

The survey asked researchers which information sources they currently use and consider essential to their research. Three areas highlighted interesting similarities and differences between the disciplines: the use of books and printed journals, the importance of electronic journals and the low use of non-text research materials.

The use of books and printed journals

Most significant was the importance of books and printed journals to the overwhelming majority of researchers: 82% of respondents across all disciplines rated books as essential to their research. Not only researchers in the humanities and social sciences require access to books. At least two-thirds of researchers in the sciences view books as essential to their work. This finding was not reflected in the literature, which provided little evidence to support the importance of books.

Less surprisingly, 95% of researchers perceived printed refereed journals as essential. The advent and popularity of electronic journals has not yet reduced the importance of the printed journal. This reliance on printed material is expected to continue across all disciplines for some time; in particular the arts and humanities community believes they will be reliant on printed material for many years.

Electronic journals

The discipline divide is very apparent in attitudes to electronic access. Medical and biological sciences research is focused heavily on journal literature and primary data and three-quarters of this group view electronic access to e-journals and electronic full-text services as essential. Timeliness and speed are the key factors, which make the use of these research sources and indexing tools in electronic formats increasingly attractive and essential to researchers. Conversely, less than a quarter of researchers in arts and humanities, area studies and languages perceive electronic access to journals as essential where fewer relevant journal titles are available in electronic form.

Low use of non-text research materials

Non-text research materials, including computerized data sets, still and moving images and artefacts, attracted surprisingly low levels of use. Although there were indications that digital images will become increasingly important to the science research community. A chemical physicist suggested 'the advent of 3D images and the gradual ability to integrate images into research work will change the way individuals perceive their work and the way in which they collaborate'.

Nature of access to research materials

Respondents were asked to choose which access and discovery methods they used and considered essential from a predefined list. The responses confirm that there are similarities between the subject disciplines in the importance of inter-library loans and document delivery, of searching library catalogues and of using library technology services. Interesting differences relate to the importance of physical access to libraries and collections and the use of library services.

Physical access to library collections and services

Respondents were asked how important it is for them to have physical access to libraries for their research. Twice as many researchers in area studies and languages and arts and humanities consider physical access to library collections essential to their research as their colleagues in the social sciences and over three times as many as researchers in the medical, biological and physical sciences. This correlates with the wide diversity of physical materials required by researchers in these fields, in comparison with those in scientific fields.

Browsing through collections of books and journals, and the serendipitous benefits this can bring to research, is essential to twice as many arts, humanities, area studies and language researchers when compared with their scientific colleagues. In contrast 80% of researchers in the medical and biological sciences identify electronic access to journals as essential.

A cause of concern for information professionals was the low use of enquiry and research assistance across all disciplines. Researchers in social sciences and humanities are more likely to use such services than their scientific colleagues. This was far from a universal vote of confidence in librarians. One participant put it very bluntly: 'People [i.e. library staff] are a rather expensive way of getting the information.'

Location of research materials

Researchers were asked which information providers they rate as essential to their work. Physical location of material is becoming a secondary issue to researchers in medical and biological sciences and physical sciences and engineering, as the widening range of essential research materials and data available electronically has an impact on research patterns in these fields.

Significant differences between subject groups appear in the importance of other university libraries in research and in the use of the British Library and other national research information providers.

Researchers' home university library

The literature suggests that researchers are now making less use of their home university library, with visits to the library in decline and a lack of awareness of what the library can and does provide (Ferguson and Crawford, 2001). Contrary to these reported trends, our survey indicates that the overwhelming majority of researchers (83%) regard their own university library as essential, the highest-rating information provider named in the survey.

But there was evidence of a growing distance from the library. Participants talked about the library in the sense of a physical building with physical holdings – and their visits to it (or not). There appeared little understanding – or acknowledgement – that the library provided many of the electronic services they used, or could use, on and off site: 'The library has lost its point. You need to take consumers back to the library or vice versa . . . I want my own librarian' and 'I tore up my library ticket five years ago and I have not visited the library since.'

Use of other university libraries

Researchers in area studies and languages are the keenest users of other university libraries but a minority of researchers in sciences and social sciences rated other university libraries essential.

The CORSALL study (Bloor, 2001) found that the level of reciprocal use between three co-operating and locally situated university libraries was low. The main barriers were summarized as 'lack of knowledge about the reciprocal access arrangements, lack of knowledge of what was available at the other libraries, and lack of time'.

Given this finding it is interesting to speculate on the likely take-up of the new SCONUL Research Extra co-operative access and borrowing scheme (Hall, 2003).

Use of the British Library and other national or regional providers

The British Library is considered essential to research by over one-third of researchers in all subject fields, and by over half of researchers in area studies and languages and arts and humanities. What is not clear from these results is whether this indicates the essentialness of actual visits to the British Library or of its inter-library loan and document delivery services.

The role of other national and regional providers of research information and resources – many of which are outside the higher education sector, such as the national museums – is not currently a particularly important one, even in arts and humanities. While a significant number of these researchers use museums and archives, few regard them as essential to their research and few outside area studies and languages regard the other copyright libraries as essential.

Focus groups expanded on the problems associated with accessing materials in other libraries, museums and archives. While many non-scientists would make use of reciprocal access agreements in areas with multiple HEIs – often essential for researchers at institutions with very limited or inappropriate local library resources – it was seen as both time and cost intensive to get (physical) access to primary materials in archives and museums. Lack of knowledge of collections is a barrier.

The 'type' of access (for example mediated by curators) allowed to researchers is also seen as a barrier. For some researchers microfilm or other surrogates provide adequate access and little need exists to have access to 'original' materials.

The RSLG report used these results to show access to external information providers beyond the 'home' institution is important for researchers in all disciplines and particularly for those in area studies and languages and arts and humanities and 'underline(s) the importance of enabling researchers to discover and access the collections of external providers efficiently'. Sadly the recommendations in the report are largely limited to the HE sector and barely mention the huge wealth of research resources held in other sectors and the substantial barriers that exist for researchers to access this material.

Access to electronic information sources and services

Web search engines and subject gateways

The internet is a significant research tool across all disciplines, as Table 20.1 shows. In arts and humanities, where use of electronic journals and information sources is still low, researchers make frequent use of generic search engines such as Google, electronic discussion lists and the websites of particularly important organizations. Concern was expressed about quality and provenance and there was even some disparagement of information sources located through use of generic web search engines. However, almost everyone admitted to making frequent use of them.

In contrast, less than a third of all researchers view mediated subject gateways, including institutional gateways and those provided as part of the Resource Discovery Network, as essential to their research. Awareness of these gateways was low: 'I feel I need to know more than I do' was the consensus. Suspicions were voiced in focus groups that subject gateways constrained freedom of choice.

Surprisingly the RSLG found this a cause for optimism: 'Comparison with an evaluation by JISC in 2000 showed just 9% of academic and research staff made regular use of mediated gateways, the results and popularity of these tools may therefore be increasing.'

Table 20.1 Electronic sources: search and discovery methods rated 'very important' by respondents (%)

	Medical & biological sciences	Physical sciences & engineering	Social sciences	Area studies & languages	Arts & humanities	All respondents
Online catalogues for your own institution's library	32	33	56	68	54	46
'Generic' web search engines	42	48	45	49	44	45
Bibliographic data-bases, abstracting & indexing services	60	44	40	38	29	43
Institutional or departmental gateways or portals	35	31	36	32	28	33
Subject gateways or portals (e.g. RDN)	26	24	27	27	21	25
Digital libraries or archives (e.g. MIMAS)	30	38	19	11	12	23
'Subject' mailing lists or alerting facilities	14	10	17	15	13	14
Personal portals	14	11	7	6	8	9
Pre-print archives	6	16	4	7	3	7

Perceived advantages and shortcomings of electronic access

The disciplines displayed significant differences on how easy it is to find, access and use information electronically compared with more traditional means, as Table 20.2 shows. Not surprisingly the science community are most at ease with electronic access with arts and humanities researchers the least confident group. Nevertheless, across all disciplines a similar pattern emerged: finding information electronically was deemed easiest; accessing the information more difficult and using it more difficult still.

Table 20.2 Finding, accessing and using information electronically: comparison with traditional, non-electronic means (%)

	Medical & biological sciences	Physical sciences & engineering	Social sciences	Area studies & languages	Arts & humanities	All respondents
Finding information electronically is a lot easier	83	77	65	48	48	66
Accessing information electronically is a lot easier	65	57	45	32	22	47
Using information electronically is a lot easier	50	35	31	22	17	32

Training, advice and guidance in using electronic sources

Training was a sensitive issue. The survey showed (see Table 20.3) that over half of all researchers either do not take up training or advice when it is offered or are unaware that it is available. Less than one-fifth of respondents had received some form of training, advice or guidance in the past two years. Even fewer researchers in the scientific community had been in receipt of training; they were also less likely to seek advice or guidance.

Table 20.3 Incidence of those using help or advice offered by their own institution's library staff (%)

	Medical & biological sciences	Physical sciences & engineering	Social sciences	Area studies & languages	Arts & humanities	All respondents
Yes, advice sought from library staff	18	17	24	28	22	21
Yes, advice, courses, updates made available by staff	9	7	16	20	14	13
No, none offered	11	12	8	10	15	11
No, offered but not used	36	40	34	33	28	35
Don't know if help/advice is available	23	18	14	9	15	17

It proved difficult to encourage focus group participants to discuss their own training needs. They consistently side-stepped the issue, as if their own training was not a pertinent topic – or something they were unwilling to share – 'I don't come into this category [of needing advice or training].'

Use of the term 'training', in connection with raising awareness of electronic sources and up-dating skills, was regarded negatively. However, awareness of aspects of electronic sources was extremely variable and there was unanimity across all disciplines about the areas they would like to know more about, including specialist online search skills and locating and filtering high-quality information sources.

These results indicate that there is an important future role for librarians in developing and maintaining awareness of electronic sources amongst academics.

Future trends in access and use of materials

There were few surprises in researchers' perceptions of the future. Responses were largely conservative. There was indication of change in three key areas: the use of research materials and sources, the use of research information providers and access and discovery methods.

The use of research materials and sources

A majority of researchers envisaged using electronic materials and sources more in the future.

The medical and biological sciences community suggested they will be using moving images more in future. Researchers in the humanities do not believe a critical mass of relevant materials is yet available electronically. They also perceived clear disadvantages in a wholesale move to an electronic future: 'Browsing is different and more difficult electronically.' There is a powerful tradition and culture of physical contact with objects and manuscripts: 'Touch and smell does matter!' Despite this these researchers are interested in electronic full texts of manuscripts and primary documents being more widely available. The potential strength of electronic access in terms of 'anywhere, anytime' was universally recognized.

Use of research information providers

Few respondents foresee any change – either increase or decrease – in the range of information providers currently used. A quarter of arts and humanities and area studies and language researchers are more likely to use other university libraries, including the British Library and those outside the UK more. But there was little evidence to suggest that other information providers, including the other copyright libraries, will be used more.

Changes in access and discovery methods

All researchers clearly expect to access e-books and e-journals more. Interestingly one-third of researchers expect to make increased use of inter-library loans and document supply, and also of library catalogues, perhaps signalling the growing importance of identifying and obtaining materials remotely from distributed collections. This will be encouraging to the embryonic Research Libraries Network, which is to drive 'much deeper collaboration between research libraries . . . in this electronic era where many functions are better carried out jointly than severally' (RSLG, 2003).

Conclusions and questions

Our survey and the RSLG report on researchers' use of and developing requirements for information resources identified four major issues:

1. The 'hybrid library': researchers in all disciplines regard both hard copy and electronic material as essential now and for the foreseeable future; but the availability of information from online sources is increasingly important for researchers in all disciplines.
2. Researchers need better tools for identifying and locating research information and increasingly expect these to emerge in electronic form.
3. Access to external providers of print resources (beyond the 'home' library) is important for researchers in all disciplines.
4. The overwhelming majority of researchers regard their own university library as essential to their research, and a significant proportion regard the British Library as an essential source for documents not in their home library.

We particularly want to highlight three issues. First, there appears to be a chasm between HE and other library and cultural heritage providers. The RSLG Report focuses, not surprisingly, on HE and the British Library but our evidence suggests that most researchers do not visit and are often ignorant of the existence of collections outside HE.

Further research is clearly necessary to identify and overcome perceived (and real) barriers to physical access targeted in particular at the arts, humanities, area studies and social sciences. The reluctance of researchers to travel to research collections means that more radical approaches may be required. These might include consideration of different economic and infrastructural models in regional and national library, museums and archival repositories, and moving materials to researchers rather than researchers to materials.

Non-HE research resource institutions need to become more effective in promoting their collections and services to academic researchers. An obvious target initially is academic librarians who may be insufficiently aware of non-HE sector sources and potentially valuable research resources, such as film and broadcast materials, photographic and art collections.

Our second area of concern is academics' preference for using generic search engines when looking for web resources. The vast majority of researchers are still not using mediated subject gateways and portals as a means of accessing electronic research resources. Either the case has not yet been made effectively or researchers are unaware of their existence.

Large sums are being spent on the development of mediated gateways and portals. Our findings would suggest that careful consideration is required by JISC and others in the research community as to how the research gateways, portals and other electronic resource discovery tools are conceived, structured, delivered and promoted to researchers.

Third, there is absolutely no mention of training and awareness in the RSLG's report despite the strong evidence of the need to develop the information literacy skills of researchers. Our study indicates that academic library services are failing to deliver the right kinds of training, advice and guidance to researchers on finding, accessing and using electronic resources. 'Maybe there's a need for a researchers' course – but not from the library. The library is useful for books.' Researchers appear unaware of existing advice and guidance opportunities and interventions are not being delivered in the most appropriate ways, at the optimum times and by the most effective people: 'The response of the librarian should be to facilitate access to all kinds of information and services. I need training in knowing what I need training in. We need librarians who are evangelists. People who will say: "Did you know about...?"' Burge's (2002) keynote paper at the Libraries Without Walls 4 conference talked about 'disintermediation': 'Librarians in the field of education [do] not behave as consistently proactive educational partners.' They need to become visible not on the librarians' territory but on the users' territory.

'What we need is people decentralized and collections centralized – subject specialist librarians are key.' The need is clear; librarians need to move out of their libraries to provide the services researchers require.

References

Bloor, I. (2001) *Collaboration in Research Support by Academic Libraries in Leicestershire, Final Report*, www.le.ac.uk/li/libservices/corsall/corsall.htm.

Burge, E. J. (2002) Behind-the-screen Thinking: key factors for librarianship in distance education. In Brophy, P., Fisher, S. and Clarke. Z. (eds), *Libraries Without Walls 4: the delivery of library services to distant users*, London, Facet Publishing.

Education For Change, Social Informatics Research Unit and Research Partnership (2002) *Researchers' Use of Libraries and other Information Sources: current patterns and future trends 2002*, http://www.rslg.ac.uk/research.

Ferguson, R., Crawford, J. (2001) The Use of Library and Information Resources by Research Staff at Glasgow Caledonian University, *Library and Information Research News*, **25** (79), 31–8.

Hall, J. (2003) SCONUL Research Extra, *SCONUL Newsletter*, **28**, Spring, 94–5.

Research Support Libraries Group (2003) *Final Report*, www.rslg.ac.uk/final/final.pdf.

Theme 5
The creation of digital resources by user communities

21

Cultural Objects in Networked Environments (COINE)

Michelle Kelly and Geoff Butters

Introduction

> For memory institutions to reach broader audiences, they need to move beyond resource discovery and offer services that also relate to people's lives. (DigiCULT, 2002)

Recent studies, such as the 2002 *DigiCULT Report (Technological landscapes for tomorrow's cultural economy: unlocking the value of cultural heritage)*, are beginning to suggest that there has been a shift in emphasis for digitization projects within museums, libraries and archives. While digitizing collections and putting information online remains the valid goal of most institutions, it is now being recognized that greater value can be added to these collections and sources of information if the role of the 'user' is more closely examined and the resources interpreted accordingly. The aim of simply creating digital content on websites and databases has been surpassed by the desire to enhance, manipulate or change the content according to the requirements of a specific audience, therefore making resources relevant to individual users. The DigiCULT Report highlights this change and the increasing demand for 'high quality, enriched digital content' (DigiCULT, 2002, 8) with an emphasis on lifelong learning and the relating of cultural resources to individual lives.

The COINE (Cultural Objects In Networked Environments) project is rooted in the idea of digital cultural heritage being driven by user communities. It embraces the possibility of there being a 'two-way' flow of information and cultural heritage resources: no longer should it only be museums, libraries and archives that create the digital content for remote users, but these institutions should also present the opportunity for the users themselves to be active in this creative process, using information technology to improve the sharing of and access to community heritage, collections and personal stories.

It is from this vision – where users are as active as institutions in the portrayal of community heritage – that the COINE project was born. Could an information system be developed that would:

- allow people to create and publish their own stories and resources?
- be suitable for people with limited experience of information and digital technology?
- perform complex searches?
- be capable of handling many hundreds of thousands of objects and narratives while still producing usable results?

Such a system could link and share stories and other research locally, regionally, nationally and internationally with this information presented in a coherent way, sidestepping the problems of inconsistency presented by the world wide web, where individuals create isolated web pages which are not usefully linked. Such a system would also offer the opportunity of uncovering private research that would normally remain hidden and inaccessible on an individual's PC.

The COINE project

The COINE project is a two-and-a-half year demonstration project with the objective of successfully creating, testing and evaluating a digital cultural domain, accessible individually or as a community, that will ultimately enable people to tell their own heritage stories and become actively involved in the sharing of and having access to local heritage. Funded by the European Commission Information Societies Technologies (IST) Programme (Framework 5), COINE seeks to provide the tools for a structured web-based environment. Digital objects (images, sound, text, video) will be captured, stored, described, linked and maintained within the COINE domain. It will also be usable as a search tool to discover other stories and research. At the time of writing, the project has been under way for 18 months. During this period the project has focused primarily on assessing user requirements, creating a functional specification and building the system. Testing of the software begins in October 2003 and will be carried out for ten months.

A European approach

COINE aims to achieve a technical infrastructure that accommodates the needs and cultures of a diverse audience and produces a universally accessible and helpful resource. The multinational approach presents opportunities for the cross-fertilization of ideas and experience with the ultimate result being the creation of a product with the widest possible appeal. It is a vital part of COINE to test the software in different social, cultural and technological environments leading to more creative solutions. With the process of modification receiving input from across Europe, the project is assured of a good range of test scenarios, heritage stories, languages and technical abilities and will produce a system that is easily transferable between different cultures, users and languages.

COINE offers an opportunity to advance the interaction of cultural heritage perspectives not just across a region but also across a country and even a continent. Much of the value of the project lies in the input and opinions of partners from different countries and their influence on the final product. Although there is a heavy emphasis on local heritage, the scheme is by no means parochial and COINE will promote the cultural links within Europe, and an understanding of different cultures, histories and ethnic identities, while simultaneously engaging a new audience in the value of information systems. The system will be suitable for all abilities and allow ordinary people to contribute to their common culture and disseminate information.

Partners in the COINE project are:

Project co-ordinator:
  CERLIM, Manchester Metropolitan University, UK
Technical partners:
  Fretwell-Downing Informatics Ltd, Sheffield, UK
  The National Microelectronics Applications Centre Ltd, Limerick, Ireland
Demonstration partners:
  CERLIM, Manchester Metropolitan University, UK
  Ennis Information Age Town, Ireland
  The Jagiellonian University, Krakow, Poland
  University of Macedonia, Thessaloniki, Greece
  Universitat Oberta de Catalunya, Barcelona, Spain.

User requirements

The role and requirements of the user are at the heart of the COINE project and, as a result, the primary stage of the project has been to investigate these issues. Sample scenarios from all countries, including those from individuals, heritage institutions, educational groups and community groups, have been put together to form a basic level of information from which to draw upon.

The study into user requirements has examined the functionality of the system: how it will work and how people will want to use it; the languages people will want to use; the generic templates that might work to help people 'tell their story'; what the process of publication will be; issues of copyright; the metadata requirements of the system and how all these will translate to a non-expert user. Test domains will be set up and populated by schools, museums, individual researchers, oral history groups, local history societies, voluntary groups and cultural institutions drawing upon groups of different ages and abilities.

The education sector is of particular interest as a future market with the possibility of a COINE system being used extensively within schools. COINE could allow children to share stories, class work or ideas within the school domain without the information being exposed on the internet. One of COINE's core features is that it can be fully functional locally and privately as well as internationally. In the UK, the process of telling a story through COINE is also highly relevant to the national curriculum. Besides the obvious links with information technology or history, COINE also engages users in processes of planning, drafting and creating narratives, all of which feature strongly in the UK's National Literacy Strategy (www.standards.dfes.gov.uk/literacy).

How will COINE work?

A 'COINE domain' in simple terms is a website, access to which is restricted to those people authorized to access it by the domain administrator through a login name and password. The administrator may operate it as a closed website allowing only authorized members to read stories, or may authorize limited access to anyone to search and read published stories. However, contributors of stories must be registered and authorized as members by the Administrator.

The domain also includes all the information about its members and its content, which is held in the database on the database server.

A domain administrator is the person who manages the use of a COINE domain, so they can add, delete or amend information about its members and its content (the stories and objects).

The COINE system will be composed primarily of a database server and a web server. The database server will host the database of the stories, the objects, the thesaurus of keywords, and so on for a domain, and information about its members. The web server will host the website for each domain, and will connect via the internet to the database server, either to deposit information in the database or to get information from the database. The two servers could be anywhere: either or both could be in the same office as the domain administrator, in another building, or anywhere in the world, connected via the internet. It is proposed that for each COINE domain the technical partner MAC houses and manages the web server, and that the technical partner FDI houses and manages the database server.

In the above case the COINE system software resides only with the technical partners and not at the COINE demonstration sites. However, it will also be possible for an organization to operate its own servers locally. In that case the technical management of the servers and software would be managed locally too. The management of the technicalities of the server computers and the software is a separate function from that of the domain administrator, but it is possible that both these roles may be carried out by the same person.

Using the COINE system

Users (both registered members and unregistered users) will use a web browser (such as Internet Explorer or Netscape) on a PC to access the website, which is the starting page for a particular COINE domain. The user can gain access from anywhere with a PC connected to the internet. Similarly domain administrators can carry out their work from any PC connected to the internet, although for the demonstration trials that is likely to be from partner sites.

A simple, easy-to-use and intuitive interface disguising sophisticated functionality lies at the heart of the COINE software system. The input of the user in designing the software is a crucial stage of the development and the terminology and appearance of the interface have changed considerably over the first 18 months of the project in response to issues raised by all the demonstration sites.

The COINE project will trial the software in many different social, cultural and technological environments representing a wide range of test scenarios, languages and technical abilities as the interface must reflect and fulfil users' needs, enabling them to tell their story easily while presenting the stories of others effectively. Though further changes are inevitable in response to the experiences of real users, some key issues have already been raised, and they are discussed below.

Terminology

The first barrier to new users is the terminology explaining the process of COINE. The initial version of the interface used rather academic terminology. It was correct in meaning but over-complicated and uninspiring to the general user. Users were encouraged to 'create a narrative' and 'choose a thesaurus term', expressions that are meaningless to many people. Although these terms would be acceptable if there was a lot of hands-on support for users, we are aiming for an intuitive system that is simple to understand without the aid of an enormous help-manual. As a consequence, a full review of terminology was carried out. Everyone agreed that the essence of COINE was 'telling stories' so the original term 'narrative' was replaced by 'story'. Now users 'create a story' and choose a 'subject term'. Figures 21.1 and 21.2 show the 'Create A Story' and 'What's your Story' web pages.

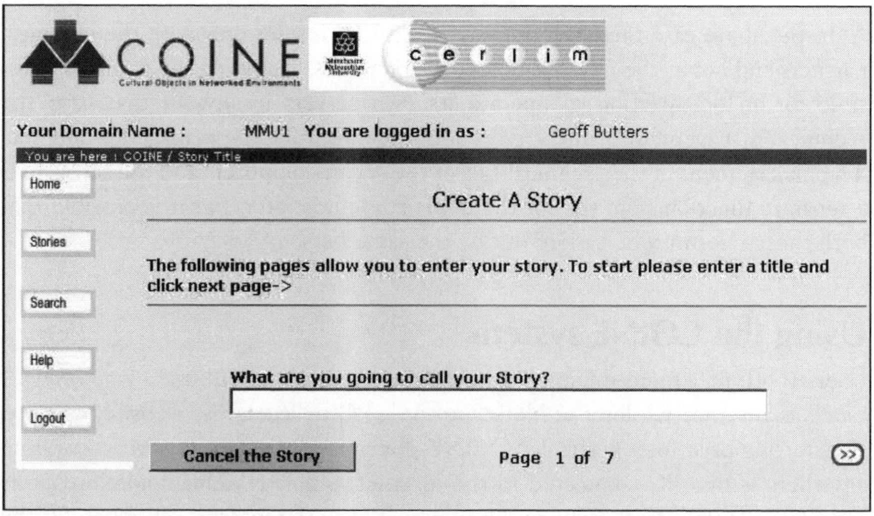

COINE
Cultural Objects in Networked Environments
cerlim
Your Domain Name : MMU1 You are logged in as : Geoff Butters
You are here : COINE / Story Title
Home
Stories
Search
Help
Logout
Create A Story
The following pages allow you to enter your story. To start please enter a title and click next page->
What are you going to call your Story?
Cancel the Story
Page 1 of 7

Figure 21.1 The first page in 'Create A Story'

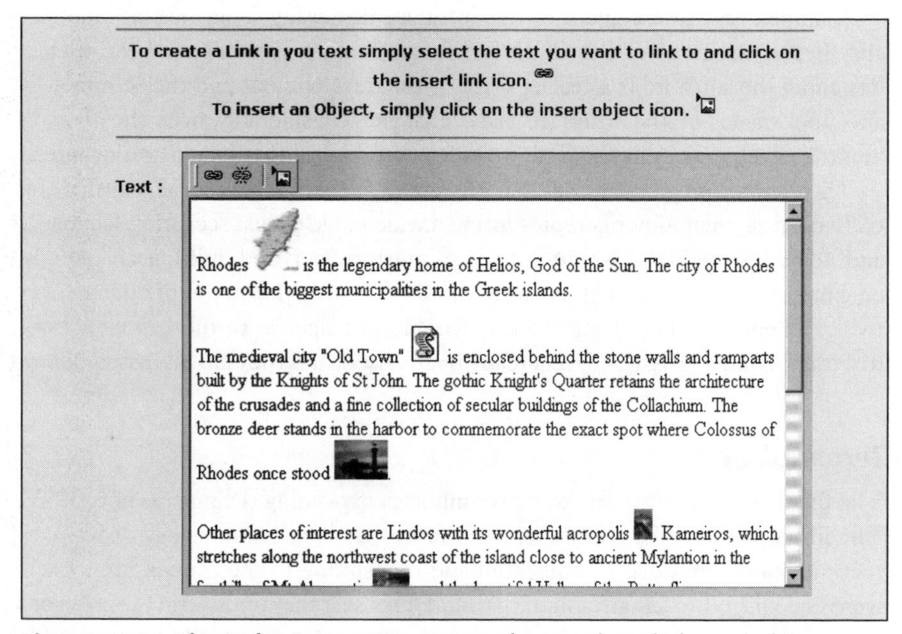

Figure 21.2 The 'What's your Story' page showing how links and objects are added

The terminology has also been personalized to give users a sense of ownership over the stories they are contributing to the system. 'Saved searches' has become 'My Ways of Finding Stories' and altering the appearance of the interface is now called 'Change My Look'. The key to attracting users to COINE lies in engaging their

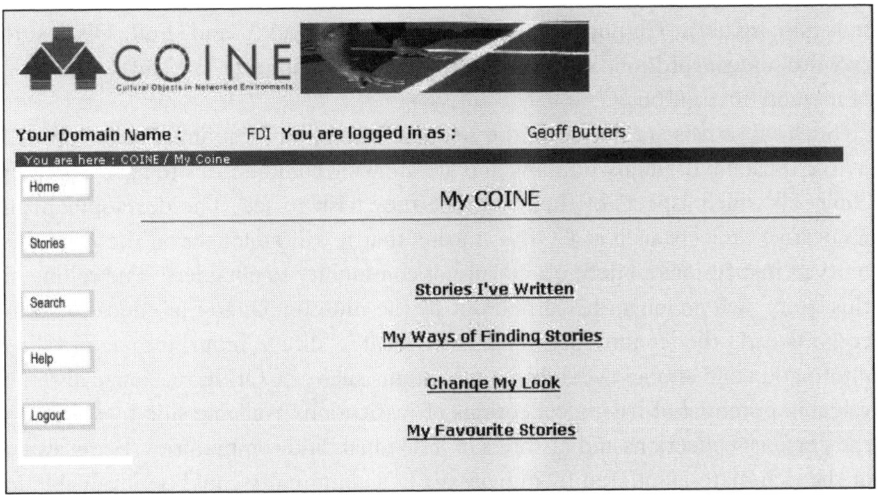

Figure 21.3 'My COINE' user's home page

interest, making them feel that their research, their story, is worth telling and sharing with others. Simplifying the terminology will help prevent the system becoming difficult to use and thus increase its accessibility, ultimately encouraging more users. Figure 21.3 shows the user's home page 'My COINE'.

Level of instruction

COINE is aiming to provide an interface that balances a clean, uncomplicated appearance with a good level of instruction and guidance. Assuming too much knowledge in a user is a common problem and the level of on-screen help has been increased where necessary. A simple 'wizard-style' set of instructions now guides the user very simply through the creative process while still maintaining a wide range of content possibilities. We have added instruction on how to add an object (an image, sound or document file) and clear correction statements if mandatory data has not been entered, for example 'please choose a language'. Demonstration trials will indicate areas where more or less instruction is needed.

The future

Cultural Objects in Networked Environments ultimately hopes to address the current limitations on accessing the collections and perspectives of the individual and to succeed in contributing to a new way of distributing and discussing our cultural heritage. There has been a strong desire in recent years for museums, libraries and archives to improve the access to and sharing of cultural heritage. Initiatives such as Culture on Line (www.cultureonline.gov.uk/), 24 Hour Museum (www.24hour-museum.org.uk/), Cornucopia (www.cornucopia.org.uk/) and Full Disclosure (www.bl.uk/concord/fulldisc-about.html) are all contributing to a shift in the role of memory institutions.

Such initiatives are removing the boundaries and physical limitations imposed by the museum or library building and are allowing communities to have a greater choice in which aspects of their heritage they wish to see. The development of innovative projects such as COINE means that it will no longer be the responsibility of institutions to define a culture or community to outsiders. The telling of this 'story' will no longer be carried out by the museum curator or education officer; instead, the community itself will have a direct input into controlling information and arranging exhibitions. Systems such as COINE recognize also the valuable potential of having collections of institutions available side by side with the personal collections and histories of individuals and communities. Being aware of the rich material offered by individuals in a community could be invaluable in raising the profile of memory institutions and securing public interest.

If successful, projects such as COINE offer a new form of cultural expression, increasing the variety of information available and giving people a greater choice. If administered by cultural heritage institutions, COINE could allow museums, libraries and archives to reach a wider audience and strengthen their role as information providers within the community.

Reference

DigiCULT (2002), *The DigiCULT Report: technological landscapes for tomorrow's cultural economy: unlocking the value of cultural heritage*, European Commission Directorate-General for the Information Society, www.digicult.info/pages/report/2002.

22

The DAEDALUS project: an open archiving initiative

Susan Ashworth and William Nixon

Introduction

Access to research materials on our campuses is dictated and constrained by the increasing cost of journals, publishers licensing arrangements and the allocation of copyright in that research to publishers. The advent of electronic journals has not increased access to research. In many cases access has, in fact, diminished, as institutions cancel hard copy holdings to subscribe to electronic journals. These are then only available to the staff and students of that institution, and often not available from off-campus locations, thereby disadvantaging the distance learner. The increasing cost of journals is often borne by institutions at the expense of provision of other materials, notably provision of monographs, to undergraduates.

The DAEDALUS (Data Providers for Academic E-content and the Disclosure of Assets for Learning, Understanding and Scholarship) project is one of a number of projects that aims to widen access to the research produced within higher education in the United Kingdom, to communities both within and without the higher education sector, by setting up open archives of that research.

The DAEDALUS project has been funded by the Joint Information Systems Committee (JISC) for three years, to set up open and freely available digital collections of the research output of Glasgow University, one of the Russell Group of research institutions in the United Kingdom. DAEDALUS is not being set up in isolation. Many institutions in the US, Europe and, increasingly, the UK are setting up institutional repositories, and protocols are being developed to enable users to cross-search these archives.

The DAEDALUS project will use three different types of software: GNU EPrints, DSpace and Virginia Tech Electronic Theses and Dissertations (ETD-db) to create collections of published and peer-reviewed articles, pre-prints and grey literature, and electronic theses. Although the technical issues surrounding the establishment of these services will be investigated, the main thrust of the project is to advocate changes to the production and dissemination of scholarly output, and to persuade researchers to make their research available to communities beyond the relatively small number with access to academic journals.

This paper will outline the trends in scholarly communications that have led to the establishment of open archiving projects in the UK; will describe the benefits to society of making academic research more freely available; will examine the obstacles to the creation of open archives, particularly the intellectual property issues and academics concerns over the Research Assessment Exercise; and will describe some of the strategies used at Glasgow University to raise the issues and persuade academics to deposit materials in the relevant archives.

Trends in scholarly communications

Research publications in science, technology and medicine (STM) are increasingly concentrated in the hands of a small number of publishers. The European Commission (EC) recently approved the purchase of Springer by investment bankers, Cinden & Candover, and the subsequent merger with Kluwer, despite pressure from organizations such as SPARC (Scholarly Publishing and Academic Resources Coalition, www.sparceurope.org) and other library organizations, which attempted to explain to the EC the dangers to the publishing market of allowing this merger to go ahead. David Prosser of SPARC Europe described in a press release how Goldman Sachs advised Cinden and Candover on the Springer sale, pointing out their emphasis on the high profits to be made out of academic research and the constant supply of publishable material. The Information Access Alliance (Susman and Carter, 2003) in the US has published a paper advocating closer examination of mergers in the serial publishing industry, stating that 'mergers of publishers of STM and legal serials have exacerbated this general trend in price increases. In the biomedical field alone, significant price increases occurred in 10 of 11 mergers over the past decade.'

The product of scholarly endeavour is increasingly owned and controlled by a small number of commercial publishers, whose priorities are driven by shareholder interests. A profit margin of 40% has been quoted by Reed Elsevier, one of the biggest STM publishers. Susman et al. (2003) have collated evidence to show that journal price increases are not justified by increased costs in publishing, and that publisher profits from STM scholarly publishing are lucrative. The two biggest STM publishers, Elsevier and Springer, are also buying up distribution mechanisms (such as library systems) thereby owning the means of disseminating content as well as the content itself.

There is significant inflation in periodical prices – running at around 15% per annum – and academic libraries, whose budgets often decrease in real terms annually, cannot maintain their collections. While world production of published scholarly research has doubled since 1980, most research libraries' journal subscriptions have actually declined by anything up to 10%. Glasgow University, a member of the Russell Group of research institutions in the UK, routinely cancels journals every year and many departments are now down to 'core' collections – a set of journals that researchers deem to be imperative for their research needs – having been forced to cancel specialist and niche journal holdings. Several faculties of the University have not purchased monograph material for several years in an attempt to maintain core collections and it is realized that holdings of textbooks and other materials required for undergraduate use have deteriorated, alarmingly in some subject areas. Figure 22.1 illustrates how the rate of journal inflation is outpacing library expenditure.

Chen et al. (2001) have shown that electronic journal publishing has not led to cheaper journal subscriptions. There are often increased costs for journals where electronic access is offered alongside the print copy, access to electronic-only journals is often more expensive than the print, and the trend to aggregate collections

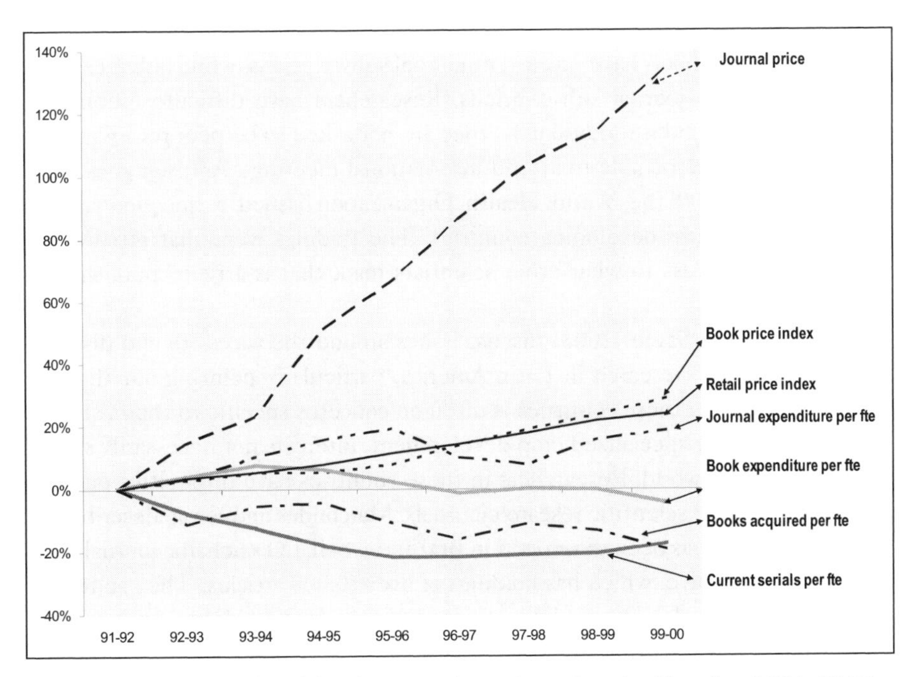

Figure 22.1 Journal and book expenditure in university libraries 1991–2000 (compiled by the Library and Information Statistics Unit, Loughborough University, from SCONUL statistics)

of journals for sale to institutions can mean that libraries have to subscribe to journals less in demand in order to get in-demand journals, while not being able to cancel selectively when budgets are under threat. Electronic publishing also raises the question of perpetual access and how, or indeed if, that is offered once cancellations are made.

Electronic journals are licensed, rather than sold outright, and these licences often limit access to staff and students of an institution only, to computers linked to campus networks only. This has meant that university libraries, often generous in their admission policies for the general public, can have difficulties allowing members of the general public to access their electronic holdings. Similarly students based off-campus often have difficulty accessing the electronic holdings of the institution to which they belong.

Access to research

It is critical to the development of healthy and financially solvent economies that a wide range of research should be accessible. Aronson (2003) states that 75 countries in the world have a gross national product (GNP) of less than $1000 per capita per annum. The lower the GNP, the higher the burden of disease. In these countries 56% of organizations such as universities, research institutions, medical institutions and schools have no current journal subscriptions, while only 21% have an average of two journal subscriptions. Researchers have difficulty publishing their work locally and internationally, they are not asked to be peer reviewers and they are unlikely to be able to attend international meetings. Aronson goes on to report that in 2000 the World Health Organization issued a questionnaire to health researchers in developing countries. The findings were that researchers' first priority is access to what other scientists read, that is articles published in journals.

Marcondes and Sayao (2003) discuss issues around the access to and dissemination of scientific research in Latin America, particularly pointing out that the focus of research in these countries is often on concerns specific to them, such as tropical diseases or specialized crop development, interests not necessarily shared by the developed world. Researchers in these countries have difficulties publishing in international scientific research journals. Marcondes and Sayao describe one open archive that has been developed in Brazil, the SciELO scientific journal gateway and open archive, which has holdings of over 10,000 articles. They state that this open archive 'plays a very important role in the worldwide dissemination of the technical and scientific literature published in developing countries, thereby increasing visibility for the literature that otherwise would only be accessible within the borders of those developing countries'.

It is not only in the developing world, however, that published research is inaccessible. Academic libraries are spending more money each year to buy fewer journals, and therefore access for researchers to scholarly communications is becoming more restricted, while the research published is available to a progressively smaller range of users. Efficacy in research is dependent on researchers having access to a wide range of information and being able to refine their inquiries through open exchange of ideas. The current publishing system mitigates against this exchange of ideas, encouraging the duplication of effort, unproductive lines of research and the slowing of innovation (Tenopir and King, 2000).

Much research is publicly funded but these research findings are routinely denied to the public. The OECD published a report in February 2003 that states that 'publicly funded research should be openly available to the maximum extent possible' (OECD, 2003).

Politically, this issue has started to garner interest in the US and the UK. There is an Act before the US Congress requiring that copyright be maintained for all papers that are generated from research substantially funded by the US Government while, in the UK, Member of Parliament Iain Gibson tabled a question to the Secretary of State for Health asking what plans he had to ensure that all public funded research is recorded and made freely available to patients, health professionals, the public and members of the scientific community' (*ACOSC Digest of Scholarly Communication News*, 2003).

The debate around the question of availability of research is beginning to reach a much wider audience than just the academic community, or even just librarians.

Institutional repositories: a response to the crisis

A number of research universities are participating in open access initiatives such as open access journals. These are journals that are usually published electronically on the internet and do not charge for access to the articles published in them. There are a number of open access journals in existence, some set up in direct competition with existing commercial journals, for example *Organic Letters*, which came out in competition with *Tetrahedron Letters* and quickly achieved a higher impact than its commercial competitor (SPARC, 2001).

Oxford University Press has recently announced that one of its flagship journals, *Nucleic Acids Research*, will move to an open access model over a period of four to five years. Lund University has established *The Directory of Open Access Journals* (www.doaj.org). This is intended to 'increase the visibility and ease of use of open access scientific journals, thereby promoting their increased usage and impact'. However, open access journals are a long way from challenging the publishing status quo, and there are many issues, not least the process of peer review, which will have to be addressed before the current scholarly publishing model will change.

Many university libraries are therefore setting up open archives or, as they are now more widely know, institutional repositories. There are a number of well-established repositories in the US, notably at the University of California, but these are still in a minority and most universities are only in the early stages of creating repositories.

Institutional repositories capture, and are considering the long-term preservation of, an institution's scholarly output, whether already published, in pre-print form or published in other ways such as departmental or technical reports. Depositing pre- or post-prints in a freely available electronic archive is a practice that has a long tradition in some subject areas, most notably ArXiv, the physics open archive (www.arxiv.org). Institutional repositories are aiming to build on this practice individually, with repositories that are compliant with the Open Archives Initiative (OAI) metadata standards being registered so that their contents can be harvested into searchable global archives.

This benefits both the institution, allowing its research output to be seen as a whole and serving as a concrete indicator of the value and benefit of that research, (which is otherwise spread across thousands of journals, conference proceedings and so on) and the individual researcher, whose research is likely to have a greater impact on the scholarly community and therefore be cited more heavily. As Lawrence (2001) points out, authors of refereed journal articles are not paid for their work but publish for the purposes of research and therefore from the author's perspective the more barriers there are to accessing these journal articles the less effect the research is likely to have. He states that 'articles freely available online are more highly cited. For greater impact and faster scientific progress, authors and publishers should aim to make research easy to access.'

Many researchers currently post copies of their articles to individual websites, but these may not be maintained if an academic leaves the institution, and if the websites are not OAI compliant; an institutional repository should have an *ipso facto* commitment from the institution to maintain and develop content that can be regularly harvested and searched.

Both of these strategies, providing open access journals and self-archiving in subject or institutional repositories, are at the heart of the Budapest Open Access Initiative.

The DAEDALUS project

The Data Providers for Academic E-content and the Disclosure of Assets for Learning, Understanding and Scholarship (DAEDALUS) project at Glasgow University has been funded by the Joint Information Systems Committee (a committee set up by the Higher Education Funding Councils within the UK) to create a range of institutional repositories, and to investigate the technical and cultural issues involved in developing these repositories. The project is part of the Focus on Access to Institutional Resources (FAIR, www.jisc.ac.uk/index.cfm?name=programme_fair) programme, which aims to 'evaluate and explore different mechanisms for the disclosure and sharing of content (and the related challenges) to fulfil the vision of a web of resources built by groups with a long term stake in the future of those resources, but made available to the whole community of learning'. FAIR is funding 14 projects across 50 institutions.

The Consortium of University Research Libraries (CURL www.curl.ac.uk) has also received funding from this programme to set up institutional repositories in other UK research universities, such as Oxford, Nottingham and Leeds. It is important to stress, particularly in discussions with academics and researchers, that open access is a principle that many big research institutions across the world support.

The DAEDALUS project is using three OAI compliant software packages: GNU Eprints for a repository of published and peer-reviewed material; DSpace for a repository of pre-prints, grey literature, departmental and technical reports; and Virginia Tech's ETD-db software for a repository of electronic doctoral theses. Nixon (2002) details the technical evolution of the Glasgow University institutional repositories and their implementation.

The decision to have three separate repositories is partly a response to academic concerns about quality, some academics not wishing to see different types of publication deposited together in an undifferentiated service, for example peer-reviewed papers alongside unreviewed preprints. Issues of quality control are clearly high on the list for many academics and software such as DSpace allows control to be devolved to 'communities' so that departments, research groups and so on can make decisions about what is deposited into the service themselves.

At Glasgow University we are offering a mediated submission service, so that we will accept documents in any format, which are then converted into PDF, with metadata being added by library staff, but we aim to allow self-submission of documents in addition to, and possibly instead of, this service at a later stage.

Clearly, the setting up of an institutional repository requires technical expertise and the commitment of resources. Although Glasgow University has received external funding, by the end of the project the University must be able to sustain the service in perpetuity. However, the greatest challenge is to fill the repositories.

Advocating change

The DAEDALUS project is undertaking a number of ongoing strategies to obtain content for the Glasgow University repositories. The project remit includes creating an open access culture across the University campus, so as well as aiming to get 750 published and peer-reviewed papers in the service by 2005, we are also engaged in a process of raising awareness of the issues involved in the open access movement and getting debate around current channels of scholarly communication and the possible alternatives.

We have established a project board with representation by a senior academic from each of the three territorial subject groups at the University. We have, by looking through departmental and personal web pages, identified authors who have posted copies of their articles on the internet and are contacting them to ask them to deposit copies in our institutional repositories. We have identified a number of journals that appear recently to have liberalized their policies concerning the use of copyrighted material by authors who publish in them, such as *Nature* and the *British Medical Journal* (*BMJ*), and we are pursuing the authors whose work is published in these journals in order to test out the journal policies.

The project staff are engaged in a long process of attending departmental, faculty and research group meetings to put the issues to academic staff and we follow up individually with those researchers who have expressed interest. The project has hosted campus events, with outside speakers, which have attracted around 50 academics at a time, who have again been contacted later in order to continue their interest and obtain content.

Many academics, some of whom are perhaps sceptical of the service on their own behalf, have been enthusiastic about their research students depositing electronic copies of their theses, and we are hopeful that an institution-wide policy decision will be taken on this matter by the end of the project. It is important for us to get endorsement for the repositories at a senior level within the University and representations are being made to senior committees.

Barriers to open access

Copyright

Many authors do not realize that when they publish their research they assign copyright in it entirely to the publisher. Publishers vary in their attitudes to allowing the deposit of a copy of a paper into an institutional repository. The Rights MEtadata for Open archiving (RoMEO) project (www.lboro.ac.uk/departments/ls/disresearch/romeo) based at Loughborough University has done detailed work examining publishers' policies. It is probably true to say that many publishers are waiting to see if institutional repositories, most of which are still fairly small, will be scalable. Should repositories become successful publisher attitudes may become more hostile. Publishers have been fairly successful for lobbying for their rights, particularly in the electronic environment, with legislation such as the various EU Directives published between 1991 and 2001 on the legal protection of databases, personal data, duration of copyright protection and others giving the industry increasing protection over access to electronic information.

The DAEDALUS project is required to act as an intermediary between authors at the University and publishers to ascertain whether or not it is possible for authors to deposit papers, but also to raise awareness about the transfer of copyright and possible alternatives to that transfer that authors might try to negotiate, for example, non-exclusive licences allowing authors to use their intellectual property more freely.

The Research Assessment Exercise

The next Research Assessment Exercise (RAE, www.rae.ac.uk) for universities in the UK will take place within this context of a far-reaching debate on the availability of research, especially research that is publicly funded, to wider communities. The principle of the open access movement is encouraging the publication of papers in electronic formats, via the internet, in open access journals or repositories of various kinds. The RAE must therefore change to accept quality research that is disseminated in a variety of ways, not just in publications that are in the commercial sector.

The current RAE places overwhelming importance on publication in peer-reviewed journals as a measure of research quality, and there appears to be a growing emphasis on journal impact factors as a measure of quality. Therefore the RAE itself could be construed as being an incentive for researchers to try and concentrate their research in these high impact journals, further encouraging monopoly control of journal ownership. Open access initiatives encourage a shift of control of the scholarly communications process away from journal publishers to institutions and individual researchers. It is also possible that the archiving of research by individual academics in institutional repositories could be an aid to the management of submissions for the next RAE.

Evidence has been submitted by various bodies, such as the Consortium of University Research Libraries (CURL), and at Glasgow University the DAEDALUS project has submitted evidence to the institutional response, encouraging the funding councils to actively support the development of open access publishing models, in individual institutions, and to state clearly that articles published outside the current monopolistic journals market will be given careful consideration and weighting in the next RAE.

It is possible to go further and to urge consideration of whether greater weight should be attached to the fact that articles published in open access journals have a much wider potential audience than articles published in expensive journals, subscription to which many libraries cannot afford, and consider judging that some of the worth of the publication of research is on the basis of how widely it will be disseminated and how freely it is available rather solely on impact factors.

Authors are increasingly driven to get their publications into a few 'top' journals, in order to maximize their chances of promotion, with pressures such as the RAE compounding these trends. As Lawrence (2003) points out, this can lead to the objective presentation of work and the accessibility of articles being compromised. Many younger researchers who might benefit most from there being greater access to their work are concerned about prior disclosure of their research making publication of it much harder.

Conclusion

Institutional repositories offer a vision of the world's research being open and available to anyone who wishes or needs to have access to it. The current scholarly communications model offers a vision of an expensive and contracting world of research open only to the few who can afford to access it.

It remains to be seen if the barriers to the scalability of institutional repositories can be overcome, but projects such as DAEDALUS, and others in the UK and elsewhere, have ambitious targets, which if reached will offer great benefits to researchers and the consumers of that research.

References

ACOSC Digest of Scholarly Communication News (2003) August, www.ucl.ac.uk/Library/scholarly-communication/acoscbull082003.doc.

Aronson, B. (2003) Open Access: what does it mean for developing countries? *Open Access to Scientific and Technical Information: state of the art and future trends, Paris 23–24 January 2003*, www.inist.fr/openaccess/en/programme.php.

Budapest Open Access Initiative, www.soros.org/openaccess/index.shtml.

Chen, F. L., Wrynn, P., Ehrman, F. L., Rieke, L. R. and French, H. E.. (2001) Electronic Journal Access: how does it affect the print subscription price?, *Bulletin of the Medical Librarians Association*, **89** (4), 363–71.

Lawrence, P. A. (2003) The Politics of Publication, *Nature*, **422** (6929) 259–61.

Lawrence, S. (2001) Free Online Availability Substantially Increases a Paper's Impact, *Nature*, **411** (6837), 521.

Marcondes, C. H. and Sayao, L. F. (2003) The SciELO Brazilian Scientific Journal Gateway and Open Archive, *D-Lib Magazine*, **9** (3).

Nixon, W. (2002) The Evolution of an Institutional E-prints Archive, *Ariadne*, **32** (June–July), www.ariadne.ac.uk /issue32/eprint-archives/intro.html.

OECD (2003) *Promoting Access to Public Research Data for Scientific, Economic and Social Development*, OECD Follow Up Group on Issues of Access to Publicly Funded Research Data.

SPARC (2001) SPARC Partner Organic Letters Surpasses Competition, www.arl.org/sparc/core/index.asp?page=f45.

Susman, T. M. and Carter, D. J. (2003) *Publisher Mergers: a consumer based approach to antitrust analysis*, Information Access Alliance, www.informationaccess.org/WhitePaperV2Final.pdf.

Tenopir, C., and King, D. (2000) *Towards Electronic Journals: realities for scientists, librarians and publishers*, Washington DC, Special Libraries Association.

23

Librarians in digital communities of practice

Andrew Cox and Anne Morris

Introduction

In *Cultivating Communities of Practice*, Etienne Wenger and his co-authors explicitly define only two member roles in a community of practice (Wenger, McDermott and Snyder, 2002). One is the co-ordinator, which is the community leadership role. The other is what they call the 'community librarian'. By this the authors refer to activities such as current awareness, making notes on meetings and subject organization of material, and boundary work – connecting members to other experts in their field (2002, 102–3).

Given the level of excitement in the business world about communities of practice, and the increasing take-up of knowledge management ideas generally in government and the non-profit sector, that an information role is seen as central by influential authors is encouraging for the profession. Perhaps this is one path for librarians to take 'out of the library into the organization', as Davenport and Prusak put it (though not necessarily, as they advocate, having first 'blown up the library'!) (Davenport and Prusak, 1993).

This paper explores the value of the 'community of practice' concept as a model of virtual work communities. It starts by defining the term and pointing to several problems with it as an ideal. It proposes, rather, that looser knit communities of interest or networks of practice are more common. Therefore, it is argued, community of practice might be better used as an 'ideal type' against which to explore social and informational dynamics, rather than as an ideal. A case study of one specialist IT community is explored to illustrate the approach. The paper concludes by arguing that if a community librarian role can contribute to user knowledge creation, it must be performed in a way that is sensitive to the specific culture that has developed in the community, with an awareness of social dynamics as well as informational issues.

What are communities of practice?

Definition

There is increasing interest in the communities of practice concept in many domains. Thus in the same month as Libraries Without Walls 5 (LWW5) was held, the annual UK learning technologists conference, Alt-C, was entitled 'Communities of Practice'. The topic was also a significant strand in the Communities and Technology conference, which was taking place at the same time as LWW5 in Amsterdam. The commercial event organizers, Ark Group, had also organized a 'Communities of Practice Masterclass' in Brussels in the same month.

The reader is probably, therefore, already broadly familiar with the concept. This is a good reason to be careful in defining it clearly here. As consultants, software companies, practitioners and academics latch onto the phrase, often in order to sell a product or repackage old ideas, there is a danger of it being 'bleached' by over-use and appropriation to particular ends (Ross, 2003).

A simple definition is not easy, however, since the most influential advocate of communities of practice, Etienne Wenger, has significantly shifted his examples and ground (Contu and Willmott, 2000; Davenport and Hall, 2002). In essence, a community of practice is a group of people with a shared interest in a subject domain – maybe even a passion for that topic – who develop a collective repertoire of work solutions, and workarounds, ideas, stories, identities. Communities of practice are said to occur naturally, to be spontaneous, self-organizing and work across formal organizational boundaries. They are also inherently rather transient.

Communities of practice, as portrayed by Wenger, are something of an information nirvana. Because of the high level of trust between members and the active mutual engagement of the group, they are very efficient at sharing information. People know who knows what and, through compressed language and frequent contacts, quickly disseminate ideas. Communities of practice have been seen as both good social structures for collaborative improvisation of solutions to immediate small problems (for example Orr, 1997), but also as capable of radical innovation, in contexts of soft problems (Por, 2003). They both support newcomers through 'legitimate peripheral participation' and are a good model for transfer of expertise or 'knowledge sharing'. Through their repertoire of ideas, workarounds, artefacts, stories and identities, the community of practice holds and develops organizational tacit knowledge and acts as an organizational memory.

Purely informational processes are interwoven with powerful social processes, such as identification and solidarity. Thus the driving motivation is to be accepted as part of the community, and a community of practice develops an idea of what it is to be a good member. There is a strong sense of community and mutual responsibility. Wenger also identifies some rather specific social processes such as 'legitimate peripheral participation', a form of learning *in situ*, from performing marginal tasks, watching and talking to other learners (Lave and Wenger, 1991). He stresses the importance of brokers and other boundary spanning activities that link the community to the outside world. Communities of practice may also have some typical communication forms such as narrative (Brown and Duguid, 2002).

Managerialist discourse?

If all this sounds a little bit too good to be true, that may be because it is. There is something 'suspicious' about the whole concept, and the way it has come to be used. Wenger's early work was analytic, bent on understanding the nature of an emergent and supposedly pervasive social phenomena. Indeed the case study used in his 1998 work, has a strong counter-cultural feel. But his latest writings are increasingly 'performative', using the community of practice as a tool for managing informal ties, for the benefit of the organization.

It is reasonable to question why management in so many blue-chip companies is so keen to try and cultivate communities of practice, using Wenger's 'gardening tips'. This is surely because communities of practice seem to offer a solution to many of the supposed problems of the modern organization: to motivate the workforce, to innovate and be 'flexible'. Yet, however light-handed the management advocated in this context is, it could be seen to reflect an organizational aspiration to extend surveillance and influence into the informal network. The questioning analytic approach gives way to simplistic universalist recipes so typical of writing about management. On close inspection, then, community of practice theory has the hallmarks of managerialist ideology. Swan and colleagues have recently shown how the concept was used in one case by management to break down professional divides and resistance to cross-organizational working (Swan, Scarborough and Robertson, 2002). This benefits the organization, but whether it is good for the employees is another question, one that community of practice writing is increasingly less likely to ask.

On an individual level the idea of being a member of a community of practice is, on first reading, exciting and inspiring. Yet to tell the truth are we prepared to put the effort and time into such intense working relationships? Do we not, in fact, find community oppressive and restrictive of individual freedom and identity? Perhaps the desire for community is a yearning for something we have no wish to have. Exploration of this paradox is beyond the scope of this paper

(Sennett's (1998) comments on the ideological nature of 'team work' are suggestive). But, if Wenger himself is very careful in his use of the concept of community, in many respects the mania for community of practice may represent its ideological force, rather than its real efficacy or value.

Networks of practice and communities of interest

Having acknowledged these problems with community of practice as an ideal, there does still seem to be some potential value in it as a model, or an 'ideal type'. Writers have contrasted communities of practice with weaker linked groupings, but done little to explore which aspects of the model apply in these looser networks. Thus Wenger, McDermott and Snyder (2002, 42) contrast the concept of a community of practice with weaker tied 'communities of interest'. The main difference seems to be a sense of intensity: the purpose of a community of practice is 'to create, expand and exchange knowledge, and to develop individual capabilities', whereas a community of interest is solely 'to be informed'. In their fuzzy boundaries, openness of membership and pattern of growth and disappearance, however, the two phenomena are similar.

Brown and Duguid (2002, 141–2) have also proposed the term 'networks of practice' to describe occupational groups or social worlds, groups with a common practice, but with indirect rather than the direct links of a community of practice. Members of such groups do not know each other. They are 'loosely coupled systems. . . . Collectively, such social systems don't take action and produce little knowledge. They can, though, share information relating to the members' common practices quite efficiently.'

Whereas there is a ballooning literature of communities of practice, little research is being published on communities of interest or networks of practice, though they are surely more common (though see Faraj and Wasko 2001; much of the literature on open source is also instructive, for instance Benkler, 2002). What needs to be more fully explored is what parts (if any) of the community of practice model fit such looser knit networks of practice. This would increase our understanding of how to maximize the benefits of information exchange and knowledge creation. It would also clarify how information professionals could most support such communities. The purpose of this paper, then, is to undertake such an analysis using an example of one such weaker-linked virtual community.

Case study

The case study presented here is of a specialist IT support discussion list. (For ethical reasons it has been given a pseudonym). The reader is probably familiar with the technology used by the list, which allows e-mails to be distributed to a group of subscribers. They are often referred to as listservs or e-mail distribution lists. In this case a web-based archive of past postings is kept.

This is a relatively 'simple' technology, but probably most long-lasting virtual communities are still text based, though they are as likely to be on Usenet or web based, as through e-mail. However, the potential for text-based communication to enable the creation of rich cultural (Baym, 2000) and empathic communities (Preece, 1999) is now well established, contrary to early predictions from media richness theory (Levy, 1998; Wellman, 1997).

IT-LIST was founded in 1994, but archives are only available since 1998. The study described here was largely based on the archive of five years, March 1998 to February 2003. In this period around 7570 messages were sent, so it is a busy list, but not cacophonous. There are an average of about 125 messages per month. No historic membership figures were available, but current membership is around 750. Of members, 80% are from ac.uk domain. Most of these are from higher education, with only 3% (N=23) from further education. Approximately 70% of members appear to be male, 25% female, with 5% unidentifiable from available data. This list was chosen as a rather successful, if loosely knit 'virtual community', which might illustrate the range of both informational and social processes identified by Wenger.

The study used a mixture of methods (a web-based questionnaire and face-to-face, telephone and electronic interviews) together with content and discourse analysis of the community archive. For the textual analysis, samples were taken of all the postings sent in five sample months, plus all the postings in threads longer than ten messages occurring in two of the years. The form of discourse analysis was genre analysis (Orlikowski and Yates, 1994; Bauman, 1999; Burnett, 2000). This involves identifying recurrent types of communication, defined by purpose and linguistic features and structure. The argument is that the character of genres that are present (or absent) and changes in their frequency are an effective way to characterize the nature of the community.

Genre analysis

The genre analysis showed that communication on IT-LIST had a very specific character. Most messages fall into a category of postings that the researchers call the question and answer genre. There are three variations on this: a request for help to solve a problem, a request for a tool to perform a task or a more general request for guidance on how to achieve some end. Many other genres of message (familiar from other discussion lists) occur in small numbers but are mostly quite rare. That this is fairly specific is revealed if one reflects on the character of most library-related lists. These are dominated by posting of announcements of events and resources. As specialists on information sources rather than content, librarians like to be alerted to new resources. On IT-LIST such announcements are unusual. The interest is far more in sharing fixes for detailed, often obscure, problems, usually based on practical experience and individual expertise.

The value of the question and answer genre is obvious. In information terms it offers the immediate and unique value of answering individual queries. Because the genre is so simple and familiar (from other lists and from IT discourse generally) new members can quickly learn how to fit in and make relevant posts. In this way the noise of irrelevant messages is kept down. The genre requires little co-ordination. The cost of participating is low, in terms of reading time (it is quick to delete irrelevant threads). Also the risk of embarrassment (implicit in not being able to answer the question for oneself) can be managed by using relative anonymity (often by removing the signature file). Yet, that is overlaid with the relative transparency of e-mail handles, which inhibits unconsidered posting, and reduces the likelihood of poor answers being sent. There is a delicate balance here between reputation and anonymity.

Despite its apparent triviality, the question–answer genre is rather rich in information terms. As well as directly offering answers to members' specific enquiries, it implicitly gives members a sense of what others in similar jobs are doing at other institutions, some sense also of the mood of the times. It acts also as an information neighbourhood, a place in which 'people may simply situate themselves . . . because it is a likely place within which to stumble across information of interest' (Burnett, 2000). This is a low cost way of keeping up to date and informed.

There are some cases in the sample of archive examined, of collaborative improvisation of fixes to relatively novel problems. One thread in particular illustrates this capability. In 24 messages in one afternoon 16 or 17 individuals collaborated to offer five separate possible solutions to a problem. The help also included several demonstration versions. The technology does support such collaborative problem solving, then, but it is relatively unusual. Generally questions are answered from the experience of having had the problem and fixed it before, or experience of using a tool, or individual expertise. This sort of answer is privileged over theoretical answers or simple links to information that may help solve the problem. More often extended discussions result from debates about good practice. The list largely construes this in terms of accessibility. It is ambiguous about whether it is a medium through which certain members promote ideas about good practice or whether the list itself has its own collective take on the topic, stressing the practical of more idealistic standards bodies.

The list is perhaps best defined by the type of genre or discussion that is rare: bantering, 'for your interest' style announcements or meta discussion about what the list should be about is unusual. Human or cultural issues of IT support, although acknowledged on a sister list to be paramount issues, are rarely mentioned. Surprisingly, also, it is rare to discuss state of the art technology. In fact, one interviewee was rather critical of the list for not being a place where big ideas were discussed. All this points to the list having a very specific character.

IT-LIST is rather successful in reducing anti-social or conflictual behaviour. Flaming and even ranting is relatively rare and, where it does occur, is often followed by an apology. Much conflict on other lists arises from individual's selfish behaviour, often linked to their desire to stake out a reputation. In some sense, the nature of expertise is to create ignorance (Huber, 1999). For an individual to prove that they are an expert they have to show that they know about a topic (though this could be more by acting out the role of expert, than knowing anything), to establish the importance (or market value) of that topic and, above all, to make others feel they do not know anything (Huber, 1999). Playing the expert is rather tedious behaviour, then. In contrast, on IT-LIST, interviewees themselves strongly objected to being thought of as experts. This is because it is a network of peers, without the presence of potential customers or employers.

It would be wrong to construe the list as purely informational in character. The list constructs what Wenger would see as a member identity. This is somewhere between a technical expert and a competent professional. The terse, quick-fire questions and answers are businesslike, shorn of explicit communication, yet they also demonstrate helpfulness directly. Overall, there is a sense of a group of busy, highly competent, often expert individuals. Although explicit statements of empathy are relatively rare, the sense of moral support is accomplished implicitly, through questioners acknowledging that local sources of information have not answered the question. Rapid, helpful responses create a sense of community, without very strong ties developing, or needing to be sustained. List members valued this sense of seeing others in the same boat as them. So it is, in some sense, a 'community of coping' (Korczynski, 2003).

In a sense, the question and answer genre is also a form of the narrative that Brown and Duguid (2002) identify as characteristic of communities of practice, if in a pared-down form. The often repeated story is: an individual has a need or problem, they ask for help, the community respond quickly, rationally, helpfully. A 'happy ending' follows.

Ideal or ideal type?

To conclude, the paper returns to the issue of the 'community librarian' role, as defined by Wenger, McDermott and Snyder (2002), in the context of IT-LIST.

Part of the librarian's role, according to Wenger and his colleagues, is to capture and organize outputs, as an aspect of stewarding the repertoire of the community. The transactions of IT-LIST are captured automatically as the list archive. Yet use of the archive is low. Hits run at a few hundred a month. There are occasional list complaints about the search interface, but the real problem may be that the fragmented nature of the discussion makes search results difficult to interpret. In fact, past discussions are rarely cited in current communications. Perhaps IT-LIST does need a librarian, then, to write summaries and excite interest in building on past work. This might move the list beyond dealing with simple questions and answers to more reflective, double-loop learning. Yet the truth is that the list is concerned with immediate problem solving, nothing more nor less. Ultimately one has to respect this as being the preferred type of knowledge creation desired by the community, however trivial and ephemeral at times it seems, for more work is being done than is apparent.

Again considering the role of the 'community librarian' as that of providing current awareness, unlike many lists, on IT-LIST there is little posting of announcements of resources that 'may be of interest'. This could be seen as a failure to engage in connecting to groups beyond the boundary of the community. However, it is also consistent with the culture of the list, which is focused on solving immediate problems and needs. Anything else is seen as noise. If one did wish to post an item relating to a current topic that might be of interest to this community, one would need to be sensitive to this specific culture and the narrowness of the scope of use.

Finally, looking at the 'librarian role' of connecting to other experts, the group does see itself as having a diversity of expertise, but reaching out to further fields might add a level of creativity. It would also potentially raise the noise level, and reduce the level of natural, tacit understanding that arises from most members sharing a background in UK higher education. Any interventions would need to be sensitive to the subtle balance that has spontaneously emerged.

In early stages of the research described here it was expected that there would be a focus on additional tools that might boost the level of engagement among list members, such as blogs to enable the expression of individual identity, document stores and annotation tools to facilitate deeper collaboration or simply chat tools to boost immediate communication. Yet there was little interest in these extra functions among IT-LIST members.

The problem is that the 'community of practice' as an ideal invites us to see IT-LIST as somehow failing because it is not intense enough, not creating new knowledge, not reflective enough. In fact IT-LIST works very well. The list is continually responsive and helpful. Low engagement means that the effort of being a member and of co-ordinating the community is low. The list shows no signs of flagging after nearly ten years of useful work; one might compare this with the transience of the community of practice. The locally developed culture shows a finely tuned adjustment to actual needs. Interventions should, then, carefully respect this, and Wenger's theory helpfully models some of the key processes that should be observed. Simplistically applied, however, the recipes of community of practice literature are probably not the right guide.

References

Bauman, M. L. (1999) The Evolution of Internet Genres, *Computers and Composition*, 16, 269–82.

Baym, N. K. (2000) *Tune in, Log on: soaps, fandom, and online community*, London, Sage.

Benkler, Y. (2002) *Coase's Penguin, or Linux and the Nature of the Firm*, www.benkler.org/CoasesPenguin.PDF.

Brown, J. S. and Duguid, P. (2002) *The Social Life of Information*, Boston, Harvard Business School.

Burnett, G. (2000) Information Exchange in Virtual Communities: a typology, *Information Research*, **5** (4), http://informationr.net/ir/5-4/paper82.html.

Contu, A. and Willmott, H. (2000) Comment on Wenger and Yanox, Knowing in Practice: a 'delicate flower' in the organizational learning field, *Organization*, **7**, 269–76.

Davenport, E. and Hall, H. (2002) Organizational Knowledge and Communities of Practice, *Annual Review of Information Science and Technology*, **36**, 171–227.

Davenport, T. H. and Prusak, L. (1993) Blow Up the Corporate Library, *International Journal of Information Management*, **13**, 405–12.

Faraj, S. and Wasko, M. M. (2001) *The Web of Knowledge: an investigation of knowledge exchange in networks of practice*, http://opensource.mit.edu/papers/Farajwasko.pdf.

Huber, B. (1999). *Experts in Organizations: the power of expertise*, Academy of business and administrative science, Barcelona, July 1999.

Korczynski, M. (2003) Communities of Coping: collective emotional labour in service work, *Organization Studies*, **10** (1), 55–79.

Lave, J. and Wenger, E. (1991) *Situated Learning: legitimate peripheral participation*, Cambridge, Cambridge University Press.

Levy, P. (1998) Perspectives on Organisational Network Communities: a review paper for library and information service managers, *Program*, **32** (4), 343–58.

Orlikowski, W. and Yates, J. (1994) Genre Repertoire: the structuring of communicative practices in organizations, *Administrative Science Quarterly*, **39**, 541–74.

Orr, J. E. (1997) *Talking about Machines: an ethnography of a modern job*, Ithaca, NY, Cornell University Press.

Por, G. (2003) *Radical Innovation with Communities of Practice*, www.communityintelligence.co.uk/reources/radino.php.

Preece, J. (1999) Empathic Communities: balancing emotional and factual communication, *Interacting with Computers*, **12**, 63–77.

Ross, A. (2003). What Can We Learn from Organic Online Communities? How communities of practice seed themselves with conflict. Paper presented at the *Virtual Communities Conference* 16–17 June, London.

Sennett, R. (1998) *The Corrosion of Character: the personal consequences of work in the new capitalism*, London, W W Norton.

Swan, J., Scarborough, H. and Robertson, M. (2002) The Construction of 'Communities of Practice' in the Management of Innovation, *Management Learning*, **33** (4), 477–96.

Wellman, B. (1997) An Electronic Group is Virtually a Social Network. In: Kiesler, S. (ed.) *Culture of the Internet*, Mahwa, NJ, Lawrence Erlbaum, 179–205.

Wenger, E., McDermott, R. and Snyder, W. M. (2002) *Cultivating Communities of Practice*, Boston, Mass., Harvard Business School Press.

24
X4L: Exchange For Learning

Susan Eales and Andrew Comrie

Introduction

This paper introduces the Joint Information Systems Committee (JISC, www.jisc.ac.uk) funded Exchange for Learning (X4L, www.jisc.ac.uk/index.cfm?name=programme_x4l) programme and highlights the approach of one particular project within the programme: Learning for a Healthier Nation.

JISC is a strategic advisory body, funded by all the UK post-16 funding councils, which provides the network infrastructure for learning, teaching and research, offers support and guidance in the use of information and communication technology (ICT), and acts as a national and international leadership body for collaboration across education and research.

The JISC Information Environment Development vision has evolved from an earlier initiative known as the Distributed National Electronic Resource (DNER) and aims to enable seamless access to a diverse range of quality resources for learning, teaching and research in a secure way. Funding has been allocated to a number of development programmes that will contribute to the realization of this vision including:

- authentication and middleware tools to bring together distributed collections of resources
- demonstrator portals, subject portals and a learning and teaching portal to allow cross-searching of these collections
- work with commercial publishers to explore the challenges and benefits to them of engaging with the information environment

- influencing the development of common standards to allow resources to be shared
- interoperability and communication with international education bodies.

X4L

X4L is part of the JISC Information Environment Development since, for the evolving information environment to be more directly useful for learning and teaching as well as research, it must be populated with suitable learning materials and case studies.

The motivation for X4L is the imperative to make the most of the considerable investment that has taken place in a range of content that has high potential value for use in learning, but needs a pedagogical framework and robust tools to ensure that it can be more easily slotted into programmes of study by the teacher or lecturer. The programme is led by 25 projects from across the UK and involves more than 100 institutions and teams from colleges, universities, libraries, JISC services, local authorities and commercial companies. X4L is a three-year programme, running from June 2002 to July 2005 with a funding allocation of around £4 million.

The programme will explore the repurposing JISC-funded content suitable for use in learning. The programme will also encompass content created by other bodies and agencies active in this area where intellectual property rights allow for educational use in further education (FE) and higher education (HE), or can be negotiated. Part of this activity is to explore the process of integration or 'plugging-in' of learning objects into virtual learning environments (VLEs) and managed learning environments (MLEs).

The four main aims of the X4L programme are to:

- use and develop the best available tools to explore whether repurposing content can become a popular, sustainable way of producing e-learning materials for the future
- increase the numbers of people in institutions with the necessary skills to repurpose learning objects
- expose and begin to tackle the challenges associated with repurposing learning objects
- begin to populate a national repository with repurposable learning materials as well as case studies and exemplars of how these have been achieved.

The programme is split into two strands. Strand A is concerned with repurposing learning objects, while Strand B is developing tools that allow materials to be repurposed and shared as easily as possible together with an assessment engine.

Strand A projects

There are 22 Strand A projects that are developing learning materials. All involve FE–HE partnerships. Subject areas for which learning materials are being repurposed include:

- English literature
- physics A level
- ESOL
- engineering
- biology A level
- key skills
- art, media and performance
- study skills
- business and business law
- music and music technology
- health and medicine
- hospitality and catering
- underpinning maths for engineering and environmental science.

Strand B tools

There are three Strand B tools projects.

The JISC learning materials repository – JORUM (Latin, a drinking bowl: its contents)

The JORUM (www.jorum.ac.uk) is being designed as an advanced tool set, allowing users to locate, preview, access and publish objects. It will also allow for repurposing and sharing content for use in multiple teaching and learning scenarios in a wide variety of educational environments. At the same time, issues around national repository provision are being explored. Challenges such as sustainability, access management, functions and scope including classification schemes and search facilities, business models, management, preservation and local and national relationships are being investigated as part of the JORUM project.

Tools for teachers with pedagogic flexibility – RELOAD

RELOAD (www.reload.ac.uk) is developing an open source content packaging tool that can be used online or offline and will be available on CD-ROM if required. This tool will allow users to break down learning materials into objects and reassemble them into new learning materials.

Tools for flexible assessment methods – TOIA

The TOIA project (www.toia.ac.uk) will develop templates and tools for authoring standards-compliant questions and assessments, a web-server-based assessment delivery system and a results reporting tool.

These tools will be made available to the FE and HE community as a whole.

Issues being explored by X4L

Two main issues being explored by the X4L programme are interoperability and intellectual property rights (IPR). Interoperability and IPR are central to enabling re-purposing of content and the functioning of a national repository.

With regard to interoperability, X4L projects are all piloting the use of the UK Learning Object Metadata (LOM) Core, developed by the JISC-funded Centre for Education Technology and Interoperability Standards (CETIS (www.cetis.ac.uk) from a sub-set of the IEEE Learning Object Metadata (LOM) specification. Projects are supported in the use of the UK LOM Core by a full-time adviser based within CETIS.

All projects are expected to contribute to our awareness in the area of IPR. Support is being provided by the JISC legal adviser and the JISC-funded Legal Information Service (JLIS) (www.jisc.ac.uk/legal). Investigations into licensing procedures are being undertaken as part of the JORUM project in order to make these as robust but as easily understandable as possible for all stakeholders when the repository is launched as a national service.

Supporting studies into other major themes that emerge will be commissioned during the programme lifetime. These will be made widely available to maximize the learning opportunities arising from project investigations.

Communities of practice

Communities of practice at all levels are beginning to develop through X4L. At national level, the number of institutions involved in the programme represents a considerable pool of expertise, collaborating and sharing good practice and resources. Regional cluster groups allow further opportunities for project staff to share experiences and ideas and also to demonstrate prototype materials. At institutional level, partnerships and relationships are developing between FE and HE staff, between subject teachers in different institutions, and between library and information staff and teachers. At project level, some projects are developing subject communities of practice, for example, in art, media and performance studies, medicine, law and study skills. Many more practitioners are being included in the X4L community by producing case studies and lesson plans using some of the outputs of the projects.

Empowering teachers, lecturers and other key staff to use technology effectively

As with all JISC development programmes, X4L does not have the production of market quality outputs as a main objective. The resources that are produced are in the form of exemplars, case studies, templates and prototype tools, which are intended to empower and inspire teachers and other key staff to create materials themselves that suit the particular needs of the syllabus or programme of study and the individual needs of their learners.

Library and information professionals' involvement and benefits

The X4L programme is providing the opportunity for teachers, learning technologists and library and information staff to work together. Skills of the information professional have proved vital in areas such as resource discovery and evaluation, staff development for teachers and liaising with commercial content providers. Several projects are producing materials and tools that will assist library and learning resources staff in their support of students and teachers in the areas of study skills and information skills training. These include Lawpaths (http://library.kent.ac.uk/library/lawpaths/), Learning to Learn (www.stir.ac.uk/daice/l2l), RDN4FE (www.rdn.ac.uk/projects/rdnfe/) and VTSX4L (www.vts.rdn.ac.uk/x4l/).

The 'Learning for a Healthier Nation' project

Overview

The Learning for a Healthier Nation project is one of the 22 projects funded under Strand A of the JISC-funded X4L programme and is concerned with identifying and repurposing electronic learning resources for use by tutors teaching on health care courses at college and university level.

The project has concentrated on resources specifically relating to 'the big four' diseases – cancer, chronic heart disease, stroke and mental illness. It has four main strands:

- Strand 1 – resource research and evaluation
- Strand 2 – repository
- Strand 3 – learning objects development
- Strand 4 – piloting and pedagogical evaluation.

Learning for a Healthier Nation started in June 2002 and will run to July 2004. This paper gives an overview of the work carried in Strands 1 and 2 of the project and a summary of conclusions reached so far. More information about work to date and future developments can be obtained from the project website at http://extranet.lauder.ac.uk/x4l.

The project is led by Lauder College in partnership with Edinburgh's Telford College, Napier University, Heriot-Watt University and the Royal National College for the Blind (RNCB). With the exception of the RNCB, all partner institutions are located in Scotland.

Project teams

Learning for a Healthier Nation is involving a range of specialists from the partner institutions including:

- librarians
- health care university tutors
- health care college tutors
- disability access specialists
- pedagogic research specialists.

Technical support is commissioned from a commercial company. Intrallect (www.intrallect.com) was formed in 2000 as a spin-out company from the University of Edinburgh and specializes in developing solutions for the new generation of e-learning systems.

Finding and evaluating resources

Strand 1 of the project has focused on finding and evaluating resources that are relevant to health care programmes delivered in UK colleges and universities. This work split into four activities: electronic resource searching, resource evaluation, metadata tagging and evaluation of accessibility of electronic resources to people with a disability.

Electronic resource search

Before the resource search activity began, the academic team specified the types of resources they were looking for. To assist this process, a 'mapping grid' was developed. Using the mapping grid, the academic staff team were invited to specify key subject areas and subheadings, keywords to be used for searching, subject areas to be excluded, course information, course level and learning outcomes. The level of the course was determined using levels four to seven of the Scottish Credit Qualifications Frameworks (SCQF). Further details of this framework can be obtained from the SCQF website (www.scqf.org.uk). The library team then used the information provided in the mapping grids as a guide to help them identify relevant resources.

It was agreed by the project's operational group that the project would not include subscription based reference or bibliographic sources, but would instead focus on resources that were freely available to all institutions from the JISC Resource Discovery Network (RDN) (www.rdn.ac.uk). The RDN subject gateways were used as the main source for locating suitable resources. The specific subject gateways used were BIOME (http://biome.ac.uk), OMNI (http://omni.ac.uk) and NMAP (http://nmap.ac.uk) for resources relating to cancer, chronic heart disease and stroke and BIOME and SOSIG (www.sosig.ac.uk) for resources relating to mental illness.

Few resources were discovered relating to mental health legislation and hypertension. Therefore, to supplement resources in these areas, the library team used the Google search engine to identify additional materials.

The resource search identified a total of 5000 resources that were relevant to the four health areas. After an evaluation where each resource was assessed for clarity, style, functionality, bias, currency, the authority of the author, level (SCQF Levels four to seven) and copyright issues, only 507 met the library team's evaluation criteria.

Resource evaluation

Each resource was passed to the academic team for further evaluation of usability in learning and teaching at college and university levels. In order to ensure resources were evaluated consistently, a resource sheet was developed using Microsoft Word. The resource sheet design was influenced by the need to:

- describe certain attributes of the resource using IMS restricted vocabularies so that metadata could be assigned consistently when the resource was added to the digital repository

- capture the information from the tutors that would be used during future strands of the project at an early stage. This included tutors' views on the type of learning activity the resource could be used for, ideas on improvements that could be made to the resource from repurposing and any issues relating to copyright restrictions and accessibility.

After academic evaluation, only 235 of the 507 resources passed to the academic team were considered to be suitable in content and level by tutors.

Metadata tagging

Even though CETIS has recently launched the UK LOM Core application profile, providing practitioners in the UK with guidelines for using learning object metadata, this remains a complex issue for tutors and librarians. One issue relates to the level of resource disaggregation to which metadata is applied. A key area of investigation for this project will be to determine who, in an educational setting, is best placed to add metadata to resources that are being uploaded to a repository. The project will produce guidelines for institutions as a result of this investigation.

Disability access evaluation

A key activity of Strand 1 of the project has been to carry out research into the way metadata can be used to provide librarians and tutors with information about the accessibility of an electronic resource to individuals with a disability. This work is ongoing and is being progressed by partners from the Royal National College of the Blind working with JISC services Techdis (www.techdis.ac.uk) and CETIS (www.cetis.ac.uk) through Techdis' accessibility metadata project (www.techdis.ac.uk/metadata), which aims to develop accessibility evaluation criteria and accessibility metadata.

The Learning for a Healthier Nation project is contributing to Techdis' work by:

- testing the accessibility evaluation criteria developed by Techdis by applying it to the resources that have been selected and evaluated by the library and academic teams
- piloting and evaluating the trial application that Techdis is developing to allow users to create accessibility metadata for learning resources.

The outcomes from this work will also be used to influence the design and development of digital repositories.

Exploring digital repositories as a new way of storing and accessing electronic learning resources

Strand 2 of the project aims to establish a digital repository of relevant health care resources. The intention is to enable librarians and tutors to:

- add health care resources to the repository using different classifications
- add metadata
- search and find good quality resources relevant to the subject and level being taught download the resources for use within a specified learning system or virtual learning environment (VLE) using a straightforward browser-based tool.

The work is divided into two activities: investigating digital repositories and identifying which classification systems to use.

Investigation into digital repositories

The project intends to use one of the digital repositories Intralibrary (www.intrallect.com) or Xtensis (www.xor.ltd.uk/xtensis) currently being investigated by the JORUM+ project (www.jorum.ac.uk). Learning for a Healthier Nation is contributing to the work of the JORUM+ project by carrying out:

- librarian and tutor evaluations of both repositories
- accessibility evaluation of both repositories
- technical evaluation of both repositories.

Following this and feedback from other X4L Strand A projects, Intralibrary and Xtensis will be amended and Strand 4 of Learning for a Healthier Nation aims to pilot the uploading of resources into one of these upgraded repositories.

Which classification systems?

Intralibrary and Xtensis currently support two levels of Dewey for classification purposes. Learning for a Healthier Nation is working with other projects to identify more appropriate classification schemes, including the MeSH (medical classification system). This will now be available in the upgraded versions of the repositories.

Project findings

To date the project has reached a number of conclusions and aims to propose solutions over the next year. The RDN was developed to improve access and use of freely available websites in learning, teaching and research by human selection, cataloguing and arranging them within subject gateways or hubs. Some major barriers still exist, however. First, the subject gateway search facilities lack sophistication making resource identification more time consuming than when using commercial search engines. Second, there are concerns about the relevance of the resources in the RDN to learning and teaching. Significant numbers of resources were rejected by librarians and tutors because they were considered to be:

- not appropriate to the level of course being taught
- US-biased
- a repeat of information found and presented in a better way elsewhere
- out of date
- of poor quality compared with resources available from other sources.

Only 8% of the resources evaluated were of value to the health care courses being delivered by the college and university partners.

These findings are being considered by the RDN Central and the JISC Content and Services Team.

Digital repositories have the potential to provide solutions to some of the problems with the existing RDN. They need further development, however, and need to address issues such as:

- ensuring that the process of adding metadata is as non-technical and simple as possible
- providing flexibility by supporting different classification taxonomies
- providing metadata indicating the level for which the resource is suitable across the FE–HE curriculum
- providing metadata relating to the type of learning and teaching activity for which the resource is appropriate
- providing metadata that gives information on disability access
- allowing users to search simply but in a variety of different ways
- determining a reasonable amount of metadata required.

Tutors will expect to assemble learning activities using the resources held in repositories and to present these activities to learners using a VLE. Further research is required into the relationship between digital repositories and VLE systems.

Adding metadata to resources is a time-consuming job requiring specialist knowledge and skills. Our investigation indicates that the knowledge base lies with both librarians and tutors. Opportunities must then arise for models that include more partnership working between librarians, teachers and repository managers, and possibly others. How this will be achieved is another question!

Conclusion

X4L is an ambitious programme that is helping resources in FE and HE to be managed for the core business of learning and teaching by providing a national repository containing learning materials that can be repurposed, as well as exploring issues such as interoperability, IPR, resource evaluation and accessibility. It is helping to build communities of practice and empower the teacher or lecturer. It is also hoping to raise the profile of the library or learning resources service and its staff within the institution, allowing information professionals to contribute to a national development programme and helping to build relationships between library and information staff, teachers and others.

INDEX

Developing Web-based Instruction

Planning, designing, managing, and evaluating for results

EDITED BY ELIZABETH A DUPUIS

Delivering effective web-based instruction is an issue that all librarians now have to consider, particularly if working in an organization that delivers an education programme. If you are responsible for delivering online instruction to users in your library, or if you are considering setting up such a facility for e-learning, then you need this practical, comprehensive book.

An array of talented librarians and educators contribute their perspectives on the current scene, and the text guides you through all the stages needed to create successful web-based instruction in your library. Anyone creating or revising learning modules – be they short online assignments, standalone tutorials or credit-bearing courses that can be delivered over the internet – will find a wealth of information and insight from those who have 'been there, done that' in this key area of development.

The book is divided into three main sections: planning and management; evaluation and assessment; and design and development. The chapters cover:

- scope, timeline and budget
- teams and partners
- audience and stakeholders
- pedagogy and andragogy
- educational technology
- statistics and metrics
- focus groups
- usability testing
- assessment of learning
- goals and objectives
- interactivity
- content organization and development
- site design
- putting content online.

The text is regularly interspersed with overviews and further sources of information, and a useful appendix gives help with how to put a project proposal together.
This book is essential reading for all those involved in delivering online learning in libraries, whether in a technical, design, educational or support role.

2003; 296pp; paperback; 1-85604-494-7; £44.95

Developing Academic Library Staff for Future Success

EDITED BY MARGARET OLDROYD

In a climate of rapid change – growth in student numbers, new e-learning methods, the need to manage resources on a value-for-money basis, and the move towards the digital library – staff development is a key area of concern for university and college library managers. Success in the development of all staff, as part of a coherent approach to human resource management, is critical in delivering the strategic and operational objectives of any forward-looking library service.

This book looks at the place of staff development in the current and future strategic management of academic libraries. It highlights how roles are changing and evaluates the implications of this for skill needs and development routes. The contributors are practising managers in education institutions, and their contributions are illustrated by drawing on their own experience, using material from case studies and relevant international initiatives. Contributions include:

- human resources for higher education in the 21st century
- rethinking professional competence for the networked environment
- developing the academic library managers of the future
- converging on staff development
- developing the academic librarian as learning facilitator
- development routes for academic library support staff
- lifelong learning at work: staff development for the flexible workforce
- delivering staff development using a virtual learning environment
- collaborative staff development
- taking the strategic approach to staff development.

This book is essential reading for all current and future academic library managers as well as institutional managers and staff developers.

The contributors
Moira Bent , Sheila Corrall, Philippa Dolphin, Biddy Fisher, Sally Neocosmos, Patrick Noon, Margaret Oldroyd, Chris Powis, Margaret Weaver, Jo Webb, Sue White.

2004; 208pp; hardback; 1-85604-478-5; £39.95